Sketches From Church History

Bishop Hugh Latimer preaching before the boy King Edward VI at Paul's Cross, 1548.
'I will speak of thy testimonies also before kings, and will not be ashamed' (Psa. 119.46)

Sketches From Church History

S. M. HOUGHTON

*Based in part
on an earlier work
by B. J. Bennink*

'Great is the Lord and greatly to be praised . . .
One generation shall praise Thy works to another,
and shall declare Thy mighty acts' (Psalm 145 : 3–4).

The Banner of Truth Trust

The Banner of Truth Trust
3 Murrayfield Road, Edinburgh EH12 6EL
P O Box 621, Carlisle, Pennsylvania 17013, U.S.A.

© *Banner of Truth Trust 1980*
First published 1980
ISBN 0 85151 317 4

Printed and bound in Great Britain by
Morrison & Gibb Ltd, London and Edinburgh

Contents

Acknowledgements

The Publishers express their gratitude to the following sources for permission to reproduce illustrations in this volume:

The Banner, Grand Rapids, Michigan, USA: *A Christian Reformed Church*, 218

Baker Book House, Grand Rapids, USA: *Abraham Kuyper*, 238

Bettmann Archive Inc., New York: *Rome in the Time of Aurelian*, 22

Bibliotheque Publique et Universitaire, Geneva: *Huguenot Church at Lyons*, 136

The British Museum: *View of Geneva in 17th Century*, 107

The British Travel and Holidays Association, London: *Merton College, Oxford*, 65

The Camera Press, London: *The Arch of Titus*, 13

The Evangelical Library, London: *Meeting of the Westminster Assembly*, 158; *The Holy Club, Oxford*, 187

Fine Arts Publishing Co., London: *Latimer Preaching before Edward VI by E. M. Board, R.A.*, frontispiece

Fox Photos Limited, London: *Hampton Court*, 151

Francois Martin, Geneva: *Monument to the Reformers at Geneva*, 111

The Free Church College, Edinburgh: *The Burning of John Huss*, 71

The Guildhall Library, London: *Burning of Martyrs at Smithfield*, 115

Paul Hamlyn Ltd.: *The Colosseum*, Rome, 15

Henry E. Huntington Library and Art Gallery, USA: *John Eliot*, 173

The Mansell Collection, London: *The Massacre of St. Bartholomew*, 133

The National Gallery, London: *St. Jerome in his Study*, 26; *Interior of Grote Kerk, Haarlem*, 167

The National Galleries of Scotland, Edinburgh: *After the Battle by Robert Hardman, R.A.*, 163

The National Library of Wales, Aberystwyth: *John Elias preaching*, 225

The National Museum of Antiquities, Edinburgh: *John Knox's Pulpit*, 127

The National Museum of Wales: *William Williams*, 201

The National Portrait Gallery, London: *Hugh Latimer*, 112; *Thomas Cranmer by G. Flicke*, 113; *Henry VIII and Edward VI*, 119; *John Bunyan*, 161; *John Wesley*, 189; *Selina, Countess of Huntingdon*, 200; *J. C. Ryle by Pellegrini*, 223

New England Mutual Life Insurance Company, Boston, USA: *The Declaration of Independence by Charles Hoffbauer*, 208

The New York Public Library: *An 18th Century View of New York from the Brooklyn Heights by William Bennett*, 180

Radio Times Hulton Picture Library, London: *George Whitefield preaching at Moorfields*, 196

Reformation Dagblad, Holland: *A Burning Christian Church*, 35

Religious News Service, New York, USA: *Mediaeval French Monastery*, 60; *Christian Martyrs in Rome*, 17

Scottish Tourist Board, Edinburgh: *St. Andrews*, 123

The Tate Gallery, London: *John Knox preaching at St. Andrews by Sir David Wilkie*, 125

Thomas Photos, Oxford: *Christ Church, Oxford*, 77

J. Topham Ltd., Sidcup, Kent: *Lindisfarne*, 29

Introduction

The publication of this book fulfils a long-cherished hope on the part of the publishers. Although many historical titles have been issued by the Banner of Truth Trust since its inception in 1957 none of these has met the need of those who, approaching church history for the first time, wished for a general coverage of the subject before they proceeded to works of greater detail. Despite frequent requests for such a book we knew of no out-of-print titles which, if reissued, would suitably meet the need. One older publication, however, *Sketches from Church History,* written by B J Bennink and printed in the United States in 1925, did, at length, provide a starting point. Bennink's work supplied both title and a plan upon which the present volume is based, but while five of his chapters have been incorporated in revised form, the rest of the work is newly prepared material by a living author.

There are a number of reasons for the decline of interest in Christian history at the popular level during the present century. In this period the teaching of history has generally been dominated by a view which would make faith in divine providence no part of our responsibility. 'Facts' without any reference to the hand of God are supposed to be the limits of the historian's province. So history, thus interpreted, becomes only the subject of the class room or the lecture hall; it ceases to inspire; the music and life, which throbs in the way in which the Bible itself teaches history, is gone; the world is all, the soul has disappeared.

Yet it is not only in the secular realm that the study of church history has thus suffered. In this present century comparatively few Christian churches have thought it needful that every Christian should know the spritual history which lies behind the present day. And therein it may be argued, lies no small part of the spiritual weakness and superficiality of contemporary religion. For church history ought to provide a standard of comparison, it ought to raise our vision of God, and it ought to show us, by countless examples, what faithfulness to Christ and his Word truly means. Significantly it was in her eras of declension that the Old Testament Church forgot her history. 'Not to know what has happened in the past is always to remain a child', and childish ignorance is no safe state for those who are called to fight against superhuman powers.

Sidney M Houghton brings to this volume the interest of sixty years' work in this field. A graduate of Manchester University, he was to teach history at Rhyl, in one of the leading Welsh Grammar Schools, from 1925 until 1960. During the same period it was through his endeavours that Rhyl Grammar School came to possess one of the finest school libraries in Wales and his own personal library also became an outstanding collection. Supposedly entering upon retirement in 1960, Mr Houghton was to become the chief literary and editorial adviser to the present publishers, personally supervising the republication of many theological and historical works. If a high standard has come to be associated with Banner of Truth publications this is in no small measure due to his keen eye. Articles from his pen have also appeared regularly in various periodicals and chiefly in *The Bible League Quarterly* which he has edited since 1970.

The scope of this book is obviously limited. Being intended for readers in the English-speaking world it focuses attention chiefly upon Britain, Europe and America. Several additional chapters would have been needed to extend the *Sketches* to the 20th century and perhaps it is still too soon to place developments in the present century in their true perspective. The breadth of these pages appears in their suitability for both young and old and in the avoidance of any denominational emphases.

Those who begin to feel the excitement of this subject will want advice on further reading and while no formal bibliography is included a list of other books from the same publishers will be found on page 247.

Iain Murray
The Banner of Truth Trust
3 Murrayfield Road
Edinburgh

October 1980

The pen of inspiration at work in the New Testament describes the events which brought the Church of the Christian era into existence—the death and resurrection of the Lord Jesus Christ, the coming of the Holy Spirit, the preaching of the gospel to the Jews of Palestine and to Jews and Gentiles scattered throughout the world. The book known as The Acts of the Apostles describes the establishment of the church, and ends with Paul, 'the apostle of the Gentiles', a prisoner in Rome and awaiting the hearing of his 'appeal to Caesar'. The period of time covered by these events is approximately 30–64 A.D.

During this period the difficulties experienced by Christians were caused chiefly by unbelieving Jews. Roman officials, some of whom are mentioned by name in the New Testament, were usually tolerant of Christianity and unwilling to try to suppress it. They seem to have realized that Christians were law-abiding citizens; they may even have heard that the followers of Jesus were commanded to pray for 'kings and for all that are in authority' (1 Tim. 2 : 2). So, during the period of time covered by the Epistles of the New Testament the Roman Emperors left Christianity untouched.

But during the reign of the Emperor Nero (54–68 A.D.) the situation began to change for the worse. Nero was a monster of wickedness, one of the vilest men ever to occupy a throne. The proverbial story that he fiddled to amuse himself while Rome was burning illustrates his callousness.

The fire broke out in Rome in the year 64. Whether justly or unjustly one cannot be certain, but Nero was suspected of deliberately causing

I

The Early Church

above Jerusalem from the North-East: '. . . beginning at Jerusalem' (Luke 24 : 47).

 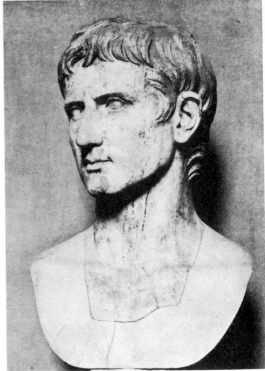

left (Caesar) Augustus (27 B.C.–14 A.D.) – the official title of Octavianus, made Roman Emperor by the senate after the death of Julius Caesar. The same title was assumed by succeeding emperors. In his own honour Augustus named the eighth month of the year after himself, following the example of Julius Caesar who had earlier given his own name to July. Augustus was Emperor when Christ was born (Luke 2.1).

right Tiberius (14 A.D.–37 A.D.), named in Luke 3.1 and Emperor when Christ was crucified.

the fire, and the Roman historian Tacitus tells us that he screened himself by putting the blame on the Christians. These are his words:

Nero punished with the utmost refinement of cruelty a class hated for their abominations who are commonly called Christians. Christus, from whom their name is derived, was executed at the hands of Pontius Pilate in the reign of Tiberius ... In Rome an immense multitude was convicted, not so much on the charge of arson as because of their hatred of the human race. Besides being put to death they were made to serve as objects of amusement; they were clad in the hides of beasts and torn to pieces by dogs; others were crucified, others set on fire to serve to illuminate the night when daylight failed.

It is obvious that the charges brought against the Christians were outrageously false. Tacitus acknowledges this and states his belief that they were 'being destroyed, not for the public good, but to gratify the cruelty of an individual'.

Suetonius, another Roman writer of the second century, speaks of the Christians as 'a set of men adhering to a novel and mischievous superstition,' but he does not give us any detailed explanation of his statement.

A much fuller reference to the early Christians is given in letters that passed about the year 112 between the Younger Pliny and the Emperor Trajan. At this time Pliny was the Governor of Bithynia (in Asia Minor: see Acts 16 : 7 and

1 Peter 1 : 1). He was perplexed as to how to deal with the Christians in the province, and he wrote to his overlord:

This is the course that I have adopted. I ask them if they are Christians. If they admit it I repeat the question a second and a third time, threatening capital punishment. If they persist I sentence them to death, for their inflexible obstinacy should certainly be punished. Christians who are Roman citizens I reserved to be sent to Rome. I discharged those who were willing to curse Christ, a thing which, it is said, genuine Christians cannot be persuaded to do.

Further, Pliny's letter also gives us an insight into Christian practice in the early second century:

On an appointed day the Christians are accustomed to meet at daybreak and to recite (or sing) a hymn to Christ, as to a god, and to bind themselves by a *sacramentum* (oath) to abstain from theft and robbery, adultery, and breach of faith. After this they depart, and meet again to take food. To find out the truth concerning them I applied torture to two maidservants who were called deaconesses. But I found nothing but a depraved and extravagant superstition.

In his reply to Pliny, Trajan told him that he had acted rightly, but he advised him not to seek out Christians for punishment. Only if they were informed against were they to be put on trial. If, on arrest, they were prepared to worship the gods approved by Rome, and to deny Christ, they could be discharged.

It is very probable that the number of Christians increased greatly during the second century, but records are scanty. We know, however, that about the year 150 a Christian could write, for the benefit of the Roman Emperor:

We are but of yesterday, and we have filled all that belongs to you—the cities, the fortresses, the free

Nero (54 A.D.–68 A.D.), his name is not actually given in Scripture, but the Augustus of Acts 25.21 is Nero. It is also possible that in 2 Timothy 4.17, where the apostle Paul speaks of his deliverance from 'the mouth of the lion', Nero is indicated.

towns, the very camps, the palace, the senate, the forum. We leave to you the temples only.

One of the most interesting of Christians at this period was Justin Martyr who was a native of Samaria and born about the year 100. Until he was thirty-two years of age he searched in vain for truth. Several non-Christian philosophies attracted him but he could not find satisfaction in any of them. Then, one day, walking by the sea-side, he fell into conversation with an old man, a Christian, who convinced him of 'the truth as it is in Jesus'. In later life he wrote several *Apologies*, that is, writings which defended the Christian faith. They describe Christian worship on the Lord's Day in some detail, mentioning the reading of Scripture, the sermon, prayers for all men, the kiss of peace (2 Cor. 13 : 12), the observance of the Lord's supper, and almsgiving. Justin met a martyr's death about the year 165. One who was martyred with him made the noble confession, 'I am a Christian, having been freed by Christ, and by the grace of Christ I partake of the same hope'.

A long-remembered event about ten years after Justin's death concerns The Thundering Legion. The reigning Emperor was Marcus Aurelius, famed for his philosophical writings, usually called his *Meditations*. He was waging a military campaign, but the enemy had succeeded in cutting off his vital water-supply, and it appeared that he might have to surrender. But we are told that the soldiers of the Twelfth Legion, who were all Christians, fell on their knees and prayed earnestly for rain. Almost before they had risen to their feet again a heavy rainstorm occurred, which threw the enemy into great confusion, and saved the situation for the Emperor who believed that a miracle had happened. He himself was no Christian, but for the moment his heart may have been softened towards the followers of Christ.

From time to time persecutions broke out, occasionally as the result of imperial policy; sometimes, however, they were due to the whims of local governors and magistrates. A Christian writer named Tertullian tells us that Christians became the scapegoats for any public disasters that occurred:

If the River Tiber rises as high as the city walls of Rome, if the River Nile does not send its waters over the fields, if there is an earthquake, or famine, or pestilence, immediately the cry is, 'The Christians to the lions'.

The wildest accusations against Christians were believed and the most inhuman punishments inflicted upon them. Traditionally there were ten great persecutions, the most severe being those that fell last of all.

It is not surprising, therefore, that Christians often met in out-of-the-way places, and used secret passwords by means of which they might recognize one another if they met for the first time. One of the commonest of such passwords was the word 'fish'. In Greek the word was 'ICHTHUS' and an acrostic well-known to Christians ran:

I esus
CH rist
TH eou (of God)
U ios (Son)
S oter (Saviour).

Hence, if a stranger introduced the word 'Ichthus' into his conversation, he was really endeavouring to find out whether he was speaking to a Christian or otherwise.

How can the persecution of Christians be explained? Historians have made a number of suggestions including the following:

(1) Roman Emperors were much opposed to 'gods' which the Empire did not recognize. The Empire had 'gods many and lords many' (1 Cor. 8 : 5) but it did not own the God of the Christians.

(2) The Christian faith preached One who was God over all the earth. It knew nothing of political frontiers. It said that the heathen gods were idols, and it denounced idolatry. It aimed at extending the kingdom of Christ into all parts of the earth. The Emperors regarded this as a very dangerous programme.

(3) Christians could not join pagans in heathen worship, nor could they take part in idolatrous acts on social or civic occasions. Also,

opposite The upper part of the Arch of Titus, showing the Jewish temple's seven-branched candlestick. When Jerusalem fell to Titus in 70 A.D., to commemorate the victory the Arch was erected in the Forum at Rome. The reliefs depict the Jewish captives and the temple spoils.

Christians met with Christians, sometimes of necessity secretly, and came to be regarded as members of a secret society, and unsociable in their behaviour. It was easy to accuse them of plotting against the State.

(4) Christians were regarded as threatening the financial, political and religious interests of various classes of people—priests, the makers of idols, the sellers of idols, salesmen of sacrificial animals, and so on.

(5) As previously mentioned, it was popularly believed that Christians aroused the anger of the Roman gods, who replied by sending famine, earthquake, military defeat, and similar punishments on the Empire.

The final persecution came in the reign of the Emperor Diocletian, and commenced in the year 303. Diocletian was at that time visiting Bithynia. He held court in Nicomedia, its capital, and passed edicts ordering the destruction of all places of Christian worship, and the burning of all Christian books throughout the Empire. Christians were to be liable to torture and were to be denied all civil rights. Shortly, other edicts followed. Eusebius, a later Christian historian, tells us that all persons without exception were required to sacrifice and make offerings to idols.

A noble reply was given by one Christian to his persecutors: 'Where are your Scriptures?' was the demand. 'In my heart' was the reply.

After the death of Diocletian, his successor Galerius carried on the persecution for six more years, until in 311 he met his death in a manner similar to that of Herod Agrippa as recorded in Acts 12.23: 'He was eaten of worms and gave up the ghost'. It deserves to be recorded that, in his dying torments, he published a decree of toleration, confessing himself baffled by the fortitude of Christians, and entreating their prayers on his behalf. Who can fight against the Almighty and prosper?

2
The Martyrs

No Christian reader of the Four Gospels can for a moment doubt that behind the opposition to Jesus and his gospel was the hostility and enmity of Satan, the 'prince of this world', and that of the demonic hosts subject to his control. Scripture describes them as 'the devil and his angels' (Matt. 25 : 41). The closing book of Scripture shows how earth is a battlefield in which two armies are engaged—the people of God, led by 'the Captain of their salvation', the hosts of darkness led by 'the dragon, that old serpent, which is the Devil, and Satan' (Rev. 20 : 2).

From the beginning to the end of Scripture, and not in the Four Gospels only, we are taught that rebel angels wage relentless war against the kingdom of God. Normally Satan, in planning his campaigns, acts through human agency. In the period when Jesus was exercising his earthly ministry we find Satan enlisting scribes and elders, Pharisees and Sadducees, in his service. Among Gentile peoples he makes use of false religions which have 'gods many and lords many' (I Cor. 8 : 5), and as these false religions are commonly allied with civic powers, if not actually

The Colosseum, Rome. Dedicated in 80 A.D., it could hold about 45,000 spectators.

founded by them, we very often find kings and governors and magistrates acting as the instruments of persecution in the endeavour to make it impossible for the true faith to be practised.

Demonic activity as related to false religion led the apostle Paul to warn Corinthian Christians—and the same necessarily applies to all Christians in all subsequent ages—against having fellowship with devils, against 'drinking of the cup of devils', and 'being partakers at the table of devils' (I Cor. 10 : 20–21). Strong words, yet fitting the circumstances! Naturally, therefore, both among Jews and Gentiles, those who rejected the preaching that Jesus of Nazareth was both Lord and Christ became infuriated against believers, and by false accusation stirred up 'the powers that be' against them.

As we have already seen, much of the information that survives about Christians in the early centuries of our era concerns their sufferings. The rulers and governors in that period of history were often willing to use the most inhuman and cruel methods to blot out Christianity. Thousands upon thousands of the early Christians sealed their faith with their blood. They were beheaded, burned at the stake, thrown to wild beasts to be torn to pieces and devoured, and cast into boiling oil. Their bodies were mutilated and tortured in as many different ways as men hostile to their beliefs could invent and devise. Yet their faith often sparkled like a precious stone as they faced their persecutors, and some of them spoke words which have echoed down the long corridors of time.

The New Testament does not record the death of the apostles of Christ except in the case of James, the brother of John, who was killed by the sword of King Herod Agrippa I, a descendant of Herod the Great (Acts 12 : 1–2). But there is little doubt that most, if not all, of the apostles were martyred. In their place came a group of men often called the 'Apostolic Fathers', the best known of them being Hermas, Ignatius of Antioch, and Polycarp of Smyrna.

Hermas is famed as the writer of a book called *The Shepherd* which was well known and much read in the early church. It has been termed the Pilgrim's Progress of the early Church, and was sometimes read in Christian assemblies.

Ignatius became a martyr early in the second century. For about forty years he was bishop of the church at Antioch (in Syria) and, apart from his violent death, is remembered for seven letters which he wrote to the churches. An ancient but unprovable tradition asserts that he was the child whom Jesus took into his arms (Matthew 18 : 2) saying, 'Whosoever shall humble himself as this little child, the same is greatest in the kingdom of heaven'.

When Ignatius was an old man, the Roman Emperor Trajan, who ruled from the year 98 to 117, paid a visit to Antioch, one of the most important cities of the East, and, being told about the bishop of the despised and hated Christians, he wished to see him. Not that Trajan had any respect for the Christian faith! Indeed he used bitter words when he spoke to Ignatius:

Trajan: 'There you are, wicked devil, deceiver of men!'
Ignatius: 'Not an evil spirit', but I have Jesus Christ in my heart'.
Trajan: 'Jesus Christ within you? Do you mean him who was crucified by Pontius Pilate?'
Ignatius: 'Yes, he was crucified for my sins'.

Whereupon the heartless Emperor, without any further procedure of a legal kind, condemned him to be transferred to Rome and to be thrown

to wild beasts, 'butchered to make a Roman holiday'.

Ignatius was therefore brought to the amphitheatre at Rome, known later as The Colosseum. It was an almost circular building, with seats in three tiers holding about 45,000 spectators. Almost daily the crowds came together to enjoy various kinds of public exhibitions, plays and games, and from time to time they took great pleasure in witnessing the death of Christian martyrs.

How often they had feasted their eyes on a spectacle such as that to be seen when Ignatius stood before them all! When Trajan sentenced him he had replied, 'I thank thee, O Lord, that thou hast vouchsafed thus to honour me'. And now, face to face with death, he said: 'I am God's grain, to be ground between the teeth of wild beasts, so that I may become a holy loaf for the Lord'. Soon after the lions were loosed upon him nothing was left but a few gnawed bones. When mourning friends later took these bones for burial

'The Christians to the lions!'

'Do you want martyr relics?' was a question once put to certain mediaeval sightseers in Rome; 'take up the dust of the Colosseum; it is all the martyrs' was the advice given. The seating of the Colosseum was in three tiers, with standing room above them.

they knew that Ignatius was 'with Christ, which is far better'. (Phil. 1 : 23).

About the year 155 the aged Christian pastor Polycarp was also martyred. He had been a disciple of the apostle John and had become the leading Christian in the church at Smyrna, one of the 'seven churches of Asia' named in chapters one and two of the Book of Revelation. In the middle of the second century this church was visited with fierce persecutions. Polycarp found refuge for a short time outside the city limits, but he was betrayed by an unfaithful servant and fell into the hands of his enemies. Calm and dignified, he surrendered himself with the words, 'God's will be done'; then, after giving food to his hungry persecutors, he poured out his heart before the Lord, praying for himself, his friends, the church of Smyrna, and also for his enemies.

The usual test applied to Christians was that they must call Caesar, the emperor, 'Lord', as if he were a divine person. Refusal to do so meant the death sentence. Taken before the Roman consul, Polycarp was required to say, on oath, that he venerated Caesar in this way. But he was firm in his refusal. 'I have wild beasts' said the consul; 'if you refuse I will throw you to them'. 'Send for them' replied Polycarp.

'If you despise the wild beasts I will send you to the fire', said the consul; 'swear and I will release you: curse the Christ'.

'Eighty and six years have I served Christ' replied Polycarp, 'and he has done me no wrong; how then can I blaspheme my King who has saved me? You threaten the fire that burns for an hour and then is quenched; but you know not of the fire of the judgment to come, and the fire of the eternal punishment. Bring what you will'.

The consul was astonished and sent a herald to announce to the people that Polycarp had confessed himself to be a Christian. When the torch was applied to the wood, and smoke and flames encircled him, again he prayed: 'Lord God, Father of our blessed Saviour, I thank thee that I have been deemed worthy to receive the crown of martyrdom, and that I may die for thee and for thy cause'.

It is recorded that all the multitude 'marvelled at the great difference between the unbelievers and the elect'. They saw what Christian obedience meant, for Jesus had said, 'Be thou faithful unto death and I will give thee a crown of life' (Rev. 2 : 10).

Mention, too, must be made of Blandina, a slave girl in Southern France, physically weak, but a heroine in faith. She refused all allegiance to heathen gods. Wild beasts, it is said, would not touch her, so she was taken to a fire, then fastened up in a net, tossed repeatedly by a furious bull, and finally died by having her throat cut.

In Carthage, North Africa, lived Vivia Perpetua, a young mother whose earthly life was bound to an aged father, and to her infant son. She had fully grasped the meaning of the words, 'He that loveth father or mother more than me is not worthy of me; and he that loveth son or daughter more than me is not worthy of me', and therefore she gave up all for Jesus, and lost her life that she might gain it.

One of the most notable of the martyrs was Cyprian of Carthage, a notable teacher of rhetoric who was converted to Christ somewhat late in life. His growth in grace and in the knowledge of his Lord was unusually rapid and within three years he became bishop in his native city. He set a splendid example of Christian living and service to his flock. Periodically persecution raged and ultimately Cyprian was condemned to death by the pro-consul Galerius:

Galerius: You are Thascius Cyprianus?

Cyprian: I am.

Galerius: You have given yourself to be bishop to people who do not give service to our Roman gods.

Cyprian: I have.

Galerius: Consider.

Cyprian: Do what you are required to do; in such a simple matter there is nothing to consider.

Galerius: Your life has long been one of sacrilege; you have constituted yourself an antagonist to the gods of Rome and to their sacred observances. As you have been a standard-bearer in heinous offences, you shall be in your own person a lesson to those who have been associated with you. Our pleasure is that Thascius Cyprianus be executed with the sword.

Cyprian: Thanks be to God!

Surrounded by an immense crowd a centurion severed his neck at one stroke. But 'the blood of the martyrs of Jesus' was not shed in vain. (Rev. 17 : 6).

From the end of the first century onwards many Roman Christians found refuge in what were termed The Catacombs, a word that appears to denote 'down the hollow'. They abound in an area near the city of Rome, and originally seem to have been cemeteries with numerous underground passages. When persecution was raging, these passages, and spaces leading out of them, became places of refuge. Many of them remain to the present day, and inscriptions, paintings, and Christian symbols—for example, the dove, fish and bread, and the palm branch—can still be seen as reminders of the time when such a dwell-

ing was needed by Christians whose lives were endangered. Worship was often conducted in them.

Even so, many thousands died as men and women faithful to Christ, but, as one of the earliest of Church historians wrote, 'The blood of the martyrs is the seed of the Church'. It is recorded that, centuries later, as certain visitors to Rome were being shown the Colosseum, their guide told them of the deaths of vast numbers of Christians within the building. They asked him whether relics of those former days could still be obtained. Turning to them he said, 'Gather dust from the Colosseum; it is all the martyrs'.

3

Constantine the Great

The year 311 saw the end of the persecution of the Christian Church. The Emperor Galerius, the last of the persecutors, died that year and for a short time there was war between rivals for supreme power, the struggle being complicated by reason of the fact that the Roman Empire was practically divided into eastern and western halves. Ultimately, however, after an important battle at Milvian Bridge, near Rome, Constantine became sole Emperor. In the struggle for the throne Constantine had lost all confidence in the national gods, and therefore he was driven to call on the God of the Christians for help. Eusebius tells us that shortly before the battle of Milvian Bridge the Emperor had seen in the sky a flaming cross with the words inscribed in Greek, 'By this, conquer'. He adopted the cross as his emblem, and beneath the standard of the cross his soldiers marched to victory.

It is very doubtful whether Constantine was ever a true convert. His predecessors had persecuted the Christians for political reasons. He favoured them on similar grounds, and showed himself willing to continue the policy of toleration which had, in fact, been introduced about a year before he won his victory. It was a turning-point in the history of the Empire, and even more so in the history of the Christian Church.

Was it a change for the better? Yes, and No! Persecutions ended, for the Emperor now became a defender of the Christian faith, although he postponed his baptism until very shortly before his death in the year 337. Churches were built for Christian worship, and bishops and preachers received liberal salaries from the State. The Christian Sunday was recognized as a day of rest on which ordinary work was forbidden and even Christian soldiers were permitted to attend the services. All this was certainly a great blessing for the people of God; it was a great calm after a severe and prolonged storm.

But with toleration came danger. It now became an honour and a distinction to be a Christian. The best positions in State and community were given to them. The Christians became leaders everywhere. It was only natural that many pagans turned to Christianity, not because their hearts were converted to the living God, but to gain position and promotion. Jesus would have said to them, 'Ye seek me because ye did eat of the loaves' (John 6 : 26); that is to say, to seek earthly gain. 'Woe unto you when all men speak well of you' (Luke 6 : 26) ran another word of warning. Most certainly worldly men were undesirable members of the Church.

And how the outward appearance of the Church changed! Instead of primitive simplicity came pride and pomp, for the reproach of the cross was turned into royal fame and glory. Christianity in its outward manifestation was promoted. Constantine granted to the Church the right to receive gifts and legacies, and he himself enriched it with gifts. From this time the Church became a rich 'corporation', and a worldly spirit entered into it. Before long bishops ruled in large cities as pagan governors had formerly done; they set an example of luxurious living, which contradicted the instruction of the Master, 'Take my yoke upon you and learn of me; for I am meek and lowly in heart'.

The greatest danger threatening Christianity was realized when the emperor decided that he himself would rule the Church. The Lord Jesus Christ is King in his Church, and no earthly power should ever be allowed to use its influence, much less its authority, in that spiritual dominion where Christ reigns supreme. But Constantine called meetings of bishops and other Church dignitaries, and such meetings were then presided over in his name.

It is small wonder that under such conditions the signs of apostasy and heresy were shortly seen. Arius, a presbyter of Alexandria, in Egypt, openly disputed the divinity of Christ, asserting that Christ was a created being, and thousands followed him in his errors. To combat this heresy God raised up Athanasius, also of Alexandria, who wrote a famous book entitled *On the Incarnation of the Word of God*, in which he defended the true biblical doctrine of the Person of Christ. He is remembered by the saying, 'Athanasius contra mundum' (Athanasius against the world), meaning that even if he were the sole upholder of the truth, he would be prepared to defend it against all its opponents. A famous creed is named after Athanasius.

On account of the great debate that took place over the heresy of Arius, Constantine called a general Council of the Church at Nicea, a city in Bithynia, close to Byzantium, the city renamed Constantinople. About 300 bishops were present, but most of them were from the eastern part of the empire. Seven only came from the West. Arianism was denounced and a formula of Christian faith adopted which is known as the Nicene Creed. The date of the Council was 325. It is a landmark in the long history of the Church, and shows the vast importance of 'the doctrine of Christ'.

Constantine reigned until 337. He is known as 'the Great'. As an instrument in God's hand he enabled Christians to worship freely; but the good that his reign brought was a mixed blessing. It had its evil as well as its good aspect. If peace came to the Church, so too did worldliness. Multitudes took up with Christianity who had no experience of conversion and of the work of the Holy Spirit in the human heart. Quality was sacrificed to quantity. The fire of persecution had kept the Church pure; toleration resulted in the introduction of elements which boded ill for the future.

Rome in the time of Aurelian (late third century A.D.). Aurelian, a noted Roman soldier, died in 275 A.D. He was known for his extreme severity. At the time of his death he was planning a renewal of the persecution of Christians.

Almost 25 years after the death of Constantine, the imperial sceptre came into the hands of Julian, who was called the Apostate because he abandoned Christianity and did his utmost to restore pagan worship. But he did not return to a policy of persecution—the sword, the fire, and the lions. His chief weapon was the pen, for he was a talented writer. He discharged all Christian officials and gave their position to unbelievers; he forbade the instruction of Christian youth and robbed the churches of their possessions, so that when at the age of 32 he was killed in battle, his death was a great relief to the Church.

The successors of Julian the Apostate restored the arrangements introduced by Constantine the Great. Furthermore they forbade the use of

divination, that is, the attempt to forecast future events by supernatural means, an art that Scripture everywhere condemns. They forbade sorcery also—the use of magic—as a great evil. The emperor Gratian (375–383) refused the title of Pontifex Maximus which marked out the emperor as the 'chief priest' of Rome's old heathen religion and the head of all the officials responsible for the carrying on of that religion. It was about this time, too, that the old religion, having lost so many of its supporters and so much of its influence, received the name of 'paganism' or 'peasants' religion', as no longer worthy of the attention of intelligent men and women. Yet it died hard.

4

Church Fathers

We must distinguish between Apostolic Fathers and Church Fathers. Some of the former, as we have already said, were the eminent men who were taught the Christian faith by the apostles themselves. We have mentioned them in the chapter on The Martyrs. These Apostolic Fathers had to fight against an enemy that destroyed limb and life, an enemy threatening the body of Christ, his Church, from without.

After them came the earlier and later Church Fathers. The outstanding ones lived in the era of external quiet, during the reign of Constantine the Great and his successors. But despite its quietness, it was also an era in which destructive and heretical doctrines were taught, for the enemy from within tried to destroy the Church by leading it into gross error. One of these enemies was Arius, previously mentioned, who denied the Godhead of the Lord Jesus; he taught that Christ was created and that he was not the eternal Son of the Father.

The Church Fathers defended the truth of God's Word against such heretical teaching. They were leaders raised up by God to preach true doctrine and practice. In their writings we find the history, teachings, and traditions of the early Church. In this chapter we shall deal with only three of them, Ambrose, Augustine, and Jerome. Athanasius we have mentioned already.

Ambrose (339–397) was the son of a Roman governor in Gaul (France). Educated in the law in Rome he entered the Emperor's service and was stationed in the province in which the city of Milan stands. While he was there the bishop of the city died and a division arose among the people over the choice of a successor. Probably certain of the people wanted a bishop who held the heresy of Arius, while others wanted a bishop who held to the doctrine formulated by the Council of Nicea. As there was the probability that a riot might ensue, Ambrose, as governor, attended the gathering and spoke to the people, urging them to conduct themselves in an orderly and Christian manner. Suddenly the voice of a child (as was supposed) was heard, saying 'Let Ambrose be our bishop'.

Ambrose was greatly loved, for he was a truly Christian man, and as his grave, eloquent and pleading words impressed the hearts of the people, they interpreted the voice as the voice of God giving them direction in the performance of his will. From all sides the cry was heard, 'Ambrose is our bishop, Ambrose is our bishop'. The startled governor responded to the call, even though he had not yet submitted to Christian baptism. He felt that it came from God; he was baptized, taken into the Christian ministry, and confirmed in the office of bishop in little more than a week.

Although gentle by nature, Ambrose had a character which remained firm in the face of the fiercest opposition. For one event in particular he is always remembered. It concerned the Emperor Theodosius who, though a professed Christian and a member of the Church, had massacred 7,000 of the city of Thessalonica, as punishment for a rebellion in which Roman officers had been killed. Ambrose wrote a letter to the Emperor but received no reply. Soon afterwards the Emperor came to worship at Milan and intended to present himself at the Lord's table. But the bishop, unwilling to receive him at the table, met him at the entrance to the church building, and said: 'How will you lift up in prayer the hands still dripping with the blood of the murdered ? How will you, with such hands, receive and bring to your mouth the body and blood of the Lord ? Get out of here, and do not dare to add another crime to the one you have already committed'.

In the outcome the Roman emperor made public confession of his sin and sought forgiveness. Eight months passed before he was received at the Lord's table. In token of his submission he also issued a law that henceforth the death sentence against a man should never be carried into effect until thirty days after it was pronounced.

We turn next to Augustine, the greatest of all the Church Fathers. He shines forth as a bright star in the firmament of early Church history. He was born in 354 in the province of Numidia, North Africa, not very far from ancient Carthage. Patricius, his father, was a pagan, but his mother, Monica, was a woman in whom all the virtues of a Christian mother were found in abundance; she excelled in the fervour of her faith, the tenderness of her affection, and the constancy of her love.

Augustine's father's only concern for his son was that he should excel in matters intellectual. He knew that his son was highly gifted. He arranged for him to complete his studies in the city of Carthage, but there Augustine found the temptations of life too much for his ardent, sensual nature. He became completely ensnared by the vanities of the world. Monica, however, prayed ceaselessly for her erring son. For long it seemed as if her prayers were not heard, and that all her entreaties, admonitions and instructions were lost upon him. It must have been a great encouragement to her much-tried faith when a good bishop living near her North Africa home assured her that a son of so many prayers and tears could not be finally lost. This comforted Monica, and in due time the bishop's words proved true.

Monica had specially prayed that her son might not be allowed to leave Africa for Italy, for she feared that temptations to sin might be even greater there than in Carthage. Yet in spite of her prayers her son went to Italy. She feared the worst, but God meant it for the best. After a time spent in Rome, Augustine went to Milan, and in the providence of God he became acquainted with Ambrose who took much interest in him. The sermons of the bishop impressed him greatly. He began to study Scripture and, by the light of the Holy Spirit, to understand the nature of sin and grace. The struggle within his heart became painful in the extreme.

At the age of thirty-one Augustine was in a garden in Milan, weeping and calling to God for deliverance from sin. He despaired of himself. Suddenly he heard the voice of a boy or girl from a neighbouring house repeating in a kind of chant, 'Take and read; take and read'. Without delay he took up the New Testament, and read Romans 13, verses 13–14, the first words on which his eyes fell: 'Let us walk honestly, as in the day; not in rioting and drunkenness, not in chambering and wantonness, not in strife and envying. But put ye on the Lord Jesus Christ and make not provision for the flesh to fulfil the lusts thereof'. Almost at once every shadow of doubt melted away. There and then Augustine passed from death to life. Immediately he went to tell his mother what had happened. She was close at hand, for she had followed him to Italy. Her mourning was now turned into joy, and she blessed the Lord who was able to do exceeding abundantly above all that she had asked or thought.

Afterwards Augustine wrote his *Confessions*, one of the most famous books of all time, in which he describes the way the Lord led him out

Augustine of Hippo Regis at prayer; by Ribera, a Spanish painter (d. 1656).
'He had a deeper spiritual insight into the Scriptures than any other of the Fathers. Never was a man more determined and fearless in the defence of the truth'. He rendered immense service to the Kingdom of God. Luther and Calvin, and indeed the whole Church, under God stand deeply in his debt.

of sin and doubt into grace and truth. In Italy he had become a teacher of rhetoric, but now he returned to Africa, intending to live in seclusion. This, however, was not the will of God for him. Instead, he was led to become bishop of a town called Hippo Regis, in Numidia, and his splendid talents were devoted to the building of the Church of God in the West. He died at Hippo in the year 430.

Augustine's influence was especially felt in the Pelagian controversy. Pelagius, a British monk, was a dangerous man, for he taught false doctrines. He denied original sin and asserted that Adam's sin did not affect the entire human race.

Jerome in his study. Born in Dalmatia, he settled in Bethlehem in 386 A.D. and ruled over a monastery there. His chief title to fame results from his translation of the Bible into Latin from the Hebrew and Greek. Its title of VULGATE denotes that it was in common or popular use. For long centuries it has been the version used by the Roman Catholic Church. Note the peacock; it was widely believed that the peacock's flesh was incorruptible; hence the bird became an emblem of the resurrection.

Man, he claimed, is not born sinful, but is able to do all that God requires of him, if he only wills to do so. Pelagius taught that the ability to be saved is found in the lost sinner's heart if he will but use it. He really denied the necessity for a 'birth from above', for the inward work of the Holy Spirit, and for the intervention of the un-merited grace of God. Salvation is 'not of works lest any man should boast' (Eph. 2 : 9) but Pelagius's teachings were virtually a denial of this great truth. Augustine was his most power-ful opponent and his writings on these themes have been influential in nearly every period of Church history since that time.

Jerome lived during the same period as Augustine. It is said that as a youth he spent time in the Catacombs around Rome translating the many inscriptions. Besides Latin, he acquired an excellent knowledge of Greek, and was one of the few western scholars who gave attention to the Hebrew language. In fact he became one of the chief scholars in the early Church. His great-est work was to translate the Bible from Hebrew and Greek into Latin. Much of this work was accomplished at Bethlehem where he settled in the year 386. It is known as the Vulgate (that is, the Bible 'in common use') and was the version used throughout the Middle Ages in the Roman Catholic Church. It was the first book to be prin-ted when movable type was invented in the middle of the 15th century. In the 16th century the famous Council of Trent termed it 'authen-tic'.

Jerome also opposed the Pelagian heresy with much vigour. He died in or about the year 420.

5

Monasticism

Monasticism refers to a life apart from the world, a life almost exclusively devoted to meditation and prayer in accordance with certain rules and regulations prescribed by the founders of the various 'Orders' of monks. In its origin, how-ever, it can be traced to the hermit's life, a hermit being a person who desires to lead a solitary life in some secluded place, without any contact with other human beings.

During the days of persecution many Chris-tians tried to find safety in seclusion, and to grow in holiness and godliness by living a life of conse-cration and self-denial. Later, during the reign of Constantine the Great, when the days of persecution had passed, and the Church and the world drew together, many more Christians thought they could please God by separating themselves as far as possible from the world and living in seclusion; not as hermits, however, for the most part, but in small companies.

Egypt was the birthplace of Monasticism, for it was there, in the middle of the third century, that a certain Antonius secluded himself from the world for religious purposes. While a young man he was so deeply impressed by the story of the rich young ruler (Mark 10 : 17–27) that he decided to apply the words of Jesus to himself—'If thou wilt be perfect, go and sell that thou hast and give to the poor, and thou shalt have treasure in heaven; and come, take up the cross, and follow me'. He sold all his valuable property and distributed the money among the poor. He then said farewell to the world, to relations and friends, and lived alone—first near his home, then in a tomb, later in a disused fort, and finally on a mountain. Twice a year his friends brought him food, which he ate with a little salt. He drank nothing but water. He decided not to comb or cut his hair, except once a year, at Easter. He never took a bath. Men of his type are often called anchorites (those who 'take to the bush'). They believe that thereby they are able to reach to higher degrees of holiness than others. Antonius, we are told, lived until he was 106 years of age.

The most misguided 'saints' of those times were the Stylites or Pillar Saints. They took their name from a certain Simeon who died in 459 at the age of about 70. 'Stylos' is the Greek word for a pillar. Simeon imagined that by living on the top of a pillar his soul would benefit. Beginning with a pillar about six feet high, and gradually increasing its height, he ended up by living for over 30 years on a pillar 60 feet high. He had many visitors and he preached to them from the top of his pillar. Some of the visitors erected pillars of their own, normally in the region of Antioch in Syria.

opposite Lindisfarne. At low water there is a causeway joining Holy Island to the mainland. The ruins which appear in the photograph are those of an eleventh-century Benedictine Priory, not of the monastery established by Aidan.

As time moved on, hermits gave place to monks who were organized on a social basis and housed in buildings known as monasteries. The earnestness of these people may have been genuine, and their intentions sincere, but the whole practice of monasticism is contrary to the words of Jesus, for he said to his disciples: 'Let your light so shine before men, that they may see your good works and glorify your Father which is in heaven' (Matt. 5 : 16). Scripture certainly tells Christians that they are not 'of the world' (John 17 : 14), and are to keep themselves from worldliness (2 Cor. 6 : 17), but to do this by means of a physical separation from unbelievers is not possible.

The head of a monastery was called the abbot (from the late Latin *abbas*: father) and the head of a nunnery (similar to a monastery, but for women) the abbess. Unhappily, while the monks withdrew themselves from the world, with its sins and temptations and allurements, in order to seek after holiness, they themselves sometimes became addicted to the most terrible sins. To correct these abuses, rules and detailed regulations were introduced, and the monks were provided with useful employment.

In the west of Europe, monasticism originated in the work of a monk named Benedict who, having lived for a time in a cave as a hermit, established a monastery near Naples in the year 529. Its members were called Benedictines. The three essential requirements or vows for these monks, as prescribed by Abbot Benedict, were poverty, chastity, and obedience. By obedience was meant strict adherence to the laws of the Church and the rules of the monastic Order. The Benedictine Order became immensely popular and widespread. To it belonged a monk named Augustine who brought forty monks to Canter-

bury in Angle-land (England) in the year 597. Of course, this Augustine and the Augustine previously mentioned as Bishop of Hippo Regis in North Africa, were totally different persons, living in different periods, but sometimes they are confused. The Augustine who came to Canterbury established a Benedictine monastery there.

There were numerous Orders of monks, distinguished one from another by the dress they wore: Carthusians, Cistercians, Franciscans (founded by the famous Francis of Assisi), Dominicans, Augustinians, Capuchins, and others. In certain ways they rendered great service in the growth of civilisation. We shall see how some of them became missionaries to barbaric peoples. Monasteries became the seats of learning and piety, especially during the Dark Ages, supplying teachers and founding schools. The monks were also employed as copyists of manuscripts during the centuries before the invention of printing. With painstaking industry they collected and transcribed ancient manuscripts and thus preserved literature which would otherwise have been lost. Furthermore, they became the almoners of the pious and the wealthy and distributed alms to the poor. Monks and nuns often cared for the sick and afflicted also. Many monasteries even engaged in the cultivation of the fields. In the later Middle Ages, however, when serious decline had set in, and piety had largely died away, slothfulness, iniquity and vice all too frequently characterized the monasteries and reformers urged their closure.

In the British Isles, one of the earliest and best-known of monks was The Venerable Bede who lived at Jarrow-on-Tyne, and is known as 'the father of English history'. So far as is known he never travelled outside the Kingdom of Northumbria. He lived from about the year 673 to the year 735, and was probably the most learned man of his age in England. He knew Latin, Greek and Hebrew, and was familiar with the classical literature of ancient Greece and Rome, and also with the writings of Ambrose, Augus-

tine and Jerome. He himself wrote *The Ecclesiastical History of the English Nation* which tells us most of the things we know about the church in England from Roman days until Bede's death.

The story of how Bede died as he was completing his translation of the Gospel of John has often been told. A boy-scribe wrote down the translation as Bede dictated it to him. 'One sentence is left unfinished', said the boy. 'Write quickly, then', said Bede. 'Now', said the boy, 'it is finished'. 'True' said the dying man, 'it is finished. Now take my head between your hands and raise me, that sitting I may call on my Father'. Then, as he breathed out the words, 'Glory be to the Father, and to the Son, and to the Holy Ghost', he passed away.

Mention must also be made of Columba, who belonged to an earlier period than Bede. He was born in Donegal, in the North of Ireland, during the sixth century. Leaving Ireland in 583 he settled in Iona, a small island off the south-west coast of Mull, from which he hoped to preach the gospel on the mainland of Scotland among the Picts. The monastery he established on Iona became a centre of learning and evangelization.

About the year 633 the King of Northumbria invited the monks of Iona to send preachers to his kingdom to teach the Christian faith. The first to be appointed met with no success, but the second was the monk Aidan whose work was well-rewarded. He established a monastery on Holy Island, very close to the Northumbrian coast. It was known as Lindisfarne, and from it gospel light beamed out over a large area of the country.

One great law of the kingdom of God is that he is greatest who serves best—'he that is chief, as he that doth serve' (Luke 22 : 26). How difficult a lesson this is for all the followers of the Master himself who said, 'I am among you as he that serveth'! A most homely and expressive application of this lesson was given by the Lord when he washed his disciples' feet just before the celebration of the last Passover, with which we associate the institution of the Lord's Supper.

In this chapter we shall note how, contrary to the example and the teaching of Christ, the spirit of selfishness and pride and seeking to be first began to show itself in the Church. Many Church officers wished to be regarded as great men, and finally the office of pope was recognized, the pope being the leader of leaders, the supreme 'father' in the Church. The word 'pope' is but another form of the Latin word 'papa', father.

The Christian Church of the New Testament knew only two permanent offices, that of elder and that of deacon. The elders were divided into two classes, those who served in preaching and teaching, and those who watched over the flock. The elders were also known as bishops, the word 'bishop' meaning overseer, supervisor, or superintendent. But after a time some bishops thought that they stood much higher in work and dignity than the other elders who, in their view, were an inferior class. This was entirely contrary to the words of the Lord, 'But be not ye called Rabbi, for one is your Master, even Christ, and all ye are brethren. And call no man your father upon earth, for one is your Father, which is in heaven'. (Matthew 23 : 8). This, of course, does not refer to the use of 'father' in family life, but to relationships in the Church of God.

If a first step is taken on the declining path, a second one soon follows, and a third, and a fourth, with increasing speed. Thus the Church went down the path of decline with astounding rapidity. Soon the bishops in large cities, who had charge of influential congregations, exalted themselves above those in the less important churches, and began to dictate to them. The bishops of Rome, Antioch, Jerusalem, Alexandria, Ephesus, Corinth and Constantinople considered themselves as possessors of the highest authority. They called themselves Patriarchs (ruling fathers), and exercised a supreme power over other churches. It is only natural that among these patriarchs a struggle for pre-eminence arose. For years there was a bitter contest, culminating in the strife between the patriarchs of Rome and Constantinople for the highest position in the Church at large.

Constantine the Great, for a variety of reasons, had transferred the seat of the Roman Empire from Rome to Byzantium on the Bosphorus, a narrow strait that separates Europe from Asia, and had re-named it after himself. After this no emperor resided in Italy, and as years passed, the bishops of Rome seized the opportunity to amass power to themselves. Claims began to be made that the apostle Peter had lived and laboured at Rome for some 25 years. The New Testament knows nothing of this. There is no evidence that Peter was ever bishop of Rome, or that he was in that city for any length of time, although it is probable that he died there. But Rome prevailed over Constantinople, at least in the West. The patriarch of Rome claimed the highest authority in the whole Church, and declared himself the successor of Peter. The name 'patriarch' was changed to 'pope' early in the sixth century. One important bishop of Rome was Innocent I (402 A.D.) who made it a rule that no important decisions must be taken

6

The rise of the Papacy

by churches in the West without the knowledge and approval of the bishop of Rome. Zosimus, the next bishop of Rome, went a step further and said that no-one had the right to question a decision taken by the Church of Rome. Leo I, bishop of Rome for 21 years from 440, a man of great ability, strengthened Rome's hold on all western churches. Another famous bishop was Gregory I (the Great), 590–604.

The emperors at Constantinople governed Italy by a man called the Exarch who lived at Ravenna, a port on the Adriatic Sea well to the north of Rome. But his rule was weak, and when the Lombards pressed into Italy from the North, it was Gregory who took chief responsibility for defending Italy against the enemy; so that in matters temporal, as well as in matters spiritual, he became very important. It was he, too, who appointed provincial bishops as his deputies or vicars, and as a mark of their authority he presented them with the pall or pallium, a coveted article of dress. Gregory also reformed church music so thoroughly that almost all the music of the Middle Ages was called by his name.

An event of great importance took place in the year 800, for Charlemagne (Charles the Great), king of the Franks, who ruled much of western and central Europe, was crowned Holy Roman Emperor by Pope Leo III in that year. The western half of the old Roman Empire had been overwhelmed by the barbarians of Northern and Eastern Europe in the fifth century. The revived Empire, very dissimilar from the old, lasted, at least in name, until it was ended by Napoleon 1000 years later. The coronation of Charles made the popes think that they had the power and right to enthrone and depose monarchs at their will.

Two famous documents, both of them forgeries, further assisted the growth of the power of the Papacy. The so-called Donation of Constantine claimed that the Emperor of that name, when he went to live at Byzantium, had granted the bishops of Rome very extensive rights in Italy, including the privilege of wearing a golden crown. Later, documents called Decretals, professing to be letters and decrees of bishops of Rome going back to apostolic days, exalted the powers of the Church in general, and assisted the bishops of Rome to establish their authority in both Church and State.

The rivalry between the popes of Rome and the patriarchs of Constantinople finally resulted in the separation of the eastern from the western part of the Church. There always had been a difference in language, the East using the Greek, the West the Latin language, but there also sprang up differences in doctrine. The most important of these concerned the Holy Spirit, for the Greek Church asserted that he proceeds from the Father alone, whereas the Roman Church rightly teaches that he proceeds from the Father and the Son. Attempts to prevent division failed, and in 1053 the breach between the two churches became final. Since that date the Roman Catholic Church and the Greek Orthodox Church have existed independently of each other. Yet in most respects they are very much alike.

But not only in the exaltation of Church dignitaries were the signs of apostasy visible; in the form and practice of public worship the difference between what we find in the New Testament and what was observable in the Churches of both East and West was amazingly great. Magnificent church buildings were erected, the Sophia church at Constantinople being the finest of them all. These buildings were lavishly furnished in harmony with a gold-covered throne for the

St Catharine's Monastery, Egypt. It occupied the lower slopes of Mt. Sinai and was built on the site of a fort built by the Emperor Justinian in 530 A.D. In the Middle Ages it probably held from 300 to 400 monks. In 1859 it was visited by Tischendorf, a German theologian, and to his amazement he discovered there in a good state of preservation a parchment manuscript of the Bible, the so-called Codex Sinaiticus, dating from the 4th Century A.D., and containing the New Testament and parts of the Old Testament. Later it came into the possession of the Czar of Russia. Finally, in 1933 it was purchased from the Soviet Government for £100,000 by the Trustees of the British Museum where it can now be seen.

bishop or patriarch. They were normally divided into three parts, one for the catechumens (candidates for baptism) or minors, one for the laity (the mass of the congregation, not holding church office), and a third for the bishop and lesser church officers. The bishop appeared in public worship in ornate and expensive apparel, consisting of a pure white garment or cloak, over which hung a brightly-coloured tunic or robe. Everything pointed to outward show and inward emptiness. It was a period of pomp and pride, of sounding brass and tinkling cymbals, without spiritual reality.

Another sign of apostasy was the praying to saints and the worship of images. It originated in the following way. The memory of the martyrs who had suffered cruel deaths under the Roman emperors lived vividly in the minds of the people. The stories of their lives and deaths were read and re-read. This might indeed have been very beneficial. But then the graves of these heroes were visited; memorial services were held; churches were named after them; and even in the days of Augustine people began to invoke deceased saints. And not only the martyrs but famous bishops were idolized. Mary, the mother of Jesus, 'blessed among women', was unduly exalted, and the time came when she was looked upon as 'the queen of heaven', and worship was paid to her. Images were placed in the churches. At first they were found only in the homes of the people, but in the 4th or 5th century they were also placed in the church-buildings.

All this was contrary to true Christian doctrine, for in the teaching of the New Testament we find nothing of superiors and inferiors in the Church of God. Peter himself tells us that all the people of the Lord belong to 'a royal priesthood, an holy nation, . . . that ye should show forth the praises of him who hath called you out of darkness into his marvellous light' (1 Peter 2 : 9). Preachers, elders, deacons, church members without office, are all alike; and although there are differences among them because of their work and service, these differences do not affect their oneness in Christ.

We shall explain later how popes claimed and exercised powers. which rendered them 'lords over God's heritage', not 'ensamples to the flock', but little if at all different from territorial kings and princes. Before the Middle Ages ended, popes and rival popes clashed with one another—at one time three popes hurled their curses at their rivals—and when the 16th-century Reformation got under way, we find the first English Protestant archbishop saying, as he was about to be burned at the stake, 'As for the Pope, I refuse him as Christ's enemy, and antichrist, with all his false doctrines'. A cogent word indeed!

7

Islam

When the Church went astray, denying him who had bought his people with his precious blood, the Lord sent trials and afflictions to correct his unfaithful children. The greatest trial of all was connected with the person named Mahomet or Muhammad, better known in western lands as Mohammed.

Mohammed was born in the year 570. His birthplace was Mecca in Arabia, and he claimed descent from the family of Hashem and the tribe of Koreish, to whom, according to their tradition, had been entrusted a famous Black Stone which was alleged to have fallen from heaven.

Mohammed was a sickly child who suffered from epilepsy and this undoubtedly influenced the whole course of his life. Being orphaned when a child he was taken into the home of his uncle, Abu Talib, whom he once accompanied on a business trip to Syria, where he visited Jewish and Christian settlements, and saw and heard many things which impressed him deeply. At the age of 25, he entered the service of Kadijah, a rich widow, and carried on her husband's trade. In this he prospered greatly and soon married Kadijah who was 14 years older than himself. In trading he became still better acquainted with

Jews and Christians and his own fellow-countrymen, and formed the conviction that a new religion was needed. He thought much on the unity of God and conceived the idea that he was a messenger of God, who had to warn his people that they could only escape condemnation by giving up their idols and turning to the worship of the one supreme God whom he knew as Allah.

In his 40th year Mohammed spent a whole month in solitude in a mountain cave near Mecca called the Cave of Hira. He said that while he was there he saw visions and received messages from heaven. He also claimed that the words were spoken to him, 'O Mahomet, of a truth thou art the prophet of God; fear not; I am his angel, Gabriel'.

He gave his new religion the name Islam, which means 'obedience' or 'surrender'. He acknowledged that Moses and Jesus were prophets, but claimed that he, Mohammed, was the greatest prophet of all. He said that Jesus was a holy man, but denied that he was the Son of God, for, he argued, God being one, could not have a Son. He also denied the virgin birth of Christ, his resurrection and ascension. Never has the Christian faith had a greater enemy than Mohammed.

When he came out of his solitude Mohammed boldly attacked the idolatry of his people, but they laughed at him and ridiculed his ideas. In the year 622 he and his followers were forced to flee for their lives from Mecca to a city called Medina. Their flight, called the Hegira, began on July 16, and that day in 622 became the first day in a new Mohammedan calendar. Eight years later Mohammed returned to Mecca in triumph and destroyed the 360 idols of that city. Over-awed by his success, the inhabitants now shouted,

'There is but one God, Allah, and Mohammed is his prophet'. No doubt his opposition to idolatry became one great means of winning the support of certain Christians called Iconoclasts or image-breakers, who detested idolatry but gave little

A burning Christian church, characteristic of the destruction introduced by Islam.

attention to other aspects of Mohammed's teaching.

The new religion taught that everything which occurs has been fore-ordained by an absolute fate, and that after death the evil will be punished and the good rewarded. Islam knows nothing of salvation by the sheer unmerited grace of God. Its chief tenets are (1) the confession of God, that there is no other God but Allah and that Mohammed is his prophet; (2) the offering up of prayer at stated intervals, five times each day, the suppliant facing Mecca; (3) the giving of alms; (4) fasting during the month of Ramadan, the 9th month of the Mohammedan year, from sunrise to sunset (as the Mohammedan year is lunar, Ramadan falls successively at all seasons of the solar year); (5) pilgrimage to Mecca at least once in a person's lifetime.

The teachings of Mohammed were collected in a book known as the Koran, many of his sayings having been first recorded on bones or palm-leaves. The name 'Koran' itself signifies 'rehearsal' or 'reading'. Mohammed claimed that its various sections came down to him from heaven during a period of 23 years. Its pages furnish Moslems with most of their prayers. Written in Arabic, and ranking as the greatest masterpiece of Arabic literature, Mohammedans claim that it was written originally on a huge table located near God's throne and called 'the preserved table'. The angel Gabriel is said to have been the agent who introduced Mohammed to divine secrets. The Koran itself claims that when reformation was required among men, God used prophets, the chief of whom were Moses and Jesus, but later Mohammed appeared as the greatest of them all. We can only add that the teachings of the Koran are very different from those of the Bible. Mohammedans flatly deny the Sonship and Deity of Jesus Christ and his resurrection from the dead. They pour scorn on his atoning death and hold to a way of salvation —if salvation it can be called—which completely excludes the unmerited grace of God. Indeed the teachings of the Bible and the Koran are poles apart.

In the Koran Mohammed allows his followers as many as four wives each, but he himself claimed to have received a revelation from God that he might take many more. He died in 632 at the age of 63, leaving no son, and only one daughter, Fatima. His body was buried in a grave dug under the bed on which he died.

Different prophets, said Mohammed, have been sent by God to illustrate his different attributes—Moses, his clemency and providence; Solomon, his wisdom, majesty and glory; Jesus Christ, his righteousness, omniscience and power. But I, the last of the prophets, he said, am sent with the sword. Let those who promulgate my faith enter into no argument or discussion, but slay all who refuse obedience to the law. Whoever fights for the true faith whether he fall or conquer, will assuredly receive a glorious reward, and be certain of entrance into paradise. Prayer, he added, leads half-way to God; fasting leads to the gateway to heaven; alms opens the door, but waging the holy war gives actual entrance into heaven.

After his conquest of Mecca, Mohammed sent messengers to emperors and kings demanding that they recognize him as 'the messenger of God', and he set about the task of propagating his religion by the sword. The leaders who succeeded him after 632 were known as Caliphs, and four of them founded the Mohammedan (or Moslem) Empire which ultimately stretched from India to the Atlantic Ocean and was even

larger than the Roman Empire. By the year 662 Syria, Egypt, Mesopotamia and Persia had been conquered. Caliph Omar took Jerusalem in the year 637 and built on the site of the old Jewish temple the mosque which has since been called by his name. It was also Omar who destroyed the world's most famous library, located at Alexandria in Egypt. He declared that no books other than the Koran were needed, and so he did away with some of the greatest literary treasures of the ancient world, including in all probability many early copies of the Christian Scriptures.

Thousands of Christian churches were destroyed or converted into mosques. Northern Africa, where once Augustine and Cyprian had laboured among flourishing Christian congregations, fell a prey to the Arabs, and Christianity was so completely destroyed there that hardly a trace of it remained. In 711 the Arab hosts entered Spain, crossing the Straits of Gibraltar, and not long afterwards they crossed the Pyrenees into France. But in the year 732, just 100

Mecca, in Saudi Arabia, which every Mohammedan is required to visit at least once in his life, and to walk around a cube-shaped building in the court of its Great Mosque. Mohammed claimed that Abraham had erected this building at the time when he arranged for his son Ishmael to be 'cast out'.

years after the death of Mohammed, the Franks, under their leader Charles Martel (the Hammer), met the Arabs on the plain of Tours, and defeated them in a six days' battle, causing them to withdraw behind the Pyrenees. But for over 700 years longer they remained in control of much of Spain. It was not until 1492 that Ferdinand of Aragon drove the Moors (as the Mohammedans were then called) out of Granada, their last stronghold in Spain, and caused them to return to Africa.

Thus we see what a chastising lash Mohammed and his followers became under the hand of the Almighty, and how the light of the gospel was extinguished in Northern Africa and large parts of Asia. Mohammedanism is the only world-religion established since the coming of our Lord Jesus Christ into the world, and it has remained the chief of all the enemies of Christianity. Converts from it to the Christian faith have invariably been few and hard-won.

It is not possible to say exactly when Christianity first came to Southern Britain. The story that Joseph of Arimathæa came to Glastonbury in Somerset and introduced the faith is mere legend without any historical foundation. It has even been asserted that the apostle Paul came to Britain, but of this there is not the slightest historical proof. It is certain, however, that long before the Roman armies left Britain in the year 410, the Christian faith had arrived. Probably the earliest Christians were Roman colonists or soldiers belonging to the army of occupation, and the natives of the land may have learned the faith from them. It must be remembered that the Romans were not in Britain for a brief time, but for three-and-a-half centuries.

Tertullian, writing early in the third century, tells us that Christians had by that time penetrated into parts of Britain which even the Romans had failed to reach. We know, too, that in the year 314 bishops from York, Lincoln and London attended a Church Council held in Gaul (France). Britain's first martyr was Alban, who lived in the city of Verulamium, later re-named St. Albans. He had given shelter to a preacher of the gospel and was so deeply impressed by the godliness of his guest that he himself became a believer, and was condemned to death. He refused to deny his Lord by casting a pinch of incense into the fire burning on a heathen altar, and said, 'I am a Christian and I worship the true God. These sacrifices of yours are made to demons who cannot answer your prayers'. On a mound outside the city, where later the Abbey of St. Albans was erected, he was executed.

The story of Christianity in Britain during these early centuries is very obscure. We have previously referred to a heresy[1] which troubled the church in the days of Augustine of North Africa, and we mention it again because its originator, Pelagius, was a British monk. Some account him of Irish descent, but it is more likely that he was a native of Wales, for his family name was Morgan, Pelagius being the name by which he became known to scholars when, about the year 400 he appeared in Rome (Morgan appears to mean 'sea-born'; the Latin 'pelagus' means 'ocean'). His erroneous teachings were condemned by the churches on the Continent of Europe, and in 429 two bishops, Germanus and Lupus, were sent from Gaul to oppose Pelagianism in Britain. Using St. Albans as their centre, they were successful in their mission, although a second visit was needed about 20 years later.

The two bishops are said to have been responsible for a famous victory obtained by the Britons over the northern Picts who had never been subdued by the Romans. The bishops, it seems, persuaded the Britons to arrange an ambush so as to take the Picts by surprise. Then, as they rushed out upon them, all were to shout (just as Joshua's men shouted at Jericho) 'Alleluia, Alleluia'. Unused to such tactics, the Picts fled in dismay. It was called the 'Alleluia Victory', and is thought to have taken place at Maes Garmon (the field of Germanus) in North-east Wales (430 A.D.).

Before taking up the story of the Christianization of England late in the 6th century, we turn to Ireland, Scotland and Wales, for the further work of the Church in these lands precedes the preaching of the gospel to the

[1] See pages 25–7.

8

The Christian Faith comes to the British Isles (1)

Jutes, Angles and Saxons after their conquest of England. Shortly before the Roman legions were recalled to Italy to resist barbaric invaders, there was born in North Britain, in the region of the Antonine Wall stretching from the Forth to the Clyde, a boy named Sucat ('warlike'). The year was 373 and the place of his birth Alcluyd, now Dumbarton ('the fort of the Britons'). In his youth he was captured in a raid by Picts and Scots and sold to a tribal leader in Antrim. His conversion to God soon followed. As a Christian he took the name of Patricius (Patrick) and was directed by the Lord to preach the gospel to the Irish people when he was about thirty years of age. He and his helpers laboured hard, 'sowing belief until he brought all the Ulstermen by the net of the gospel to the harbour of life'. Armagh later became the chief centre of his work. Church Histories sometimes speak as if the whole of Ireland was covered by his work, but it was the northern part that he chiefly benefited. The date of Patrick's death has caused much controversy, but it is probable that it occurred in the year 463, when he was 90 years of age.

Associated with Patrick as its author is a hymn entitled 'Breastplate' of which in the late 19th century, Mrs. C. F. Alexander supplied the popular version:

I bind unto myself today
The strong Name of the Trinity,
By invocation of the same,
The Three in One and One in Three.
I bind this day to me for ever,
By power of faith, Christ's incarnation:
His baptism in Jordan river,
His death on cross for my salvation.

His bursting from the spicèd tomb;
His riding up the heavenly way;

His coming at the day of doom:
I bind unto myself to-day;
Of God all nature hath creation,
Eternal Father, Spirit, Word;
Praise to the Lord of my salvation:
Salvation is of Christ the Lord.

Just as parts of Ireland were Christianized by a man born in Scotland, so were parts of Scotland Christianized by a man born in Ireland. Columba of Donegal was not the first of preachers in Scotland, for Bede tells us of the labours of Ninian during the early 5th century, chiefly among the northern Picts who lived in the area south of the Grampians; but of him little historical information is recorded.

Columba and his monastery in Iona were mentioned in an earlier chapter. Those who lived in the monastery were divided into three groups and allotted different duties. One group conducted the daily services of worship; a second received instruction so that they might become preachers of the Word; the members of the third group worked with their hands both indoors and out-of-doors. From Iona Columba undertook an important journey. It was his ambition to preach the gospel of Christ to the northern Picts, and in or about 565 he set out for Inverness where their king, named Brude, lived. Monkish histories record many so-called miracles, and we are told that on this occasion the gates of Brude's palace opened to Columba of their own accord, whereupon the astonished king professed conversion. It is clear that, whatever else happened or did not happen, Columba's mission met with success. Certainly Scotland benefited greatly. Iona became Scotland's 'Canterbury' and her kings from this time onwards were usually buried there.

A contemporary of Columba was Kentigern,

St. Asaph, North Wales: the cathedral in the background.

but he is much better known by his other name, Mungo. We have very little reliable information about him, but it is certain that Glasgow was his chief centre of witness; its cathedral is named after him.

One other name must be recorded, that of Cuthbert who belonged to Lothian, that is to say, the area between Edinburgh and Berwick-on-Tweed. As a boy he kept sheep near Melrose. Later he became a monk and also bishop of Lindisfarne. By his efforts the gospel was made known throughout Lothian. Later in his life his labours extended as far westwards as Carlisle, but the desires of his heart were for a strict monastic life. In consequence he made for himself a cell on one of the Farne Islands, near Bamborough, and died there in the year 687.

As for the Christian Faith in Wales, little can be profitably said. Such records as survive from ancient days are so full of monkish legends that no reliance can be placed on them. Mention, however, can be made of David, the traditional date of whose death is 601. He was probably born in Ceredigion, which in later centuries became Cardiganshire. In his youth he became a monk and soon enjoyed a great reputation. He may have made the most westerly part of Pembrokeshire his place of settlement, for it is there that the Cathedral Church of St. David is located. One incident will illustrate the type of story associated with his name. In connection with the Pelagian heresy a vast company of bishops, presbyters,

Ruins of the Bishop's Palace at
St. David's, Pembrokeshire
(*from a drawing by H.
Gastineau*).

abbots, kings and princes assembled at Brefi
(later called Llanddewi Brefi) to denounce the
heresy. Preaching to the vast throng was essential, but no-one could be found able to attempt
the task. David, who was not present, was sent
for, and he consented to attend. A handkerchief
was placed beneath his feet by a boy whom he
had restored to life on his journey to Brefi. At once
the ground rose under him and became a hill;
from its summit David was able to address the
multitude. Certainly we can place no reliance on
monkish 'lives of the saints'. In North Wales a
chief centre was Llanelwy (the church on the
Elwy), otherwise St. Asaph. Kentigern of Glasgow is said to have visited North Wales and to
have instituted his disciple, Asaph, as bishop of
the area, and also as abbot of a very large
monastery.

When the heathen Angles, Jutes and Saxons invaded Britain in the fifth century and conquered large parts of it, the Britons took refuge in the mountainous west—Cornwall (called West Wales), Wales (called North Wales), and Cumbria—but they apparently took no steps to preach the gospel to their conquerors. The evangelization of Angle-land—Kent, Wessex, Mercia, Northumbria, and other areas—came from two different directions. Monks, and Aidan in particular, came from Iona into Bernicia, the northern part of the kingdom of Northumbria, and met with much success. The Celtic Church to which they belonged was independent of Rome.

Another group of preachers, led by a Benedictine monk, named Augustine, was sent to England in 597 by Pope Gregory I who had seen several fair-haired boys on sale as slaves in one of Rome's market-places. He pitied their ignorance of the Christian faith and inquired to what nation they belonged. 'They are Angles', he was told. 'Not Angles, but angels', he replied as he looked into their faces. 'But to which province in Angle-land do they belong?' he next inquired. 'To Deira', he was informed. 'Well, then, we must pluck them *de ira* (from the wrath of God)' was his reply. 'And who rules Deira?' he next asked. 'Their king is Alla' was the reply. 'Then', said Gregory, 'Alla's people must sing Alleluia in the land of Alla'. When he became Pope he remembered the slave-boys and sent Augustine to preach the Christian faith in England.

Naturally the Roman missionaries, forty in all, set foot first in Kent, where Ethelbert was king. It so happened that the latter had previously married Bertha, the Christian daughter of a Frankish king living in Paris. She had been permitted by her husband to carry on Christian worship in the ruined church of St. Martin, outside Canterbury, which survived from Roman times. Augustine was well received, and very soon many professed belief in Christ. Canterbury now became the Christian centre, and before long Augustine was appointed 'bishop of the English' by Pope Gregory.

Before his death in 604 Augustine decided to get into touch with the Christians who had been driven into Wales by the Angles and Saxons. He wanted them to submit to the traditions and customs of his own church, for in certain ways the Celtic church in Wales followed traditions of which he disapproved. It was agreed that the place of meeting should be a spot called in Bede's time Augustine's Oak, now identified with Aust on the River Severn. Before the arrival of the Kentish monks the Welsh leaders had come to an agreement that if Augustine rose from his seat to greet them on equal terms as they approached him, they would give consideration to what he had to say, but if he kept to his seat it would show that he regarded the Roman Church as superior to the Celtic Church, in which case they would not show friendliness. In other words, they agreed to take Augustine's behaviour as a sign of his pride or his humility. In the event Augustine remained seated and this ruined the conference from the start. Nothing came of it.

About the time the conference with the Welsh was held the king ruling over a part of Northern England was Edwin, whose father had ruled over Deira. Deira and Bernicia together formed the larger unit of Northumbria. Unhappily the ruler of Bernicia had wrongfully taken possession of Deira. But Edwin bestirred himself, recaptured Deira, and extended his conquests as far north as Edinburgh, a city which ever afterwards commemorated his name. Edwin also extended his

9

The Christian Faith comes to the British Isles (2)

The Venerable Bede dictating his translation of the Gospel of John shortly before his death in 735 at the age of sixty-two. 'Bede loved to meditate and make notes on the Scriptures,' usually in a stone hut where he was free from interruption.

conquests into south Lancashire, and even as far as Chester, Anglesey and the Isle of Man. Indeed, before he died, he ruled over almost all parts of England except Kent.

But our chief interest in Edwin lies in his marriage and his subsequent conversion to Christianity. Kent had become a Christian kingdom, as we have seen. Edwin, while still a pagan, asked Ethelburh, the daughter of the king converted to Christianity during Augustine's mission, to marry him. Naturally there were difficul-

ties, for Christians were forbidden by Scripture to marry non-Christians, and the king of Kent rightly objected. But ultimately consent was given when Edwin made two promises; first, the bride and her attendants were to have full liberty to practise Christianity; second, Edwin would give serious consideration to the gospel of Christ.

Ethelburh was accompanied to Northumbria by a Roman monk, Paulinus of Canterbury, and before long Edwin called his counsellors together —the king's council was known as the Witan—

and Paulinus preached to them. Almost all that we know of the events of the period is derived from Bede's *Ecclesiastical History*, formerly mentioned. He tells us that Coifi, the organizer of the old pagan worship, spoke in favour of the acceptance of Christianity. But probably a much deeper impression was made upon the listeners by one of the king's chief nobles. We give Bede's own account of his speech:

O king, the present life of man, it seems to me, can be compared to the swift flying of a sparrow across the hall in which you sit at supper during the winter, together with your captains and ministers. A good fire blazes in our midst, while the storms of rain and snow are heard and felt around. As we thus sit, a sparrow, I say, comes flying in at one opening and almost at once it flies out at another. While the bird is within it is sheltered from storm and rain. But very quickly, after this time of "fair weather", it vanishes out of our sight into the dark winter from which it had come. Similarly this life of man appears for a short space of time, but of what went before, or what is to follow, we are utterly ignorant. If, however, this new teaching can give us certainty, it is but right that we should receive and follow it.

The outcome, says Bede, was that 'all that were fore-ordained to eternal life believed' and were baptized. The baptisms took place on Easter Day, 12th April, 627, in a wooden church building which Edwin had erected at York. Coifi immediately began the work of destroying the altars and idols which belonged to pagan worship, and as he did so he said, 'Who can more properly than myself destroy those things which I worshipped through ignorance, for an example to all others, through the wisdom which has been given me by the true God?' Paulinus remained for six years preaching the gospel of Christ.

In this way Deira, the southern part of Northumbria, agreed to accept the teaching from Canterbury, and so from Rome. But Bernicia, the northern part of the kingdom, had already accepted the teaching of Aidan of Lindisfarne, and so of Iona, and the Celtic and Roman Churches were by no means in full agreement. What was to be done?

In the year 664, Oswy, then king of Northumbria, called a Conference or Synod at Whitby. He himself had been brought up in the Celtic tradition, but he was prepared to listen to Wilfred, the abbot of Ripon, who represented Canterbury. On the Celtic side the chief speaker was Colman of Lindisfarne, the successor of Aidan. Also present was Hilda, Abbess of Whitby, a lady of royal blood. Wilfred's arguments seemed to the king to be more forceful than those of Colman, and after much debate the latter withdrew, shortly afterwards leaving Lindisfarne with thirty of his monks and returning to his home in Ireland. It was not long before most of England accepted the views of the Roman Church.

In 668 Theodore of Tarsus, a Greek monk, was made Archbishop of Canterbury by the Pope. Very soon he invited all English bishops to a Council held at Hertford, the first Council of the whole Church in England, and it was decided to divide the country into dioceses, each having its own bishop. From Rome there also came to England John, the 'arch-chanter', to teach the rude Anglo-Saxons how to sing the praises of God, and how to appreciate Church music. It was not long before missionaries began to leave England for work on the Continent of Europe, and two of these will be mentioned in our next chapter.

Two other names—Caedmon and Alfred—from the Anglo-Saxon period are worthy of mention. Bede's *Ecclesiastical History*, devotes a chapter to Caedmon who was a farm labourer of Northumbria. In his days it was customary for all persons to sing in turn as the harp was passed around their halls at supper. This Caedmon could never do, so he always retired from the company at the first opportunity. One night, however, after he had laid down to sleep in the stable where he was taking care of the horses, he had a vision; but let Bede himself take up the story:

A person appeared to Caedmon in his sleep, and greeting him by name, said, 'Caedmon, sing some song to me'. 'I cannot sing' he replied 'and that was the reason why I left the hall'. The other answered, 'However, you shall sing'. 'What shall I sing?', said Caedmon. 'Sing the beginning of created beings', said the visitor. Caedmon at once began to sing verses to the praise of the Creator, and the deeds of the Father of glory. When he awoke from sleep he remembered all that he had sung in his dream, and added much more to it. Soon he was taken to the abbess Hilda of Whitby and asked to tell her his dream. He was also given passages of Scripture, both historical and doctrinal, and he very quickly put them into excellent verse. The abbess and the learned men of the kingdom now believed that heavenly grace had been conferred on Caedmon by the Lord.

Our second name—that of Alfred, King of Wessex (West Saxons) 871–899—is memorable because of the efforts Alfred made to give Christian education to those over whom he ruled. He invited learned men from the Continent of Europe to assist him in establishing schools and it was his special endeavour to instruct his people in the elements of the Christian faith. He himself engaged in the work of translation. Bede's *History*, originally written in Latin, he translated into Anglo-Saxon. He also translated many of the Psalms. A Preface which he wrote for one of the books he translated includes the following words:

These are the waters which the Lord of hosts promised for our comfort, and his will is that these ever-living waters should flow into all the world from all who truly believe in him; and their wellspring is the Holy Spirit.

To encourage the clergy of England in the performance of their duties Alfred presented the chief of them with copies of Pope Gregory's *Pastoral Care*. It taught the clergy how to minister to the needs of the souls of men. Asser, a learned Welshman whom Alfred kept at his court, tells us that the king himself was barely able to read English and Latin manuscripts until he was 38 years of age. In consequence he repeatedly asked Asser to copy out texts of Scripture for him into his pocket-book.

Alfred also revised the laws made by earlier kings and supplied them with a preface in which he included a part of the law of Moses as found in Exodus chapters 20 to 28. He also informed his judges that Christ came into the world not to destroy but to fulfil the law of God. They must therefore show mercy and mild-heartedness, and teach men to do to others that which they would have men do to them.

King Alfred well deserved his title of 'the Great'.

Charlemagne (768–814). King of the Franks and first mediaeval Roman Emperor, crowned by the Pope at Rome in 800. He promoted a revival of learning at Aachen, one of his capital cities, and thereby established 'the common culture of the West'. His ancient biographer wrote of him: 'He is delighted with the books of St. Augustine, especially with those entitled *Of the City of God.*' His influence on both Church and State was undoubtedly profound.

10

Early Missionaries in Europe

Under the rule of the Roman emperor who followed Constantine, the countries in Europe along the River Rhine and the River Danube were evangelized, but much of the work had to be repeated in later years.

One of the famous missionaries of the seventh and eighth centuries was Willibrord, born in Northumbria in 658, a tall, dignified man, grave but cheerful. When only seven years old he had been sent by his parents to the monastery at Ripon. At the age of twenty, he went over to Ireland to a college of which Egbert was the head. Eleven years later he wanted to lead a band of missionaries into Europe and Egbert gave him leave. He had obtained the consent of the Pope to labour among the Frisians, a name applied to all the Dutch tribes of those days. Probably Frisia was much larger than present-day Holland, for during the long centuries much territory has been engulfed by the sea. It is not without good reason that Frisian lands have been called The Low Countries.

In due course Willibrord arrived at Utrecht, where in 631 the first Christian church had been built, and did not spare himself in his efforts to spread the knowledge of the gospel throughout the land. In fact he may be called 'the apostle of the Dutch'. On one occasion he arrived in Zeeland, a part of Frisia, and saw several people kneeling before a stone idol. Immediately he felt as the apostle Paul felt when, in Athens, he saw men 'wholly given to idolatry'. Willibrord placed himself before the clumsy image. The people were amazed. What business had the stranger there? Beginning to preach, he rebuked the people for their foolishness. 'Your gods', said he, 'have eyes but they see not, and ears but they hear not. And now I shall show you that I am right'. Then, taking up a club, he smashed the idol to pieces. The crowd fled in terror, but a priest of the pagan worship, standing near and fearing that he would be robbed of his authority and influence, drew a sword and bruised Willibrord's head. Happily, the wound was not serious, and the missionary carried on fearlessly with his work.

During his travels he came to a village named Heilo in the north of the country. There had been a prolonged drought and nowhere was there water to be had. Exhausted, the little band of gospel workers sat down, their thirst all but unbearable. Willibrord knelt in prayer, asking God for his help. Then he took a spade and began to dig. His helpers joined him and soon they found a spring of cool fresh water. To this very day the spring, known as 'Willibrord's put' can be seen at Heilo. After fifty years of faithful labour in the gospel, Willibrord died and was buried at Echternach in Luxembourg.

Another worker from England, accounted greater than Willibrord, and about 20 years younger than he, was soon at work. His name was Winfred, better known as Boniface, and he has been termed 'the apostle of Germany'. He was born at Crediton in the English county of Devon in the year 680. By his own desire he was brought up in a monastery at Exeter, and quite early in life he resolved to become a missionary. In 716 he went to join the aged Willibrord in Frisia, but there was war in the land and as it seemed impossible to engage in missionary work he returned to England. Shortly, however, he went to Rome and received a commission from the Pope to labour among the heathen tribes of Germany. He preached in Saxony, Bavaria, Thuringia, and Hesse, and in 745 he was appointed Archbishop of Mainz.

While in Hesse he came near the city of Geismar, where he found a great oak sacred to

Thor, the German god of thunder. The people regarded this oak with feelings of awe and deepest reverence. It was under its shadow that they met to worship. In vain Boniface preached to them on the vanity of idols; finally he decided to teach them an object-lesson. With some of his helpers he approached the tree with a large axe. The pagan people stood around in great excitement and consternation, and when the first blow fell on the sacred tree they expected that Thor would strike Boniface dead. Instead, an ancient story runs that a sudden gust of powerful wind rent the tree into four parts, which Boniface cut up into planks for the building of a church. The people's faith in the power of the dreaded idol vanished away, and no longer could they believe in the teachings of their priests. With redoubled efforts Boniface and his friends continued to preach to them, and many accepted the gospel of the Lord Jesus Christ. A monastery was built at Fulda and before Boniface died 400 monks were working there.

In the year 754 Boniface went for a second time to Frisia, where his efforts to preach the gospel met with great success. But the enemies of the Christian faith were wide awake and knowing that near the village of Murmerwoude many converts were to be baptized, they marched to the spot early in the morning of the appointed day and began to make trouble. The Christians wanted to defend their beloved leader and prepared to fight. But Boniface admonished them, saying, 'My children, do not fight; let us follow the example of our Lord in Gethsemane. We shall soon see him in his glory. I have longed to see him, and to be with him. Let us pray'. They all knelt in prayer, but as they did so, the mob, yelling and shrieking passionately, fell upon them and killed Boniface and 51 of his companions.

Close to Frisia is Flanders, and a missionary who brought the gospel to that area was Eligius, called by the French (for he was a Frenchman) St. Eloy. By trade he was a goldsmith and in that craft he displayed remarkable skill. The king of France gave him an order for a gold chair, adorned with precious stones, and Eligius performed the work so well that he was generally recognized as perhaps the most skilful goldsmith of his time. He became a very rich man, but by the grace of God he learned to value the treasures of heaven far above the fleeting riches of this world. Eligius used much of his wealth to liberate people who had been enslaved as prisoners of war. He ransomed many of them at great cost, and then allowed them to return to their home and country.

But Eligius wanted to do more. In his heart was the longing not only to free men from the chains of earthly prisons; he wished to deliver their souls from the powers of sin in which Satan held them. He wanted to tell those who were spiritually bound with fetters how they might be freed by the love of a Saviour who had overpowered Satan. Eligius' desire was fulfilled. He was made a bishop and soon he set out as a missionary to the heathen of Flanders and the Low Countries. During 18 years he laboured among them with great zeal and consecration. He died in the year 659 at the age of seventy.

Almost a century and a half after Elisius died, Ansgar (or Anskar), known as 'The Apostle of the North' was born in northern France. When a boy of five he entered a Benedictine monastery and in due course became a monk. But he had a strong missionary zeal, and when the opportunity came he gladly went to Denmark with the hope of introducing the gospel there. It so happened that Harold, king of Denmark, had been driven from his throne, and had sought refuge at the court of Louis I (the Pious), king of the Franks. While resident with Louis he heard and believed the gospel, and was baptized. When able to return to Denmark he wished to take Christian preachers with him and one of them was Ansgar, who readily responded to the call with the words, 'Send me, Lord'. With his own money Ansgar bought several Danish youths, who were slaves, in order to educate them to labour among their own countrymen. At Hedeby he was able to build a small wooden church. But when king Harold was again expelled from Denmark, Ansgar also was compelled to leave the country and he returned to his own land.

Before long a request for help was received from Bjorn, king of Sweden, so Ansgar went there. But he found it necessary to establish a centre on the mainland of the European Continent from which work in Scandinavia could be carried on, and in 831 he became archbishop of Hamburg. Gospel work was now carried on with vigour, but the difficulties were many. It was a time when the Vikings or Norsemen were active in raiding, plundering, and burning the coastal cities of northern Europe and of the West, and in 840 they destroyed all religious buildings in Hamburg, Ansgar himself narrowly escaping with his life.

The king of Sweden still called for gospel workers, and Ansgar was again ready to go. Two helpers joined him, but while crossing the Baltic Sea, the vessel was plundered by pirates, and the Christians arrived empty-handed at the king's residence. He received them kindly, and soon the first Christian church in Sweden was built. But opposition was fierce, and progress was slow. Trouble was also caused by the heathen people of Denmark. The king of Sweden finally placed the question whether or not Christianity should be preached, before an assembly of the people. At a crisis in the deliberations an old Swede arose and with strong conviction said that the God of the Christians was stronger than Thor. This decided the matter and the missionaries were permitted to preach without being molested. Ansgar died in the year 865.

How is it possible, we may ask, that these Christian workers did not give up in despair? The secret is that they did not work with an eye to success, and much less for personal gain or glory, but first and last and always they complied with the command of the Lord, 'Go ye into all the world, and preach the gospel to every creature' (Mark 16 : 15).

Pope and Emperor

The Pope represented the spiritual power as head of the Church, and the emperor the temporal power as head of the Empire. Different theories were held about the relation existing between these two powers. One was that each was independently commissioned by God, the Pope to rule the souls of men, the Emperor to rule their bodies. Neither was set above the other, but the two were to co-operate and help each other.

Another theory was that the emperor was superior to the pope in secular affairs; and a third, the one held by the papal party, maintained that the relation of the two powers as ordained by God included the subordination of temporal to spiritual authority, even in civil affairs. The pope and his supporters argued that as God had set in the heavens two lights, the sun and the moon, so also had he established on earth two powers, the spiritual and the temporal. But as the moon is inferior to the sun, and receives its light from the sun, so the emperor is inferior to the pope, and receives all power from him. It was never forgotten that a pope had crowned the emperor Charlemagne in Rome in the year 800.

The strife was mainly caused by the unlimited ambition of the pope for power. For centuries this sinful strife threw Europe into political disorder and dragged the Church through the mire of darkest crimes. One pope followed another in rapid succession, some being deposed, others cast into prison, and still others murdered.

Pope John XII (955–963) was charged by a Roman Synod with almost every crime of which depraved human nature is capable. He was said to have drunk to the devil's health, and to have invoked the help of heathen gods and various demons as he threw dice. All in the Synod agreed that he was a monster of iniquity. To them John replied, 'If you wish to set up another pope, by Almighty God I excommunicate you, so that you will not have power to perform mass or to ordain anyone'. Pope Boniface VII, who put his predecessor to death by strangulation in 974, is described by a Synod as 'a papal monster, who in his abject depravity exceeds all mortals'. Now if this was said of popes, what was the condition of the lesser clergy? 'Evil communications corrupt good manners'.

In 1073 Hildebrand, the son of an Italian carpenter, became pope. He was a man of masterful spirit and inexhaustible energy, and he wanted to remodel the Church and the Christian world. His aim was to establish the supremacy of the pope over the Church, and the supremacy of the Church over the State. To accomplish his purpose he abolished simony and the right of the clergy to marry, and, above all, he determined to settle the disputed question of investiture.

Simony, named after Simon the magician of whom we read in Acts 8, is the buying and selling for money of offices in the Church. In those days there were ministers (known unscripturally as 'priests') who could neither read nor write, because without any preparation their ordination to office had been bought with money.

Investiture was concerned with the claim of kings and rulers to appoint bishops and abbots. Hildebrand asserted that any person holding office in the church committed sin if he received that office from the hands of a lay-man, that is, a man not ordained to church office. On the other hand kings and rulers could not overlook the fact that very extensive estates belonged to the Church—in France and Germany half of the land and wealth was in the hands of bishops and abbots—and the right to tax and to require military aid would pass from the State if temporal princes failed to assert their rights over land by means of investiture. The question to be resolved was whether bishops and abbots were servants of the Church or of the king.

As soon as Hildebrand, with the title of Gregory VII, ascended the papal throne he began to enforce his reformations, and as a result came into conflict with the Holy Roman Emperor, Henry IV, who lived in Germany, and who frequently sold ecclesiastical positions or appointed his favourites to them. The pope pronounced his ban against five privy councillors of the Emperor as guilty of simony, which meant that they were expelled from the Church. This naturally enraged the Emperor. The Pope knew however, that Henry had many enemies and this encouraged him to take a firm stand for what he regarded as his rights.

When the papal decrees were disregarded Gregory summoned Henry to Rome; but instead of waiting on the Pope, Henry, in turn, pronounced the Pope deposed. Gregory replied in kind by excommunicating Henry and declaring *him* deposed. At the same time he pronounced the sentence of interdict against his subjects; that is to say, all Church services and practices were to cease. But the fight between the two men went on; time would tell who would prove the stronger. The spiritual weapons of the Church were keen-edged. A person excommunicated was cut off from all relations with his fellow men. Anyone showing him the least kindness or favour, giving him food or shelter, incurred the wrath of the Church. Living, he was to be shunned as the plague, and dead he was to be buried like a beast.

As for the interdict, regions under the ban were, in a sense, excommunicated too. Churches were closed; no bell could be tolled; no marriage could be celebrated; all church services came to an end; no burial ceremony could be performed.

No wonder, then, that the lesser rulers of Germany, although subject to the Emperor, with whom they had long been dissatisfied, now required him to give way to the Pope. Henry became alarmed. His authority seemed to be slipping out of his hands, and his kingdom on the point of going to pieces. Finally he decided that there was only one thing to do; he must submit to Gregory, accept his requirements, humbly sue for pardon, and ask for reinstatement in the favour of the Church.

What followed is one of the most notable events in the history of Europe. With his wife and child Henry set out in midwinter to cross the Alps, braving all the discomforts of wind and weather, to present himself at the feet of the Pope. He found Gregory at Canossa, a stronghold of Countess Matilda of Tuscany. But the Pope refused to admit him to his presence. He intended to humble the Emperor to the dust. In the cold and snow of winter, and on three successive days, Henry stood with bare feet and the white garment of a penitent, in the snow of the courtyard of the castle, waiting for the Pope to grant him permission to kneel at his feet and ask forgiveness. On the fourth day the Pope consented to receive him, and the sentence of excommunication and the interdict were removed.

But the reconciliation was not worth much on either side; it was neither lasting nor sincere. There was a vast difference between the spirit of the two men on the one hand and the meekness and lowliness of heart of the Lord Jesus Christ on the other. The so-called representative of Christ, which the Pope claimed to be, was filled with pride and arrogance, while the penitent Emperor cherished hatred and revenge in his

Penance of Henry IV at the gate of Canossa.

heart. Henry descended upon Rome with an army seven years later and finally succeeded in driving Gregory VII into exile at Salerno, a little to the south of Naples, where he died in 1085 with the claim on his lips, 'I have loved justice and hated iniquity; therefore I die in exile'.

Even then the quarrel between Church and State did not end; indeed it continued for centuries. Henry was excommunicated a second time. In 1106 he died, dethroned by an unnatural son whom the enmity of another Pope had raised in rebellion against him.

12

The Crusades

By European Christians Palestine was always regarded as the Holy Land and Jerusalem as the Holy City. The emperor Constantine built a costly church in Jerusalem, and his mother Helena acted similarly in Bethlehem and on the Mount of Olives. From time to time pilgrimages to the Holy Land took place. When the Mohammedans captured Palestine and took possession of Jerusalem pilgrims were still allowed to visit the Land, but certain restrictions were to be observed; there were to be no processions, nor any public demonstrations in favour of Christianity, nor were any more churches to be built.

In the 11th century, however, a fierce pagan race known as the Seljuk Turks, who came from the Caucasus region, conquered the Holy Land. There they were persuaded to become followers of Mohammed and under their rule Christian pilgrims were subjected to harsh treatment and severe oppression. A cry went up from Christendom that the Turks should be dislodged by force. Pope Gregory VII himself hoped to raise an army and attack the Turks, but his quarrels with the Emperor Henry IV prevented the carrying out of his plans. In any case, however, the Popes thought it would be a good thing to persuade men of the West to turn eastwards and fight the Turks, instead of fighting one another, as they were so prone to do. Attempts had earlier been made to introduce what was called The Truce of God in Christendom, to prevent wars between Christians, but it had not been at all successful.

Then came Peter the Hermit who, having been on pilgrimage to Palestine and having experienced cruel treatment from the Turks, decided to use all his influence to stir up Christians against them. He first went to see the Pope, Urban II, who sympathized with his plans and gave him official sanction to preach a crusade (a war on behalf of the Cross) against the oppressors of the pilgrims. Peter, on his donkey, then went from city to city throughout Italy and France, and wherever he appeared the people were deeply moved. Enthusiasm for a 'holy war' was stirred up everywhere. Taking advantage of this, Urban proceeded to call a Church Council at Clermont in Southern France. He there made a fiery appeal to all Christians to engage in war under the standard of the Cross. With one voice the people exclaimed, 'It is the will of God; it is the will of God'.

Thousands enlisted in the cause, and had a red cross affixed to their right shoulder as a badge of honour. Princes and dukes, knights and squires, and even women and children were among them. To all who participated in the enterprise the pope promised the forgiveness of sins. Bishops in their dioceses everywhere preached the crusade and before many weeks had passed Christendom was stirred to its depths. Thus began a movement which lasted for two centuries and which cost Europe nearly five million lives. In the end, every hope and purpose cherished by the crusaders was frustrated. The whole movement was based on sentiment and superstition, not upon faith.

We cannot here describe the crusades in detail, or even outline, and shall only mention several of the outstanding events. Large numbers joined the First Crusade, and advanced towards Constantinople in several companies. It was their intention to cross the Bosphorus into Asia, and to march southwards into Palestine, Peter the Hermit leading one of the companies. But most of those who first set out were untrained and unprepared for warfare. The Turks met them at Nicea, the place at which Constantine had held a great Church Council in the year 325, and killed most of them. But the early groups were followed later by men trained in warfare, who laid siege to Nicea and captured it. They then marched into Syria and after a difficult siege captured Antioch. Ultimately, two years after the capture of Nicea, they succeeded in taking Jerusalem. Duke Godfrey of Bouillon was offered the title of king, but he refused to accept it. The date was July, 1099. A horrible massacre followed the capture of the city in which all the Turks were killed, including the women and children. Not till the gruesome act had been accomplished did the Christians realize how merciless they had been. For nearly 50 years the new kingdom remained intact, but it was under constant threat by Turkish forces.

In 1147, Bernard of Clairvaux, perhaps the most famous monk of his time and the writer of Christian hymns, preached a second crusade to support the kingdom of Jerusalem. As a result two enormous armies, one led by the King of France and another by the Emperor of Germany marched for the Holy Land. Again it took the route through Constantinople, capital of the Eastern Roman Empire, but it met with severe reverses in Asia Minor, and after failing to take Damascus, the capital of Syria, the remnants of the original armies returned home again. Encouraged by their successes, the Mohammedans, now led by the famous leader known as Saladin, laid siege to Jerusalem and captured it in the year 1187.

Western Europe was ablaze with indignation, and three kings determined to take action— Frederick Barbarossa, Emperor of Germany, Philip Augustus, King of France, and Richard Coeur-de-Lion, King of England. The Third Crusade had begun. The German Emperor travelled overland but was drowned as he was

crossing a river in Asia Minor; Philip and Richard went by sea. They laid siege to Acre, on the coast of Palestine, but ill-health struck them and their forces. Worse still, the two leaders quarrelled;

The storming of Antioch, June 3rd, 1098.

Philip returned to France; Richard remained to carry on alone. He reached Emmaus, only some seven miles from Jerusalem, but realizing that he could not possibly capture the Holy City, he came to terms with Saladin, whereby Christian pilgrims were no longer to be molested or taxed when they visited Jerusalem, and then took ship for England.

Next came what is known as The Children's Crusade. Stephen, a French boy, claimed that Christ had appeared to him and that what the kings and knights of Christendom had failed to do, children would accomplish by the Lord's promised help. He said that, if an army of children assembled in a southern port of France, the sea would divide before them, as it had done when the Israelites crossed the Red Sea, and thus make possible their arrival in the Holy Land. Another boy in Germany, named Nicholas, spread the news, and thousands of children, the average age being about twelve, marched up the Rhine valley to join the French boys. Some girls, too, joined the crusade. As they travelled they sang:

> Fair are the meadows,
> Fairer still the woodlands,
> Robed in the pleasant garb of spring;
> Jesus is fairer, Jesus is purer,
> He makes the grieving heart to sing.

Many of the marchers died in crossing the snowy Alps, but a considerable number finally reached the sea, as also did the French marchers. But the sea did not divide before them. Many returned home, but some 5,000 were taken on board seven merchant ships, with the promise of conveyance to Palestine. Two of the ships struck rocks and sank; the owners of the other five proved to be slave-dealers who sold the children to Mohammedans, and Europe saw them no more.

Sixth and Seventh crusades were promoted by the French king known as St. Louis, in the 13th century. The Sixth ended dismally. Louis was captured by the Sultan of Egypt and only obtained his liberty by paying a heavy ransom. In the Seventh, he was joined by Prince Edward of England, who later became King Edward I. On this occasion Louis went to Tunis in the hope of seeing its ruler baptized as a Christian, but in Tunis he died. Edward soon returned to England, nothing having been accomplished.

Christendom seemed unable to realize that the cause of Christ is not to be promoted by the use of the world's weapons. The weapons of our warfare, said the apostle Paul, are not carnal [swords made of steel], but mighty through God to the throwing down of strongholds (2 Cor. 10 : 4). Carnal weapons can never accomplish spiritual work. 'If my kingdom were of this world', said Jesus, 'then would my servants fight, but my kingdom does not come in that way' (John 18 : 36).

13

The Papacy at its Height

The aim of Pope Gregory VII (Hildebrand) to extend the power of the popes over the secular as well as the ecclesiastical sphere of life was shared by his successors, of whom the most eminent were Alexander III (1159-81) and Innocent III (1198–1216). Under them the power of the papacy was at its height.

We have already seen how Gregory VII humiliated the Emperor Henry IV at Canossa. The next great triumph of this kind for the Pope was achieved at the expense of the Emperor Frederick Barbarossa (who died during the Third Crusade).

Frederick had several tussles with occupants of the papal throne. When he had first visited Rome he had refused to hold the Pope's stirrup, but was compelled to do so—a symbolic act of courtesy—on threat of the Pope's refusal of the imperial crown. Later, the Pope wished to take supreme control in Rome, in matters civil as well as ecclesiastical. Frederick refused to agree and said, 'Since by the appointment of God I both am called and am Roman Emperor, in nothing but name shall I appear to be ruler if the control of the city of Rome be wrested from my hands'. In 1159, when Pope Hadrian IV died, Frederick proposed to call a general Council of the Church to appoint his successor, but the plan failed. After this there were twenty years of dispute between Frederick and Pope Alexander III. To bring the two together, the Doge of Venice offered to act as mediator. A meeting took place in the porch of St. Mark's Cathedral, Venice, and 'three slabs of red marble point out the spot where Frederick knelt in sudden awe, and the Pope with tears of joy raised him and gave the kiss of peace. A later legend [of which there is no historical proof] tells how the pontiff [Pope] set his foot on the neck of the prostrate King, with the words, "The young lion and the dragon shalt thou trample under feet" '.[1]

During the reign of Henry II in England, the struggle between the King and Thomas Becket, Archbishop of Canterbury, also illustrates the power of the Church. The contest between the two men chiefly concerned the punishment of 'criminous clerks', that is to say, men in 'holy orders' who were guilty of crimes under the civil law. Becket contended that it was sufficient punishment for the ordained man to be 'unfrocked', that is, deprived of his 'orders', but the King demanded that such a man should not only be unfrocked, but also brought into the civil court, after being unfrocked, for trial and punishment as a layman. At first Becket seemed to give way to the king's view, but he soon changed his mind and refused assent. When Henry, in a fit of temper, said that he wished some-one would rid him of 'this low-born cleric', four knights hastened to Canterbury and killed Becket in the cathedral. The country regarded him as a martyr, and the King thought it needful to do abject penance for what had happened. Becket's death strengthened the Church and weakened the power of the State.

Nearly half a century after Becket's death Pope Innocent III won a victory over King John of England. It followed the death of Hubert Walter, Archbishop of Canterbury, in 1205, an event which caused John to exclaim, 'Now for the first time I am King of England'. John also decided that he himself would make sure that the monks of Canterbury elected as the new archbishop the man whom he would himself name, John de Gray, Bishop of Norwich. When news of this matter reached the ears of Pope Innocent

[1] Quoted from James Bryce, *The Holy Roman Empire*, MacMillan (edition of 1930, p 168).

The Roman Sacrament of extreme unction. (see footnote, p. 75) A stone carving from a pre-reformation building in Edinburgh vividly depicting the dependence of the population upon the priest and the church.

III he let John know that the new appointment must go, not to de Gray, but to Stephen Langton, a Cardinal of English birth. John was furious; he refused to let the monks elect Langton, and entered into a long contest with the Pope. Innocent III promptly excommunicated John, placed the entire realm of England under an interdict, and told the king of France that he was free to take the English crown to himself. The French king prepared to invade England, but before he could cross the English Channel John submitted to the Pope on the Pope's conditions. They included the requirement that John must surrender his kingdom to the Pope who would then allow John to govern it as his vassal for a rent of 1000 marks per annum.

In the year 1215—the year in which English barons, headed by Stephen Langton, required

King John to sign Magna Carta—Innocent III called a General (Lateran) Council at Rome to which all the Christian rulers sent their representatives. 412 bishops and 800 abbots were present, and besides there were delegates from the patriarchs at Alexandria and Antioch. The patriarchs of Constantinople and Jerusalem appeared in person. Innocent in his opening address to the Council told them that the Lord had given to Peter, not only the headship of the Church on earth, but also dominion over the whole world, and as every knee must bow before Christ, so must all render obedience to Peter and to his papal successors. No prince, he said, has the right to rule unless he serves Peter (and so the papacy) with reverence and full submission. At the same time Innocent III put forward the doctrine of transubstantiation which lies at the very centre of the service called 'the mass', and which asserts that, by the words of the priest, the bread and wine in the Lord's Supper (they are sometimes called 'the elements') cease to be bread and wine, and literally and actually become the body and blood of Christ. Hence they are to be worshipped. The Council accepted the doctrine and thereby legislated idolatry.

Under Innocent III the papacy was at the height of its power and its supposed glory. The Church and the world were at its feet. Kings fell down before it, rendering homage. Most of Europe was subject to its sway. But not all men were caught in its mighty current. Christ had his 7,000 who had not bowed the knee to Baal. There was even an Elijah in those days, a real servant of the Lord whose name was Bernard of Clairvaux. We have already mentioned him as a promoter of the second crusade. Although he was subject to the popes and erred in many ways, in his heart there was the unquenchable fire of God's grace and the dominating power of conviction compelling him to testify to the truth as far as it was revealed to him by the Word of God. Successively he had been appointed bishop of Genoa, Milan and Rheims, but he declined these honours, 'for', said he, 'the Word of God teaches me not to strive after great things'.

Many of Bernard's followers became men of fame and held high positions. One of them even became Pope, and when this happened Bernard admonished him with the words: 'Remember that you are a successor of him who said, "Silver and gold have I none". Gold and silk and pearls and soldiers you have not received of Christ, but they came to you from Constantine. Never strive after these things. Would to God that before I die I might see the Church as it was in olden times when the apostles cast their nets, not to catch gold and silver but the souls of men!'

Bernard, himself a monk, founded many monasteries, and his advice was sought by men of rank and influence. He wrote Latin hymns, some of which have been translated into English and other languages. Shortly before his death he said, 'There are three things on which I base my hopes for eternity: the love of God for his children, the certainty of his promises, and the power by which he will make these promises come true'. Such a hope does not rest on quicksand but on the Rock of Ages. Martin Luther said of him, 'If there ever has been a pious, God-fearing monk, then it was Bernard, whom I esteem much higher than all other monks and priests through the globe. I never heard or read of his equal'.

The condition of the Church in the Middle Ages was pitiful. The masses of the people had a blind faith in the doctrines and traditions of the Church and never inquired whether they were in harmony with the Scriptures. Few could read,

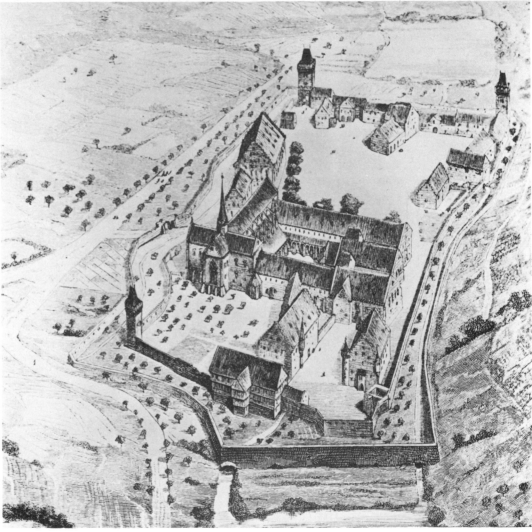

Mediaeval French monastery. The chief parts of a monastery were the chapel, cloisters and cloister garth, dining hall, kitchen, scriptorium, lavatory (wash basins), dormitories, guest rooms and library.

books were scarce; it was a rare thing for a man to have any real acquaintance with the Word of God. Superstition increased alarmingly. The doctrine of indulgences[1] gained general acceptance. The Church taught that forgiveness of sins might be obtained by the rendering of service to the Church, and in the 13th century indulgences were even sold for money.

[1] Indulgence: Defined by the Roman Church as 'the remission in whole or in part of the temporal punishment due to sin'. It usually had reference to sufferings in purgatory.

The Roman Church taught the doctrine of purgatory, purgatory being a place which all Christians entered after death so that they might be purged of, or cleansed from, the sin which rendered them unfit for heaven. On earth also, sin made necessary the performance of penance, but indulgences, whether bought or earned, enabled a man to escape penance or at least a part of it. Thus were men deluded in regard to salvation.

Occasionally feeble attempts were made to introduce reform, but such movements were soon checked. In the 13th century bishops were required by the Council of Toulouse to employ men whose sole duty was to hunt out heretics and hand them over to specially convened tribunals to be punished. Whoever shielded a heretic was to lose his property. This was the origin of what came to be known as The Inquisition.

While the demand for a drastic reformation of the Church became stronger as years passed by, every attempt to bring it about failed, mainly because it proceeded from a wrong principle. External abuses were to be corrected, but corrupt doctrine was to remain untouched. There was no appeal to the Word of God, no turning to the old paths, no repentance from dead works, and no belief in the basic doctrine of justification by faith. Dark was the night, and more than human power was needed to drive away the thick clouds. But, as we shall see, in God's time dawn came.

14

The Waldenses

The Waldensian Valleys. It was in these valleys, chiefly of Savoy and Piedmont, that a witness to the truth of the Gospel was maintained for centuries, despite the most savage of persecutions by adherents of the Roman Catholic Church. These persecutions continued for several centuries. In 1655 Oliver Cromwell declared 'a solemn fast' in England on behalf of the sufferers. His threat of active military intervention proved effective in his day, and for a few years persecution ceased. Cromwell himself headed a subscription list for the Waldensians with a personal gift of £2,000 and urged their cause so heartily that, in all, half a million pounds is said to have been subscribed. He also thought of sending Blake's redoubtable commonwealth navy to the Mediterranean to strike a blow on behalf of the Protestant cause. The mere threat sufficed to ease the strain.

Early in the 12th century there lived in Lyons, a city in the Rhone Valley in France, a wealthy merchant named Peter Waldo. In or about 1170 he employed a priest to translate from Latin into French the Four Gospels together with certain other books of Scripture. By the grace of God he saw the truths of God's Word and wanted to practise them. He began to realize that the Scriptures alone are to be the basis of faith, and not the word of any human being, be he priest or bishop or pope. He learned that there is but one Mediator, that saints should not be worshipped, and that two sacraments and two only—baptism and the Lord's Supper—were instituted by the Lord Jesus Christ. Waldo embraced these and other related truths, and in 1177 he organized a society of men and women who were willing to help him bring Bible truth before their fellows. The members of this Society are known in Church history by the name of Waldenses, or Waldensians, so called after their eminent instructor and leader. They are also known as 'the poor men of Lyons'. The call had come to them, as it once came to the seventy: 'Go your way, behold I send you forth as lambs among wolves. Carry neither scrip nor shoes . . .' (Luke 10 : 1–17); and in obedience to this command they went out 'two and two into every city and place'. Occasionally they were called Sabotati because they wore wooden shoes (sabots).

The Waldenses were 'harmless as doves' but also 'wise as serpents', for disguised as pedlars they canvassed the country trying to sell knick-knacks, but they never left a home without offering 'the pearl of great price'. They attacked the false teachings of the priests and the traditions of the Church frankly and openly, and wherever they found a listening ear they preached the Word of God boldly and fearlessly.

They visited all parts of southern France, they penetrated into Switzerland and Northern Italy, and usually they were well received. They gathered like-minded people to worship in secluded places, visited them in their homes, preached to them, and always left behind translations of parts of the Bible and devotional literature.

At first the Church authorities were lenient towards them, but when they began to realize the dangers of the movement to themselves, they placed the Waldenses under a ban. The Council of Valencia (1229) forbade men who were not priests to read the Bible, whether in Latin or in the vernacular, the only exception being that they might have 'a psalter or breviary for divine service', or 'the hours of the blessed Mary' but only in Latin. The Bible itself was placed on The Index of Forbidden Books.

Soon every kind of persecution was raised against the Waldenses as well as against other sects which protested against the corruption of the Church. The Inquisition was resorted to, and a murderous campaign was carried on against them for many years. Many thousands of them were slain, many were tortured with great cruelty, and their country was periodically transformed into a desert. Even mothers with infants were rolled down the rocks. This was especially the case in the area known as Piedmont. The believers fled to the mountains for safety. At one time 400 women and children were housed in a cave while the men were away. When this hiding-place was discovered the enemies lit a fire at the opening of the cave and all who were within perished. Dominican monks were appointed by Pope Gregory IX (1227–41) to the work of the tribunals of the Inquisition, and many were the acts of cruelty against the Waldenses for which they were responsible.

As Peter Waldo lived in southern France, that was the chief area covered by the Waldenses' testimony at the outset. The Counts of Toulouse and Foix gave them protection. But when persecution arose a number fled to Spain, Savoy, and Piedmont. Although soon driven out of Spain, they survived in France until the 16th century. Some fled to southern Italy but they were not welcomed there. Western Piedmont was the area where, in the southern Alps, they chiefly found refuge, and there they founded a distinct church which survives to the present day, free from persecution. Even in the city of Rome itself they now have a congregation. Their bitterest enemies could never deny the purity of their morals and the sincerity of their convictions.

Of them the world was not worthy. They loved not their lives unto the death. By faith they overcame the world, and we do well to remember the testimony to truth and the steadfastness under grievous tribulation which characterized their lives.

A persecution of the Waldensians which took place during the 17th Century has been made famous by a sonnet written by John Milton, secretary to Oliver Cromwell. It was Cromwell's vigorous remonstrance and threat of naval and military action that brought the persecution to a close. Milton's lines are worthy of remembrance:

On the late massacre in Piedmont
(1655)

Avenge, O Lord, thy slaughtered saints, whose bones
Lie scattered on the Alpine mountains cold;
Even them who kept thy truth so pure of old
When all our fathers worshipped stocks and stones,
Forget not: in thy book record their groans
Who were thy sheep, and in their ancient fold
Slain by the bloody Piedmontese, that rolled
Mother with infant down the rocks. Their moans
The vales redoubled to the hills, and they
To heaven. Their martyred blood and ashes sow
O'er all the Italian fields, where still doth sway
The triple tyrant; that from these may grow
A hundredfold, who, having learnt thy way,
Early may fly the Babylonian woe.[1]

---

[1] Milton has Revelation 16:19 and 17:5 in mind. To him Babylon represented the Church of Rome. He calls the Pope 'the Babylonian high-priest'.

Opposite Merton Street, Oxford, with Merton College on the right. Merton is the oldest college in Oxford. It dates from 1264. Its library is the oldest in the city.

In the 14th Century a young man was enrolled at the University of Oxford, of whom his teachers had great expectations. John Wycliffe, for such was his name, had a brilliant mind, undaunted courage, and a silver tongue. He also developed great skill with the pen. The date of his birth and the precise spot where it took place are not known, but in all probability it was during the period 1320–24, and in or near the village of Old Richmond in Yorkshire. He would doubtless be about 16 years old when he went to Oxford but to which of its colleges is uncertain. He remained in association with the University for the rest of his life, becoming first a Fellow, and then in 1361 the Master of Balliol College. He became a Doctor of Theology there also.

Wycliffe never forgot the terrible results of the plague that came to England in the year 1349.

15

John Wycliffe

His writings mention it frequently. It was called the Black Death and probably killed off one third or even a half of the population. Among the clergy mortality was very high. In the West Riding of Wycliffe's native county, more than two thirds of them died. A village in North Oxfordshire had six rectors between 1349 and 1354.

In 1366 Wycliffe came to the notice of King Edward III in connection with the refusal of the King to pay tribute to the Pope; he wrote a pamphlet containing the arguments which seven lords used in Parliament when the matter was debated. Wycliffe argued that the Pope had no right to require the King to collect money from the church in England to be sent to Rome. The Pope was probably angry because England had long ceased to pay the annual tribute of 1,000 marks which Pope Innocent III had exacted from King John in 1213. During the 1360's, when Pope Urban V had tried to recover the arrears, Edward III had consulted Parliament, with the result that the tribute was emphatically and finally repudiated.

In the year 1374 Wycliffe represented his country and king at a meeting with papal officers at Bruges, and further earned the king's gratitude. In the same year he was appointed to the Crown 'living' of Lutterworth in the county of Leicester. But if the king became an admirer of Wycliffe, it was not so with many of the clergy and the mendicant monks, who hated him bitterly and tried to bring about his downfall. He sharply criticized the monks for their indolence, for their habit of begging, and for their perversion of religion. The worship of images and relics he called foolishness, and in no uncertain terms he denounced the sale of indul-

¹ See page 59.

gences, masses for the dead, and processions and pilgrimages. The pope he denounced as Antichrist, 'the proud, worldly priest of Rome, the most accursed of clippers and purse-curvers' (robbers).

The bishops of the Church of England were greatly alarmed, and summoned Wycliffe to appear before the Convocation of the Church at St. Paul's, London, in the year 1377. He did so, and was savagely attacked by his opponents, but protected by the king's son, John of Gaunt, Duke of Lancaster. In that same year the Pope issued five Bulls (decrees) against him, and condemned him on nineteen different charges taken from his writings.

The great crisis of Wycliffe's life, however, came four years later when he attacked the Roman doctrine of transubstantiation, that is, the teaching that in the Eucharist (Lord's Supper) the bread and wine are changed into the body and blood of Christ.¹ As all priests claimed the power to perform this so-called miracle, it raised them, in the eyes of the Church, high above princes. Wycliffe's attitude in this matter aroused the greatest opposition, the king began to withdraw his support, and as for the University of Oxford, the heads and fellows of its various colleges were also in opposition to him. But he was so popular with the common people that his enemies feared to molest him. Possibly he might have brought about a better state of things in the church had he used more moderation and had he possessed more patience. But he wished to overthrow with one blow the false teachings of Rome and to re-establish the pure, undiluted gospel. Yet he discovered, as time passed, that reformation could not be brought about in one year or in ten; it required long effort and much patience.

Wycliffe's position was made more difficult because of the Peasants' Revolt of 1381, for he and his followers were blamed for it, although they were in no way responsible. John of Gaunt's Palace of the Savoy (London) was attacked, and finally the young king Richard II appeared in person to face the rebels, who were quelled and dispersed. John of Gaunt advised Wycliffe to abandon his work of reform; instead he published a further confession of faith.

At this point Parliament asked the Archbishop of Canterbury to call a church council to deal with matters in dispute. This he did, the council becoming known as the Earthquake Council because of the quake that occurred while it was in session. Wycliffe's followers looked upon this as a sign of divine intervention in their favour. Nevertheless Wycliffe's doctrine was condemned. Very soon he was summoned to appear before the Pope, but he refused to go to Rome. Actually, at this time there were two Popes, each calling the other Anti-christ. Although Wycliffe's followers and friends suffered persecution, Wycliffe himself remained untouched. He retired to Lutterworth, and lived a quiet but active life there until his death on the last day of the year 1384.

Towards the end of his life Wycliffe organized an Order of Poor Priests or preachers, who diffused his teachings among the people. Pitying their ignorance and spiritual blindness, he endeavoured to bring the truth of the gospel to them by means of these preachers, who travelled around clad in long reddish-brown gowns. The clergy derided them, but they became a formidable force, to be reckoned with by their opponents. As a result of their work many became believers. Wycliffe's enemies called them Lollards, a word whose origin is uncertain. Some consider it a term of scorn meaning 'idle folk', others that it refers to their habit of singing in praise of God.

However, the greatest of all the works accomplished by Wycliffe has still to be mentioned. He translated the Bible into English, so that all who were able to read, or listen to the Word when read, could learn the truth of God.

Of the Book that had been the sealed-up Book
  He tore the clasps, that the nation
With eyes unbandaged might look thereon
    And therein find salvation.

The Roman Church used the Latin Bible only, in the version called the Vulgate, and refused to have it translated into the language of the people. Wycliffe did not know either the Hebrew or Greek of the original Scriptures; he had to make his translation from the Latin, and so it was not as accurate as could be wished: but still it proved to be a great blessing to the people. Also all Scripture had to be written by hand for as yet there was no printing press. The poor preachers took portions of it with them in their travels and read them to men and women in cities and hamlets, wherever they could get an audience. Wycliffe's was the first English translation of the whole Bible. Probably he had helpers in his work, but to what extent is not fully known.

Early the following century two dreadful steps were taken by Parliament and Church. A law for the burning of heretics—and Lollards (Wycliffites) were called heretics—was passed in 1401, and it did not remain a dead letter, the most notable sufferer being Sir John Oldcastle (Lord Cobham) in 1417; also the Convocation of the Church condemned Wycliffe's translation of the Bible.

The hatred of the Roman Church for John Wycliffe is perhaps best shown by an event which took place about forty years after his death. By order of the Council of Constance (1415) the reformer's bones were to be dug up from their grave and refused reburial. This was carried out in 1428 when the Bishop of Lincoln burned the remains, and scattered the ashes upon the waters of the River Swift which runs through Lutterworth. It has been well said that, as the ashes were carried by the Swift to the Avon, by the Avon to the Severn, by the Severn to the 'narrow seas', and by the 'narrow seas' to the ocean, so the reformer's teachings and message reached out into all England, and from England into far-distant lands. Indeed, Wycliffe was 'The Morning Star of the Reformation' which commenced in the 16th century.

And though his bones from the grave were torn
Long after his life was ended,
The sound of his words, to times unborn,
Like a trumpet-call descended.

16

John Huss

John Huss was the most important of the fore-runners of the Reformation on the Continent of Europe. He was born of peasant stock in or about 1369 in the village of Husinetz (from which he seems to have derived his name) in Bohemia.

During the boyhood of Huss the books of John Wycliffe were reaching Bohemia and having strong influence there. In the providence of God, in 1382, King Richard II of England married Anne of Bohemia who had a remarkable love for the Word of God, and this assisted the writings of the English reformer to enter Bohemia. Huss never attained to the grasp of truth that was characteristic of Wycliffe, but he longed to purify the Church of his day and to bring it back to New Testament teaching.

The father of John Huss died when his son was still very young, so his early education was under the guidance of his mother; and she in her poverty was helped by a rich nobleman whose heart God moved to pay all the expenses of the young student's schooling. Such were his scholastic gifts that rewards came thick and fast, and by the time he was 34 years old he had been appointed Rector of Prague University. The world seemed to be at his feet.

But it was not God's will that Huss should content himself with academic fame. As a faithful student of the Word of God his mind became troubled about many things. He continually humbled himself for sins known only to himself and the Lord. He even became troubled by the fact that when he played the game of chess he was liable to lose his temper when beaten. He read the writings of John Wycliffe and, in addition, was keenly impressed by two cartoons. One of them represented the Lord Jesus wearing the crown of thorns, and the Pope wearing a crown of gold, and clothing of rich purple and silk. The second showed a picture of the woman to whom the Lord Jesus said, 'Thy sins are forgiven thee', and on its reverse side the Pope was depicted selling indulgences to the people. The truth which these cartoons so eloquently proclaimed opened the eyes of Huss to see clearly the sad condition of the Church.

In Prague was a Chapel known as the Bethlehem Chapel which had been erected for the special purpose of giving the people the opportunity of hearing the Christian message in their own tongue instead of in Latin, which, of course, few of them understood. In this Chapel Huss became the preacher. With outspoken earnestness he exposed the superstitions of men and the sins of the clergy, and fed the hungry with the bread of life. Many who saw this pale, thin man with serious countenance, and were acquainted with his pure, strict life, were persuaded that he was a true messenger of God. But the Archbishop of Prague opposed him strongly and denounced both his and Wycliffe's books. These books were collected and with his own hand the Archbishop set fire to them in the courtyard of his palace, while a loud Te Deum was sung by the clergy present on the occasion.

Huss was asked whether he was prepared to obey the Pope's commands. 'Yes', he replied, 'so far as they agree with the doctrine of Christ, but when I see the contrary I will not obey them, even though you burn my body'. The word 'contrary' as here used is important. It was Wycliffe's teaching that if Pope or clergy or any other men 'contraried' Christ, then they were the enemies of Christ and must be resisted. 'To contrary Christ' was an expression much on the lips of Wycliffe's followers, for obedience to Christ was at the very heart of their teaching.

In the outcome, the Pope excommunicated

Huss and placed the city of Prague under an interdict as long as it sheltered the heretic and his adherents. Huss therefore moved to another place. But the persecution continued unabated. In 1414 the General Council of Constance was held and Huss was summoned to appear for trial before it. The Emperor Sigismund promised him a safe conduct so he set out for Constance, fully trusting in the justice of his cause. The Council was a very splendid affair. It included the Emperor, kings, magnates of the Empire, prelates, bishops and priests. A month after his arrival Huss was arrested and imprisoned in a dungeon close to the outlet of the city sewer. Soon his trial began. But matters were complicated by the sudden flight from the city of Pope John XXIII, fearful lest an enquiry should be instituted into his intolerably wicked life and works.

When the trial of Huss opened and the reformer complained of his imprisonment, despite the safe-conduct promised by the Emperor, Sigismund hung his head and blushed shamefacedly. It soon became clear that the condemnation of Huss had virtually been predetermined. When he began to speak he was shouted down and was quite unable to make himself heard. At one point he was accused of the monstrous blasphemy of proclaiming himself a fourth person in the Holy Trinity. 'Let that person be named who has given evidence against me', said the reformer, but no reply was forthcoming. In vain he protested his belief in orthodox Christian doctrine. Sentence was passed upon him; he and his books were to be publicly burned. Kneeling down in the presence of all, Huss prayed, 'Lord Jesus, pardon all my enemies for the sake of thy great mercy. Thou knowest that they have falsely accused me, brought forward false witnesses, and concocted false charges against me. Pardon them for the sake of thine infinite mercy'.

The Archbishop of Milan and six other bishops were appointed to perform the ceremony of taking from Huss the office of priest. This done, the words rang out, 'We commit thy soul to the devil'. 'And I commit it to the Lord Jesus Christ' cried the prisoner. As they hurried him to the place of burning 'a crown of blasphemy' was put on his head, bearing the words, 'This is an arch-heretic', and depicting devils tearing his soul. Falling to his knees Huss uttered repeatedly, 'Into thy hands, O Lord, I commend my spirit', for Christ strengthened him marvellously. 'I am willing', he said, 'patiently and publicly to endure this dreadful, shameful and cruel death for the sake of thy gospel and the preaching of thy Word'.

Wood and straw were piled up around him and lighted, as he continued to call loudly upon God. Soon, life was extinct, for he choked in the smoke. The officers then gathered up the ashes, dug up the very earth around the stake lest contamination should remain, and flung them, ashes and earth, into the river Rhine, just as, a few years later, Wycliffe's ashes were to be cast into an English stream.

The Bohemian delegates to the Council returned from Constance eager for revenge, for in their opinion Huss had been murdered. Before long many of the nobles of Bohemia took the lead, armed thousands of their fellow-countrymen, and under the command of Ziska, a one-eyed man, they were ready to use force to achieve their freedom. In history they are known as the Hussites. At Prague they demanded religious toleration and the liberation of their friends who had been cast into prison. When

this was denied them they threw thirteen of the members of the city council out of the windows of the council-room. A war lasting 15 years now broke out. The Hussites had their headquarters on a mountain which they named Tabor. The Emperor Sigismund, however, had at hand at least 80,000 men under arms. Even so, Ziska and his force seemed to be invincible. But in 1421 Ziska died and a sharp contention arose among the Hussites, some of whom were prepared to compromise with the papacy. So the wars ended.

But many of the Hussites retained their faith. First called Taborites, they were later known as the Bohemian or Moravian Brethren, and

The Burning of John Huss.

of them we shall read more in a later chapter.

Huss was the Bohemian name for 'goose' and sometimes his foes used this fact to deride him. But on one occasion he replied to them: 'Instead of a silly goose the truth will hereafter send forth eagles and falcons with piercing looks.' This came about in the 16th-Century Reformation.

17

Savonarola

John Wycliffe was an Englishman, John Huss a Bohemian, and Jerome Savonarola, another of the forerunners of the Reformation, was an Italian. But whereas Wycliffe and Huss were involved in attacking the unbiblical teachings of the Roman Catholic Church, Savonarola was not a doctrinal reformer. He was a man who attacked the evil lives and immoral habits of many of his fellow-countrymen. God had used the writings of Augustine of Hippo to open his eyes to the moral apostasy in the Church. Being a man of influence through his position and intellectual qualities, he began to think about the necessity of reformation.

Born in the Italian city of Ferrara in 1452, Savonarola even as a boy was intensely serious-minded. For a time he lived in a Dominican monastery, and at the age of 38 he went to the city of Florence, a centre of science and art but shrouded in spiritual darkness and ignorance. Here he began to preach and lecture, but his voice was harsh and unmusical and few gave heed to him. Surprisingly, however, it was not long before he became a celebrated orator, and vast crowds gathered to hear his denunciations of the corruption prevalent among clergy and laity alike. Large crowds filled the majestic cathedral of the city, never tiring of hearing about repentance from sin, which Savonarola urged with glowing earnestness. The effect was marvellous. Many a hardened sinner was aroused and led to conversion from an evil life. Florence became the centre of a great revival, even though the teachings of Romanism still held sway, and the reformer became for a time the idol of the people of the city. His influence seemed unbounded.

In those days Florence was under the rule of the House of Medici, and more particularly under the rule of Lorenzo de Medici who feared the increasing power of the bold preacher. It was under Lorenzo, called the Magnificent, that a new movement known to scholars as The Renaissance was flourishing. It was a new birth of art, literature and philosophy, and Florence was its great cultural centre. An interest in ancient Greek literature began to show itself, for in 1453 the Ottoman Turks had captured Constantinople, and scholars fled westwards taking valuable manuscripts with them. But the

Renaissance was pagan rather than Christian at this time, and the Medici family had no sympathy with the teachings and high morals of Savonarola. For a time Lorenzo showed the reformer favours and gave him valuable presents, possibly hoping to silence his preaching. But in vain. When Lorenzo was 44 years of age he fell ill. Realizing that his end was near, he sent for Savonarola, but when the latter found that he had no inclination to repent of his sins, he refused him the blessing which it was his custom to grant to the dying.

Lorenzo was succeeded by his son, but the people ousted him and Savonarola was unanimously chosen as ruler of Florence. He accepted the honour thinking it would render his work of reform easier, but in this he was mistaken. For three years Savonarola governed Florence and he certainly gave it good government. But many people began to resent the strictness of the new ruler. As Savonarola intended the city to become the model of a Christian commonwealth in which God was the Ruler and his gospel the sovereign law, the haunts of vice were abolished, gambling was outlawed, vanities of dress both male and female were to be restrained, and godly living was to be promoted. Cards, dice, costumes used in carnivals, and licentious books and pictures were to be destroyed in a 'bonfire of vanities'. The men who loved these things, however, soon began to create an opposition and to stir up the people against their ruler. Rather foolishly, Savonarola claimed to have the gift of prophecy and he actually predicted that certain things would happen. But his prophecies failed and even his supporters began to mistrust him. In consequence his influence waned.

At the same time the Pope, a man of notoriously evil life named Alexander Borgia—he was

Savonarola: forerunner of the Reformation. *From a painting by Fra Bartolommeo.*

the sixth of the papal Alexanders—took the lead in attacking the reformer of Florence. He was a Spaniard and one of the most wicked men who ever occupied 'the throne of Peter'. When he became Pope he had five children and it was his aim to use his power to promote their temporal welfare. It has been said that 'how the pope would proceed, in regard to marriages, endowments, and the advance of his children, became a question affecting the politics of all Europe'. He held no moral principles that would have obstructed his aims. He was completely unscrupulous, and was quite willing to engage in murder and the use of poison if his schemes could thereby be helped forward.

First of all Alexander VI tried bribery with

Savonarola. He offered to make him a cardinal. Cardinals rank next to the Pope as the highest dignitaries in the Roman Catholic Church. The Pope is chosen by them and from their number. Savonarola, however, rejected the glittering prize, saying, 'I do not desire any other crown than the crown of a martyr'.

The Pope therefore used other tactics to belittle the power of the reformer. The monks were persuaded to speak against him and to undermine his authority, and then the Pope excommunicated and imprisoned him. The citizens who had formerly acclaimed him now allowed him to be tortured in order to make him recant his teaching, and finally they joined in the cries of condemnation. But Savonarola remained unmoved. He could not be shaken in his convictions, and when the pains caused by the tortures of the Inquisition became unbearable, his lips uttered in anguish, 'It is enough, Lord, now take my soul'.

In May, 1498 the reformer was put to death by burning. Great crowds had gathered in the central square of the city of Florence. With two of his friends he was led to the stake. Like Huss, he was stripped of his priestly robes in public while the crowd yelled, 'Now prophet, show thy power and work a miracle'. But Savonarola kept still. Had not his Saviour endured the same mockery and rejection? A bishop of the church now approached him, and said in faltering tones, 'I separate thee from the church militant and triumphant'. 'Militant, not triumphant', said the reformer, 'for you have no power to separate me from the church triumphant to which I go'. And so Savonarola died, at the age of 45. Some few, from the enormous crowd present, pressed forward to collect, if possible, some relic of the martyr, but the guards resisted them and carried out the instructions of those in authority, that the remains of the victims (three had been put to death) were to be borne away in carts and cast into the river Arno which flowed through the city.

Luther regarded Savonarola as a pioneer of the Reformation, but it is clear that his work was largely confined to the reform of public morals. It had no link with the reform of doctrine which began, though not in Italy, about twenty years after his death.

It is true that, in nature, it is darkest just before the dawn. Similarly in the Church thick darkness prevailed during the close of the 15th and the first decades of the 16th century. There was practically nothing of the simple faith, the earnest hope, and the fervent love so characteristic of the Church of the apostolic age. There was pomp and outward show in abundance, but worship was hollow and without true content. The ritual was mere formality; the preaching was sounding brass; the priests with few exceptions were selfish seekers of worldly pleasures; the people were abandoned to ignorance and superstition.

Beautiful church buildings had been erected in the Middle Ages, of which the cathedral at Cologne in Germany was one of the most magnificent, but within these buildings the great truths of God's Word were not preached. Sermons were little better than 'profane and vain babblings' in the Latin language, which remained the official language of the Church although none but scholars understood it. No food was served to hungry souls. The greatest errors were taught. In addition to the two sacraments which Christ had instituted—baptism and the Lord's Supper—Rome had appointed five others—confirmation, penance, marriage, orders, and extreme unction.[1] It was also taught that, at death, the Christian passed into purgatory, a place for purifying his soul so that he might in time become fit to enter heaven. As for little children who died unbaptized, it was taught that there was a special place called *Limbus infantum* (*limbus* meaning 'border') provided for them, but into heaven itself they could not enter.

18

The Approach of Dawn

Desiderius Erasmus

Prayers to the saints—and there were almost as many saints and saints' days as there are days in the year—were encouraged, for many of them supposedly had a surplus of good works with which they might benefit people on earth. In the homage paid to saints, or to Mary, the mother of Jesus, people forgot the worship due to God alone. Every business, calling, age and station had its patron saint; nations had their patron saints; and for every misfortune or sickness there was some special mediator to whom one could apply for relief. It was forgotten that 'there is *one* God, and *one* mediator between God and men, the man Christ Jesus'. (I Timothy 2 : 5).

Men expected to obtain salvation through baptism, attendance at mass, indulgences, and

[1] 'orders': the ordination of priests and consecration of nuns; 'extreme unction': the anointing with oil of a person thought to be about to die.

good works. Heathenism had vanished, but the superstitions of heathenism were retained. People believed in witchcraft, fairies, and good and bad omens. At Canterbury in England, as in most cathedrals, it was incredible what a world of bones, skulls, chins, teeth, hands, fingers, and whole arms were preserved as sacred relics. Shrines, such as that of Thomas Becket, were visited by multitudes, and the priests or monks in charge of them would produce relics by the hundred; for example, a finger of the martyr Stephen, hair of Mary Magdalene, blood of the apostles John and Thomas, a lock of the Virgin Mary's hair, a fragment of Christ's seamless robe. In Gloucestershire was shown Christ's blood in a vial. To support the doctrine of transubstantiation, bleeding wafers were here and there exhibited. Imposture, in fact, was everywhere. The power of the Church was, in part, built upon it. And by it the Church became enormously wealthy as the simple-minded parted with their money. Dark, very dark, is the picture of the Church in the early 16th Century.

But the day had at last arrived when God was to demonstrate his power and to begin a thorough reform of his Church. He himself came with 'his fan in his hand to purge his floor thoroughly, to gather the wheat into his garner, and to burn up the chaff with fire unquenchable'. This great event in history is known as the Reformation. It is the most important epoch in the history of the world since the events of which we read in the New Testament.

Various causes are usually given for the Reformation. The real power lay in the gospel of grace and the preaching of it, and the direct cause was the raising up by God of a number of men whom he had chosen to take the leading part in this work. Then, too, there were remote or external causes by which the work was prepared and its execution made easier. This is God's method of governing the realm of nature. He, the Sovereign, the Omnipotent, works out his purposes in all their tremendous intricacy through cause and effect, and he applies this same method in matters that concern salvation and his Church.

One of the most important of the external causes of the Reformation was the movement known to us as the Renaissance, or The Rebirth of Learning. It prepared the minds of men to throw off the yoke of illiteracy and serfdom, the agents by which the clergy kept the masses of men under their authority. One of the foremost men of the Renaissance was Erasmus of Rotterdam (c. 1466–1536). He was the son of a priest (and priests were denied by the Church the right to become fathers) and educated by the 'Brethren of the Common Life' at Deventer and at the Hague. The Brethren existed to promote piety, to provide education for boys in need, and to engage in good works generally. One of their pupils was Thomas à Kempis, who wrote a famous book of devotion entitled *The Imitation of Christ*.

Although forced to enter a monastery, Erasmus was afterwards set free from the usual vows, and he resolved to devote himself to study and the pursuit of knowledge. He attended several of the chief universities of western Europe, and spent a considerable time at Oxford where he met a scholar named John Colet who persuaded him to turn his attention from secular scholarship to biblical studies. Yet Erasmus, though a man of profound learning, was not really a reformer. He was not without a Christian consciousness, but possessed neither the purity nor strength of faith necessary in a

opposite Christ Church, Oxford. The most extensive and magnificent of Oxford Colleges, it was founded in 1525 by Cardinal Thomas Wolsey as Cardinal's College. To meet his vast expenses Wolsey received from King Henry VIII the endowments of more than 40 monasteries. He intended it to be (as Foxe, in his *Book of Martyrs*, tells us) 'marvellously sumptuous', in fact, the finest College in Christendom. But Wolsey lost the king's favour through his failure to get the royal marriage with Catherine of Aragon annulled by the Pope. Much of his property, including the College, was taken from him by the king who, afterwards, refounded the College. Its building was finished by 1546.

reformer. He was, however, a promoter of the Reformation in two chief ways.

First of all, he exposed the abuses in the Church by writing against the moral corruption of all ranks, and by unsparingly denouncing the ignorance, idleness, and dissoluteness of the monks. In one of his books called, ironically, *In Praise of Folly*, he tells how most men 'rested their hopes for salvation on a strict conformity to religious ceremonies, little thinking that the Judge of all the earth at the last day would say, Who hath required these things at your hands?' In this book we read:

It will be pretty to hear their pleas before the great tribunal. One will brag how he mortified his carnal appetite by feeding only upon fish; another will tell how many days he fasted and what severe penance he imposed upon himself; another will produce on his own behalf as many ceremonies as would load a fleet of merchantmen; another will plead that in threescore years he never so much as touched a piece of money, except he fingered it through a thick pair of gloves; another will testify his humility by producing his sacred hood, so old and nasty that any seaman had rather stand bareheaded on the deck than put it on to defend his ears in the sharpest storms; another will tell his Judge he has lost his voice by singing holy hymns and anthems; and still another, that he has forgotten how to speak by having kept perpetual silence, in obedience to the Psalmist's injunction to take heed lest he should offend with his tongue. But the Saviour will set aside their fine excuses by saying, "Woe unto you, scribes and Pharisees, hypocrites; verily I know you not".

The second contribution made by Erasmus to the Reformation was his editing of the first printed Greek New Testament in the year 1516. This called scholars' attention to the true gospel of Christ, and to that gospel as explained by the apostles of Christ. It reminded men of the way in which the Church was founded, and taught them the essential requirements of God. Above all, it taught that salvation was by grace and not by works. The Bible was, as it were, taken from under a bushel and placed upon a candlestick to shed its light in the world of men. The Scriptures were soon translated into various European languages, and the printing press, invented about 1454 in Germany, made them available in large numbers at a price which many were able to afford. As Erasmus stated in his most famous lines:

I would to God that the ploughman would sing a text of the Scriptures at his plough, and that the weaver would hum them to the tune of his shuttle . . . I wish that the traveller would beguile the tediousness of his journey with this pastime. All communication of the Christian should be of the Scriptures.

In these ways Erasmus helped to introduce reformation, but he lacked the convicting power of truth. He loved peace so well that he would sacrifice a part of truth rather than cause dissension. The reformer Luther said of him: 'He has pointed out the evil, but he is unable to point out the good and to lead into the promised land. Perhaps he will at length die with Moses in the fields of Moab, for he does not lead into the better studies of God's Word, those which concern piety'. Yet the saying, too, is memorable, that 'Erasmus laid the egg, but Luther hatched it'; in other words, Erasmus by his literary work prepared the way for the Reformation, but it was the work of others to re-establish the truth of God, through the Scriptures, in the souls of men. With Erasmus dawn set in; with the later reformers the light of divine truth reached its zenith.

Martin Luther, the Reformer, belonged to a peasant family in Saxony, Germany. 'My father, grandfather, all of my ancestors were thorough peasants', said Luther. His father bore the name of Hans (John), his mother was Gretha (Margaret). They lived in Eisleben where Hans Luther earned his livelihood by mining, specially for copper which was abundant in the hills. Their son was born on the 10th November, 1483, and as the following day was the feast of St. Martin, as observed by the Roman Catholic Church, he was named after that saint. Half a year after his birth the family moved to Mansfield, about six miles from Eisleben.

At home and in school little Martin was brought up in a simple but strict manner. Occasionally harshness was seen in the home. On one occasion his mother whipped him till the blood flowed, for stealing a hazel-nut. At school his teacher ruled his class with an iron hand, and Martin, a bright and diligent boy, but also full of boyish pranks, felt he was sometimes unreasonably and over-severely punished. Once, he tells us, he was whipped fifteen times during a single morning for no fault of his own. Indeed, in later years he spoke of the school as 'the Mansfield purgatory'.

At the age of fourteen the boy was sent to a school at Magdeburg, and the following year to Eisenach, where his parents hoped that his mother's relations would provide him with board and lodging. Sometimes he would sing from door to door with his friends, to obtain sustenance. 'I was once a poor mendicant' he said later, 'seeking my bread at people's houses, particularly at Eisenach—my own dear Eisenach!' One good lady who took pity on him was Frau (Mrs.) Ursula Cotta; she welcomed him to her table and exerted a good influence upon his soul. He was introduced by her to a refined home circle and learned to move in a higher rank of society than that to which his parents belonged.

At the age of eighteen Luther entered the University of Erfurt where he greatly distinguished himself in study. A light-hearted young fellow, full of buoyant life, he little realized that even at this time God was preparing him for a career of activity which was to astonish Europe, and which was to shake a proud and polluted Church to its foundations. But God's chosen vessels are often hidden in obscurity until the time of 'their showing unto Israel'. One day while studying at Erfurt, Luther came across a copy of the Bible. He had never set eyes upon the Book before, but as he read he was deeply stirred. The story of Hannah and Samuel, and above all, Samuel's calling, impressed him deeply.

At the age of twenty-two Luther had completed his course at the University, and then there came a turning point in his life. One of his best friends was killed in a student brawl, and he could not refrain from asking himself, 'What if I had been killed instead of my friend?' On another occasion, as he was travelling home from Erfurt, a rapier he was carrying accidentally severed a main artery in one of his legs. He called upon the Virgin Mary for aid while a friend ran for helpers who bound up the wound and saved his life. On yet another occasion a terrible thunder-storm broke over his head. Stricken with fear he fell prostrate to the ground, crying out, 'Help, Anna, beloved saint, I will become a monk'.

Luther kept his vow. After gathering with his

19

Martin Luther the Student

student-friends for frolic and song in a farewell party, the next day he presented himself at the door of an Augustinian monastery and asked for admission. He was received with open arms, for his university learning commended him to the head of the monastery. But his father was very angry, for he had hoped that Martin, as his eldest son, would obtain a high legal position, whereas as a monk he would achieve no fame or worldly wealth.

Luther wanted peace with God; he yearned and craved for it. He had realized that the world could not grant his heart's desire, and he hoped to find it in the cloister. He certainly did his utmost to obtain it. He obeyed the monastic rules scrupulously, performed the most menial services, and went about begging on behalf of the monastery. He was perhaps the most sincere, conscientious monk who ever tried in genuine earnestness to merit salvation by human effort. He even became proud of his humility! 'A proud saint', he declared later, described his condition at this time. To gain salvation he sacrificed everything. He observed every detail of discipline, praying, fasting, watching, confessing his sins; he literally tortured his body to obtain peace for his soul.

But peace and rest he failed to find, for he learned that it was impossible to merit the favour of God by such means. He almost despaired of salvation, and his physical strength began to waste away. His fellow-monks could not help him, for they were spiritually blind and could not see the crying needs of their younger brother. Nor could departed saints help him. He appealed to twenty-one of them, and directed his prayers to three every morning so as to include them all in his week's devotions. Often, Luther tells us, he endured such agony of mind that, had it lasted for half-an-hour or even five minutes, he must have died under the strain. Once for a whole fortnight he neither ate, nor drank, nor slept. And still peace did not come to him.

But there was one who brought help and consolation to the troubled man. John von Staupitz, the head of the Augustinian Order in Germany, from time to time visited the Erfurt monastery. Between Luther and himself a friendship sprang up. 'Oh, my sins! my sins! my sins!' cried the young monk to Staupitz. 'Remember that Christ came into the world for the pardon of our sins' replied the latter. At another time the very thought of Christ terrified Luther, for he thought of the Lord primarily as the one who punishes sin. 'Your thoughts are not according to Christ; Christ does not terrify, he consoles', said Staupitz to him. 'Look at the wounds of Christ, and you will there see shining clearly the purpose of God towards men. We cannot understand God out of Christ.' Such sayings sank into Luther's mind. Gradually the light of truth dawned upon him.

Luther's chief struggle had to do with the phrase 'the righteousness of God'. He was convinced that in Romans 1 : 17 and elsewhere these words referred to the awful holiness of God, and his unchanging hatred of sin and sinners. How could he, Martin Luther, ever achieve the kind of holiness that would turn away the anger of God against him?

He did not yet understand Paul's words in Romans that the gospel is the saving power of God to everyone who believes in Christ, *because* it reveals the righteousness of God. This righteousness of God is nothing other than Christ's perfect obedience to his Father's will in life and death, 'even the death of the cross'—obedience which God counts as belonging to all those in whose place Christ died. Just as the punishment of the believer's sin was borne by Christ so it is because of Christ's righteousness that the same believer, though ungodly in himself, is pronounced 'just' or righteous in the sight of God. In this way, Paul says, faith receives the righteousness of God: 'To him that worketh not but believeth on him that justifies the ungodly, his faith is counted for righteousness' (Romans 4 : 5).

When the Holy Spirit revealed this to Luther, and he learned that it was by faith alone that he could be saved, and not by his own good works, the light of the truth shone with such brilliance, and brought such deliverance into his spirit, that he felt Paul's words, 'The just shall live by faith', were the very gate of Paradise itself. And so this great truth, THE JUST SHALL LIVE BY FAITH . . . became the fundamental truth of the Reformation. In other words, a wonderful reformation came personally to Luther before God used him as the instrument of the Reformation in Europe.

Staupitz persuaded Luther to enter the Roman priesthood and recommended him to Frederick the Wise, Elector of Saxony, as a man suitable for a professorship of Theology in the University that Frederick had founded at Wittenberg. In the post Luther found great happiness. His mind was clear and his heart satisfied. He rejoiced in salvation, not by works of the law performed by the sinner, not by ceremonies and penances and similar observances prescribed by the Roman Catholic Church, but by the life and death and resurrection of Jesus Christ. New light was shed upon the entire Bible, which became to him a book of life and comfort, and of wisdom from above. All the blessings and benefits of redemption through 'the precious blood of Christ' came to him; he breathed the

opposite Luther as a student

fresh air of God's redeeming love.

Luther now wanted to spread to all men the saving truth that had brought him out of darkness into light. He longed to preach justification by faith far and wide and gradually he became conscious of the great work that awaited him. Difficulties abounded, but he learned to say, as did the apostle Paul, 'I can do all things through Christ who strengthens me'. The future, though dark, was at the same time bright with hope.

20

Luther and the Church

Although Luther was now a professor at the University of Wittenberg, he still lived in a monastery. In the year 1510 he was commissioned to go to Rome in the interests of the Augustinian Order. He was delighted with his mission, for up to this time he held the conviction that the Roman Catholic Church was *the* Church, that the Pope was the holy vicar of Christ upon earth, and that Rome, 'the eternal city', was the supreme seat of holiness. But he was miserably disappointed. The nearer he approached the 'holy city' the more wickedness he observed on every hand, and while in Rome he heard about the wicked deeds of popes and other high dignitaries.

In addition to this experience Luther discovered everywhere on his journey from monastery to monastery that the priests were deplorably ignorant, and given to the grossest superstitions, many of them even being unbelievers and blasphemers. He spent four weeks in Rome. Julius II, the Pope at the time, was scarcely anything more than a scheming statesman, greedy of gain, and willing to achieve his ends by fair means or foul. He was also engaged in a war with the French. Luther went hither and thither seeking blessing. 'I remember', he says, 'that when I went to Rome I ran about like a madman to all the churches, all the convents, all the places of note of every kind. I implicitly believed every tale about all of them that imposture had invented. I said a dozen masses, and I almost regretted that my father and mother were not dead so that I might have availed myself of the opportunity to draw their souls out of purgatory by a dozen or more masses and other good works of a similar description. . . . We did these things then, knowing no better. It is the Pope's interest to encourage such lies'.

All accounts of Luther mention an event which occurred on what is termed Pilate's staircase, being supposedly the staircase on which Pilate stood when Jesus was brought before him for trial. It was claimed that it had been miraculously brought from Jerusalem to Rome and that whoever climbed it on his bare knees would receive

The Leipzig Disputation, 1519.
In this very important debate between John Eck, Roman Catholic spokesman, and Luther, here for the first time German Christendom breaks away from Roman Christendom by insisting upon the priesthood of all believers and the right of each Christian to judge in all things according to his conscience, enlightened by the Word of God and the Holy Spirit. It was at Leipzig that Luther realized that he had now broken with Rome, and that, in truth, the fight was on.

remission of sins. Luther certainly climbed the staircase, but accounts as to what happened vary. One account, written by Paul Luther, the reformer's youngest son, tells us that as his father repeated his prayers on the staircase, the words of the prophet Habakkuk came into his mind, 'The just shall live by faith'; which caused him to realize the worthlessness of the stair-climbing. Another account, found in a sermon of Luther's, says: 'At Rome I wished to liberate my grandfather from purgatory, and went up the staircase of Pilate, praying a *pater noster* on each step; for I was convinced that he who prayed thus could redeem his soul. But when I

Luther in 1520

right The Castle Church in Wittenberg as it appeared when Luther nailed his 95 theses to its door in 1517.

1515 he began to preach in the parish church. This brought him into close touch with the people, who liked to hear Dr. Luther because he began to unfold Christian truth as no other priest or preacher had ever done in their hearing. But all this was only preliminary. God in his wise counsel was so guiding persons and circumstances that Luther's conscience soon forced him to raise a strong protest against the errors and deceitful tactics of the Church. It happened in the following way.

The popes had decided that St. Peter's Cathedral at Rome should be rebuilt. The enormous expense was to be met by contributions from all areas where the Church held sway, and with a view to promoting the inflow of money to Rome special indulgences were to be sold. Tetzel, a monk from Leipzig, was one of those who toured the German states to effect their sale, and he had a graduated scale of payments based upon social rank and upon sins committed. Some Germans, it appears, were even prepared to buy an indulgence (to secure exemption from years in purgatory) for sins they had not yet committed at the time of purchase. People were also told that they could make payments which would deliver their loved ones who had died from their purgatorial torments. 'The moment the money tinkles in my box', said Tetzel, 'that moment the soul springs up out of purgatory'.

Another matter, too, was involved. Albert, an ambitious young prince of the House of Hohenzollern, had secured appointment to two archbishoprics and a bishopric. But at a price! He had paid a huge sum of money to the Pope, and an equivalent amount in fees at the three inauguration ceremonies. He had borrowed the money from the financial House of Fugger, a House in close touch with Rome, and by arrange-

came to the top step, the thought kept coming to me, "Who knows whether this is true ?" '

The visit to Rome was a landmark in Luther's life. On seeing Rome from a distance, as he reached the city from Germany, he had fallen upon his knees, exclaiming, 'Hail, holy Rome, thrice holy for the blood of martyrs shed here'. But at the end of his stay he had learned to see the city in another light. He was prepared to say, 'If there is a hell, Rome is built over it'. Later he said, 'I would not have missed seeing Rome for 100,000 florins. I should have felt always an uneasy doubt whether I was not, after all, doing injustice to the Pope. As it is, I am quite satisfied on the point'.

Returning to Wittenberg, Luther soon received the degree of Doctor of Divinity, and in ment with Rome he was allowed to engage Tetzel as chief agent for the sale of indulgences, so that he might repay the Fuggers.

Luther's anger was unbounded. He preached vehemently against Tetzel and his ecclesiastical wares, but soon decided to take more vigorous action, for men in general had no conscience against purchasing indulgences which guaranteed the remission of purgatorial pains. Luther, therefore, wrote 95 theses, tersely stating the evils of indulgences; and on the 31st October, 1517, at the hour of noon, he nailed them to the door of the Castle Church at Wittenberg. This was the beginning of the Reformation; October 31st is its birthday. The following day was 'All Saints' Day' when multitudes flocked to the church. The theses attracted great public attention. They were read, copied, printed and distributed all over Germany, and soon, as on wings, carried over all Europe. Many rejoiced in Luther's boldness and hoped that good would come of it.

As for the Pope, he first treated the matter of the theses lightly, but he quickly changed his mind when he found out how serious was the threat to his authority and to the doctrine of the Church. He demanded that Luther should recant, and summoned him to appear in Rome. He also demanded that Frederick the Wise should deliver up this 'child of the devil' to the papal legate. In response Frederick suggested that the pope should send a delegate before whom Luther might appear and plead his cause, and to this the pope finally agreed. He sent Cardinal Cajetan to Germany and Luther duly appeared before him.

The Cardinal treated the reformer courteously and demanded the retraction of his errors. Luther replied that what the Cardinal termed his errors

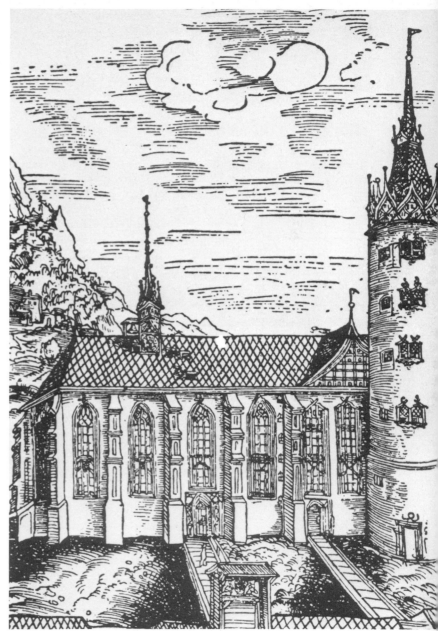

were not errors but truths of God's Word, and that he could and would do nothing against his conscience. Cajetan dismissed him with the words, 'Recant, or do not come into my presence again'. He wanted to have nothing more to do with the rebellious monk with the deep-sunken eyes and strange thoughts in his soul. Secretly he gave orders that Luther must be taken captive, but Luther received a timely warning and escaped his hands.

It was not long before the pope made another attempt to demonstrate the power of Rome, but as he now realized, flies are more easily caught with molasses than with vinegar, and so he sent his agent, a friendly, good-natured man named Karl von Miltitz, to Frederick the Wise, to present to him a golden rose, a costly gift which conveyed to its recipient fatherly love and special goodwill. The divine fragrance of this flower was to permeate the heart of Frederick and to lead him to do what the pope wanted, namely, to withdraw support from Luther and to induce the reformer to bow to the papal will. At first it appeared as if this policy would succeed. Luther apologized for his vehemence and undertook to abstain from further disputing if his opponents also remained silent. Miltitz then kissed Luther and returned to his master.

Luther soon made it clear, however, that he was not prepared to depart from his fundamental doctrinal principles, and the rift between him and the pope grew steadily wider as months went by. Another papal agent reported to Rome that the reformer was a very stubborn and dangerous heretic, and ultimately the pope excommunicated him. A bull (Latin 'bulla'=a seal) dated 15th June, 1520, was issued from Rome condemning the reformer and ordering the burning of his writings. Luther on his part formally renounced the papacy by burning a copy of the papal bull in the presence of a great crowd, among whom were students and professors. As he cast the bull into the flames he said, 'As thou (the Pope) hast vexed the Holy One of the Lord (Christ), may eternal fire vex thee'. Soon afterwards in his writings he denounced the pope as Antichrist. The reformation was well and truly under way.

When David was persecuted by King Saul he found a real friend in Jonathan, who was of great service to the troubled fugitive. In a similar way Philip Melanchthon was Luther's Jonathan during the days of struggle and persecution. He had become so fully convinced of the truths explained and proclaimed by Luther that their two souls were knit together in lifelong friendship. But Melanchthon was a very modest man; he had none of the boldness and daring of Luther. Nevertheless he was a great help to the reformer, for he was a man of deep scholarship. At the age of sixteen he published a Greek grammar; and five years later he became professor of Greek in the University of Wittenberg, the very place where Luther himself taught. He might have hesitated a long time before acknowledging himself to be a friend and admirer of Luther, but God's providence pushed him to the front as a witness to the truth.

The remarkable talents, vast knowledge, great learning, and fine culture of Melanchthon led to his being called 'the teacher of Germany'. Luther owed much to the calmness, gentleness and wise counsel of his colleague who did his best to keep the reformer's zeal and fervour within proper bounds.

Melanchthon's birth-name was Schwartzerd, meaning 'black earth', his father being known as 'the Heidelberg armourer'. When, in his youth, he became an outstanding scholar, Reuchlin, himself one of the greatest scholars of Germany, considered 'Schwartzerd' far too homely a name for him, and persuaded him to adopt 'Melanchthon' as its Greek equivalent, although, in actual fact, he usually wrote it 'Melanthon'. Normally he signed himself simply as 'Philippus'. He rendered excellent service to the work of reform in Germany, being second to Luther himself. He

21

Luther and the Pope

Pope Leo X (1513–21). He expended papal revenues on art, letters, and music. Under him the Italian Renaissance reached its greatest splendour.

lived until 1560, by which time he was 'weary of life and anxious to depart'.

But we must return to Luther. The burning of the papal bull was an act from which there could be no retreat. The reformer had set his foot on the way from which he could not return; he was now on the road leading to victory or defeat. The various powers of Europe—emperor, kings, princelings, cardinals, monks, abbots, and all—concentrated their attention on the conflict between the son of a German peasant and the man who wore the triple crown of the papacy. What would be the outcome?

The greatest monarch of his time was the Emperor Charles V. He had been elected to the throne of the Holy Roman Empire in the year 1519, at the age of nineteen. He was the grandson of Isabella and Ferdinand, the rulers of Castile and Aragon respectively, and claimed much of the New World of America as well as extensive territories in Europe. As he was a devoted son of the Roman Catholic Church, he was requested to deal with the case of Luther in a diet to be held in the city of Worms, and this he consented to do. He ordered Luther to appear before him. The reformer's friends warned him not to go, reminding him that the safe-conduct given to John Huss just over a century earlier had not been honoured. But Luther replied to them, 'If there are as many devils in Worms as tiles on the housetops I will still go there'. The most famous hymn that Luther ever wrote—and he composed a number of hymns—is said by some to have been written on the occasion of his entry into Worms, but this is incorrect. Nevertheless the lines are so typical of the man, and so appropriate for the Diet of Worms that we give the first and last verses:

A safe stronghold our God is still,
A trusty shield and weapon;
He'll help us clear from all the ill
That hath us now o'ertaken.
The ancient prince of hell
Hath risen with purpose fell;
Strong mail of craft and power
He weareth in this hour—
On earth is not his fellow.

God's Word, for all their craft and force,
One moment will not linger,
But, spite of hell, shall have its course,
'Tis written by his finger.
And though they take our life,
Goods, honour, children, wife,
Yet is their profit small,
These things shall vanish all,
The city of God remaineth.

On the 16th April, 1521, Luther arrived at Worms. The streets were crowded with people, all waiting to see the strange man who, as many of the people thought, was the devil personified. Windows and even rooftops were filled with spectators, for the occasion was indeed historic. A single man had risen in revolt against the religious ideas of Church and State, and all the forces of Church and State were invoked to quell him. Henry VIII, the king of England, was himself engaged in writing a book against Luther. Indeed, all States in which Roman doctrine held sway looked with unconcealed wrath upon 'the German beast' who set Pope and Church alike at defiance.

So dense were the crowds that, on April 17, the day fixed for the first meeting of the Diet, it was extremely difficult for the reformer and his supporters to reach the conference hall. Ultimately they did so. At the entrance stood a valiant knight, a famous army commander, who said to him, 'My poor monk, my poor monk, you are on your way to make such a stand as I and many of my knights have never done in our toughest battles. If you are sure of the justice of your cause, then forward in the Name of God, and be of good courage—God will not forsake you'.

When Luther entered the hall of assembly, he was astounded to see such pomp and brilliancy before him. The Emperor occupied the principal seat, of course, but his brother was also present, besides six electors of the empire, 24 dukes, and 8 margraves, all representing worldly power, and all of them allies of the Church. In addition there were 30 archbishops, bishops and abbots, 7 ambassadors, papal nuncios, and the deputies of free cities. In all there were 206 persons of rank. The Presiding Officer, Johann von Eck, opened the proceedings by asking Luther whether he was the author of the writings displayed on the table before them; secondly, he asked whether

Luther was willing to retract the doctrines contained in the books of which the Church disapproved. In reply, the reformer, having examined the pile of books, acknowledged that he was indeed their author, but as for the second question he asked for time for reflection, that he might not act imprudently but give an answer without offending against the Word of God. The request was granted, and Dr. Eck, in the Emperor's name, adjourned the proceedings until the following day.

Luther spent much of the night in prayer. One of his friends gives us a specimen of his supplications: 'O God, my God, be with me and protect me against my enemies of the world. Thou must do it, Thou alone, for in me is no strength. It is thy cause, O God, not mine. On thee I rely, not on man, for that would be in vain. O God, dost Thou not hear? Do not hide thy face from me.

Thou hast called me, now be my stay. I ask it in the Name of thy Son, Jesus Christ, my protector, my shield and my defence.'

April 18, 1521, was the greatest day in Luther's life. The occasion has been described as 'one of the sublimest scenes which earth ever witnessed, and most pregnant with blessing'. Again the streets were crowded with spectators; again the assembly hall was filled with notables. There was a delay of about two hours before he was brought before the Emperor; and again Dr. Eck put to him the question as to whether he would defend the books he had written or withdraw them in whole or in part. Luther made his reply—'the speech that shook the world'—first in Latin, then in the German language, and it ended thus:

Unless I am convinced by testimonies of the Scriptures or by clear arguments that I am in error—for popes and councils have often erred and contradicted themselves—I cannot withdraw, for I am subject to the Scriptures I have quoted; my conscience is captive to the Word of God. It is unsafe and dangerous to do anything against one's conscience. Here I stand; I cannot do otherwise. So help me God.

These bold and uncompromising words caused a measure of pandemonium in the Diet. Everyone was speaking simultaneously. Above the uproar Dr. Eck tried to make himself heard as he warned the reformer that General Councils of the church were a much safer guide to truth than the individual conscience. The Emperor, for his part, showed little patience with Luther's doctrine and person. Rising from his seat in anger he informed those about him that he had had enough of such talk, and thereupon he went out from the Diet. On the following day he told his courtiers that 'he could not see how a single

left Printer Johann Froben (d. 1527). In Basel he established a printing house about 1491 and became noted for the skill and accuracy with which he performed his work. He printed books for Erasmus, including his edition of the Greek New Testament in 1516. In consequence Basel became the centre of the German book trade. Froben also planned to print editions of the Greek Christian Fathers, but this was largely carried out by his son-in-law. In all, Froben printed about 300 books, including the Latin Vulgate.

monk could be right and the testimony of a thousand years of Christendom be wrong'.

Luther was escorted back to his lodgings, the Emperor's safe-conduct holding good. On April 25th he was allowed to leave Worms. Certain Spaniards followed at his heels, railing and mocking, and imitating the cries of wild beasts in pursuit of their prey, but the reformer left the city and set out on his journey back to Wittenberg. Before many days had passed he was placed under the ban of the Empire. He was declared an outlaw, and thereafter any who lodged him or gave him food and drink were liable to be charged with high treason against the Emperor.

22

Luther at the Wartburg

When Luther left Worms he anticipated a speedy journey to Wittenberg, but the unexpected happened. At a considerable distance from Worms the path entered a glen, thickly forested even to the tops of the surrounding hills. Suddenly there emerged from the woods a company of horsemen, armed to the teeth. They surrounded the carriage in which the reformer was riding, seized him and hurried him away. Their journey ended at a stately castle some eight miles distant from the scene of the attack. Its name was the Wartburg and it occupied the top of a hill overlooking Eisenach.

The friends of Luther, and Frederick the Wise in particular, had arranged for this to happen, so that the reformer might be taken from the busy and hostile world for a time and provided with a safe retreat where his foes could not find him or molest him. For almost a year therefore the world lost sight of Luther, not knowing his whereabouts. But to him, the Wartburg was a Patmos, a place of banishment indeed, yet not so unpleasing as was the real Patmos to John the apostle. He was to remain in hiding until the storm had somewhat abated. He was dressed in the garb of a knight, was addressed as Squire George, and having grown a beard and with a sword in his belt, was left to his own sweet will.

How was he to spend his time? Mainly in the study of the Scriptures, but, in addition, in the work of translating them into the German tongue. The printing press had been set up in Germany in 1454, and the first book printed was the Gutenberg Bible, but as this was in Latin it was of little use to the mass of the German people. Nine years later a Strassburg printer produced the so-called Mentel Bible in the German language, but it had two great defects; it was a translation from a translation, that is, from the Latin Vulgate, and not from the Hebrew and Greek originals; also it was clumsily worded and partly incomprehensible.

Luther was ideally qualified for the work of translation. He had given close attention to Hebrew and Greek for a number of years, and he was supremely gifted in the use of his own German language. It was said of him that 'no one wrote or spoke the German language as well as he'. At this point the Greek New Testament edited by Erasmus in 1516 proved immensely useful. Working at a tremendous pace Luther completed the first draft of the German New Testament in eleven weeks, and with the help of Melanchthon he gave it a thorough revision. By 1522 it was on sale in German shops for a sum equivalent to the week's wage of a carpenter or similar workman; and it sold at lightning speed. Next came the translation of the Old Testament, which was published in parts and completed by 1534, Luther having been helped by his friends Bugenhagen, Cruciger, and Justus Jonas, as well as by Melanchthon.

In the seclusion of the Wartburg, Luther was able to take a little recreation occasionally. During some of his walks he used to look for strawberries, and on occasion he found his heart troubled by the sufferings of hares and partridges which were being hunted. Once, he says, 'I saved alive a poor little hare which I picked up, all trembling from its pursuers. After keeping it in my sleeve for some time, I set it down, and the creature was running off to secure its liberty when the dogs getting scent of it, ran up, broke its leg, and then pitilessly killed it. The dogs were the Pope and Satan, destroying the souls which I seek to save, as I sought to save the poor little hare'.

After spending ten months at the Wartburg

Luther heard of disturbances which had broken out at Wittenberg, so without waiting for permission from Frederick he hurried to that city,

Luther working on the translation of the New Testament at the Wartburg.

The Wartburg.

greatly to the joy of his friends. Unhappily, however, social unrest and a rising of peasants against princes occurred at this time, and Luther, a strong supporter of princely power, did not always write and speak wisely about the peasants' demands. The rising was not suppressed without bloodshed. Until agitation died down the progress of the Reformation was much hindered.

In 1525 Luther believed that the time had come for him to marry. His choice of wife fell upon an escaped nun, Catherine von Bora, and his subsequent home and family life gave him much joy. It was a special joy to Luther that, at the marriage ceremony, his parents, Hans and Greta Luther, were present, and particularly because they believed the truths which God had used their son to proclaim so loudly and effectively. Sometimes the reformer called his wife, his 'dear rib', in allusion to Genesis 2 : 21. Luther himself was generous almost to a fault, but his wife seems to have exercised a restraining influence upon him in domestic matters, much as Melanchthon did in more public matters. Catherine even set to work rearing pigs and making a small fishpond, all for the good of her household.

By means of his numerous publications Luther might have become rich, for there was always a ready market for his books through northern and western Europe. But the reformer did not look for his reward in gold. He received but a meagre salary and was very liberal, often giving away more than he could well afford to the cause of the Reformation and to the poor, so that he often lacked money to buy ordinary necessities for his family. But Catherine and he were supremely happy in each other. In his will, he described her as his 'pious, faithful and devoted wife, always loving, worthy and beautiful'. She cared for his health and his general well-being. Melanchthon tells us that, to his knowledge, in earlier times Luther's bed had not been made for a whole year—he was too busy to make it—and was 'mildewed with perspiration'. 'I was tired out' said Luther, 'and worked myself nearly to death, so that I fell into bed and knew nothing about it'. Catherine must have come to him as a domestic reformer!

Luther remained a busy man to the end of his days. It is indeed marvellous how much he wrote in the space of about 25 years. To transcribe his works would take a rapid writer an average lifetime if he worked at the rate of ten hours a day. It is a striking fact that many of Luther's writings have been translated into English and can be purchased in an American edition at the present day in 55 volumes. His best known books are his *Large and Small Catechisms*. Both treat of Christian doctrine as he found it in the Scriptures. The first was written for ministers and teachers of the Word, the second for students in school and at home. They were translated into many languages. In certain respects his greatest book was *The Bondage of the Will*, which was written against the teaching of Erasmus who held, with the Roman Catholic Church, that man's will was not totally depraved by the Fall but was able to

Catherine Von Bora, Luther's wife.

contribute something to salvation. In his book Luther uses an illustration taken from the writings of Augustine:

Man's will is like a beast standing between two riders. If God rides, it wills and goes where God wills; if Satan rides, it wills and goes where Satan wills. Nor may it choose to which rider it will run, or which it will seek, but the riders themselves fight to decide who shall have and hold it.

Luther was also a musician and a poet. One of his hymns has already been quoted; it has been called the battle-song of the Reformation—'A safe stronghold our God is still', or, in another translation, 'A mighty fortress is our God'.

Luther died in the year 1546 in Eisleben, the city in which he was born. He had returned to Eisleben because two brothers, the Counts of Mansfield, had asked him to arbitrate for them in their family difficulties. He had the great satisfaction of seeing the Counts reconciled. Although he suffered much pain from ill health during the last few years of his life, his final illness was of short duration. He fervently prayed at intervals and exclaimed three times in quick succession, 'Father, into thy hands I commit my spirit, for thou hast redeemed me, thou God of truth'. Then Justus Jonas, one of his trusted friends and fellow-workers, asked him whether he remained determined to stand fast in Christ and in the doctrine which he had preached! To which he gave a distinct 'Yes' in reply. He was buried in the castle church at Wittenberg, on the door of which, 29 years before, he had nailed his famous 95 theses.

In the summer of the following year, the emperor Charles V stood at Luther's grave. One of his captains, standing by his side, asked him whether it would not be fitting for the bones of the arch-heretic to be burned. But Charles replied, 'I make war upon the living, not upon the dead. Let this man rest until the day of resurrection and of judgment'.

23

The Protestants in Germany

In our last four chapters attention has been centred upon Martin Luther, but before we turn from Germany to deal with the Reformation in other countries, it is desirable to take a further look at events from the Diet of Worms in 1521 to what is known as the Peace of Augsburg in 1555. The Emperor Charles V was checked in his fanatical zeal to crush the Reformation by political intrigue. His dominions were so extensive and his problems so numerous and varied that it was impossible for him to give his undivided attention to German affairs. If only the faithful ally of the Pope had had his hands free! But God rules his Church from on high, and he makes even the princes of the world subservient to the development of his kingdom, 'since all creatures are so held in His hand, that without His will they cannot so much as move'.

In 1526 the Emperor called a Diet to meet at Spires in which favourable action was taken with respect to the evangelical cause, for religious liberty was granted to all until a council should re-establish unity. How mild, how lenient did Charles V show himself now! The friends of the Reformation rejoiced, the Catholics were chagrined.

Three years later the tables were turned: another diet was to meet at Spires. Here the action of the former Diet was reversed and the Emperor demanded unconditional submission to the papal yoke. The princes were divided; six of them, together with a large number of German cities, declared that in matters concerning the glory of God and the salvation of souls their consciences required them to reverence God above all, and that it was not possible for them to yield to the Emperor's demands. Because of this protest they and their followers were called Protestants.

In 1530 the Emperor summoned another Diet to meet at Augsburg in Bavaria. He himself planned to attend in the hope of restoring peace among his subjects through a discussion of religious differences. Luther did not attend, for he was still under the ban of the Empire, and therefore it was not safe for him to leave the territory of the Protestant Elector of Saxony. Melanchthon was the chief reformed theologian present at the Diet, and with Luther's help he had drawn up a series of articles of belief crystallizing the Protestant position. These articles are called the Augsburg Confession. The Emperor demanded that the Confession should be read to

the diet in Latin. 'No', said John, Elector of Saxony, 'we are Germans and on German soil I hope your Majesty will allow us to speak German'. And in German the Confession was read, the result being that the great doctrines of Scripture, including justification by faith, were much more vividly presented to the assembled company than would have been possible in Latin.

The whole assembly was visibly moved by the reading. It was also made evident to all that the strength of Protestantism lay in its reliance upon Scripture and in its requirement that the truth taught in Scripture should be given to men in the languages which they understood and spoke. The Roman theologians claimed that they could refute the Confession by quotations from the Church Fathers, which caused one of the princes, Duke George of Saxony, although an enemy of Luther, to reply: 'Then the Lutherans are firmly entrenched in the Scriptures, and we are entrenched outside of them'. He stated the matter well.

The deliberations at the Diet were protracted, but finally the Emperor gave the Protestants until April 1531 to reconsider their position. He believed that, under pressure, Melanchthon was at times inclined to yield points to his opponents, and he hoped that this would now happen, and that the Confession would prove worthless. His Majesty was disappointed. The princes refused to give way, and soon they formed the League of Schmalkald in order to present a united front to Charles. But the Emperor had no wish to engage in war with them so long as the Turks and the French engaged his armies. Instead he assisted the Catholic party in Germany to form a league of their own. During the 1530's the two Leagues contended together but war was avoided. On their part the Protestants hesitated to engage in hostile acts, for they wished to remain on the defensive, not to take the offensive.

The uneasy peace continued until the death of Luther in 1546. By that time the Emperor had inflicted a crushing defeat on the French king and thus felt able to take up the Protestant challenge. On their part the Protestant princes were enfeebled. One of their leaders, Maurice, Duke of Saxony, the nephew of Duke George, proved treacherous and this enabled Charles V to gain an easy and apparently decisive victory. But he soon learned that, without the continued use of Spanish troops, he could not enforce his will upon the German people. Years passed. Resistance to the Emperor again grew stronger. Finally, the same Maurice, an able soldier, turned against him also, and almost succeeded in capturing him. By this time Charles was weary of war and he decided to abdicate. At the same time (1555) the Peace of Augsburg was concluded.

The Peace of Augsburg was based upon the principle of *cujus regio ejus religio*, meaning, 'to whom the rule, of him the religion'. In other words, each prince would determine the religion of his people. If the ruler was Catholic, his people were to be Catholic; if Protestant, his people were to be Protestant. And Protestant, in Germany, meant Lutheran. Other forms of Protestantism were not recognized by the Peace. This was one reason for the Thirty Years' War of the following century. But for the time being a measure of tranquillity descended upon the numerous German states and cities. Germany was at peace, but was divided.

But before we turn from Germany to see what happened in other States of Europe, we give stress again to the influence exercised by Luther through his writings in which he expounds the basic principles of the Christian faith. We have already mentioned the weakness of the doctrinal position taken by Erasmus, in whose view men qualified for salvation by their own efforts and attainments, weak and scanty though those efforts might be in themselves. On the contrary Luther urged that salvation is and from God, through Christ, by the sheer unmerited grace of God. He proved that the will of the unsaved man is a will in bondage to sin; that the natural man is powerless to do anything to deserve salvation; and, in short that 'it is not of him that willeth, nor of him that runneth, but of God who showeth mercy'. Casting aside all human subtleties, he showed from Scripture that faith is not man's meritorious act, and that a full justification from sin, as before God, is of grace and faith alone, through Jesus Christ.

And in such a view, all the Protestant Reformers—and we are about to look at the work of several others—were at one. Differ as they might and did in certain lesser matters, they were undivided in the belief that the salvation of the soul is the free and sovereign act of the Triune God. To his salvation man contributes nothing; his salvation is 'of God, through God, and to God' (Romans 11 : 36).

As for Luther's Commentaries on books of Scripture, the best-known is undoubtedly that on Paul's Epistle to the Galatians. Many have testified to its outstanding value. Charles Wesley, for example, after being introduced to Luther's Commentary by a friend who described it to him as 'a very precious treasure', writes in his *Journal* (May 17, 1738): 'I spent some hours this evening in private with Martin Luther, who was greatly blessed to me, especially his conclusion of the second chapter'. But the best-known of all such commendations is that found

Luther and his children.

in John Bunyan's *Grace Abounding*, where (in Sections 129–130), after speaking about his perplexity of mind produced by temptations, he writes:

'But before I got thus far out of these my temptations, I did greatly long to see some ancient godly man's experience who had writ some hundred of years before I was born. . . . Well, after many such longings in my mind, the God in whose hands are all our days and ways, did cast into my hand, one day, a book of Martin Luther, his comment on the Galatians, so old that it was ready to fall piece by piece, if I did but turn it over. Now I was pleased much that such an old book had fallen into my hand; the which, when I had but a little way perused, I found my condition in his experience, so largely and profoundly handled, as if his book had been written out of my heart. This made me marvel, for thus thought I, this man could not know anything of the state of Christians now, but must needs write and speak of the experience of former days . . . I must let fall before all men, I do prefer this book of Mr. Luther upon the Galatians (excepting the Holy Bible) before all the books that ever I have seen, as most fit for a wounded conscience'.

And so it comes about, when we find men of

Philip Melanchthon (1497–1560). Appointed Professor of Greek in Wittenberg in 1518 (when a mere 21 years of age) he came into contact with Luther and became his co-worker in the furtherance of the Gospel. Sweet-tempered and gentle in argument, he balanced Luther's vehemence. In 1521 he wrote the first Protestant work on dogmatic theology. It passed through over 50 editions while its author lived. 'By his calm wisdom. Melanchthon did much to save the Reformation from those excesses that would have made progress impossible'. His work as a scholar and public teacher gives him a high place in the history of learning and education. His contemporaries seem to have regarded him as only second to Erasmus in scholarship.

the 17th and 18th centuries telling their fellows of the amazing value of the writings of a Christian of the 16th century concerning the salvation of God, that the Scripture is fulfilled, 'Great is the Lord . . . One generation shall praise thy works to another, and shall declare thy mighty acts'. (Ps. 145 : 3–4).

Having looked at the history of the Reformation as it began and made progress in Germany, we now turn to surrounding lands, and first of all to Switzerland, where in the northern part the people were mostly German in language and customs, in distinction from those parts which were geographically and in certain other respects linked with France.

Ulrich Zwingli led the Reformation movement in the northern part of Switzerland. He was born in the village of Wildhaus in 1484. Like Luther he was of lowly birth, but he was brought up in more favourable circumstances than Luther and was educated in a school at Basel and at the University of Vienna. He was an altogether different type of man from Luther, but the teaching of the Spirit of God led both of them in the same direction. Zwingli became more and more convinced of the sad condition of the Church, and as he was a very earnest and diligent student of the Bible, he also became convinced that between many of the teachings and practices of the Roman Catholic Church and those of the Scriptures there was a world of difference. At the same time he read the writings of the early Fathers, and the books of Wycliffe and Huss. When a colleague of Tetzel, Bernardin Samson, sold indulgences in Switzerland, Zwingli raised a protest, but he was not as bold as Luther, nor was Samson as boisterous as Tetzel, so there was not such a violent clash in Switzerland as there was in Germany.

In 1519 Zwingli—he had become a priest in 1506—was invited to become preacher in Zurich and he accepted on condition that he would be left free to preach the pure gospel of Christ. In this city striking things were to happen. Great crowds came to hear his sermons, and from all sides was heard the comment, 'Such preaching we greatly need; he tells us the way of salvation'. Zwingli showed himself a true shepherd to his flock. This became especially evident during the days in which plague came to the city. It proved very severe, for 2500 died of it out of a total population of only 17,000. Zwingli, ignoring all danger of infection, visited the stricken families, and comforted the dying. He himself fell a victim to the plague and for about three months he was very ill indeed. Finally he recovered and wrote a famous 'Christian song' to commemorate the event.

Three years after his arrival in Zurich, Zwingli expressed himself very clearly and frankly about fasting, especially during the season of Lent, and this plunged him into a contention with the bishop of Constance. The debate was in public and was heard by a crowded audience, including the Mayor and Council of the city. The spokesman for the bishop claimed that the antiquity of the custom of fasting during Lent was in itself a plain proof that it was inspired and required by the Holy Spirit. Zwingli spoke against the custom but urged the people not to act rashly, and to exercise patience. Like Luther at that time, he told the people to await the coming reformation. But the bishop remained highly dissatisfied with such words, and did his utmost to suppress all preaching of Reformation doctrines. Zurich, however, declared itself firmly in favour of Zwingli's preaching and teaching, and the influence of the city became widespread.

Luther and Zwingli agreed on many points of Bible doctrine, but they also differed on some

ULRIC ZWINGLE

important points, including the doctrine pertaining to the Lord's Supper. One of the German princes, Philip, Landgrave of Hesse, was anxious to bring about a union between the two men and their respective adherents, and for this purpose he called a conference at Marburg in 1529. But success was not achieved. It is not our purpose here to explain the doctrinal differences between the two men; it can only be said that on both sides views were tenaciously held, even though both claimed to hold strictly to the teaching of Scripture. With tears in his eyes Zwingli said, 'There are no people on earth with whom I would rather be in harmony than with the Wittenbergers' (that is, with the followers of Luther). But Luther would not bend to Zwingli's teaching and would only receive the Swiss reformer and his followers as friends, not as brethren and members of the Church of Christ. He said to Zwingli, 'You have a different spirit'.

Before long the Swiss brethren formed a new religious organization which they called the Reformed Church, in distinction from what came to be called the Lutheran Church. Reformation now made rapid progress. Switzerland is a country divided into cantons and many of these accepted the new doctrine; others, however, remained strictly Catholic, and even formed a league with Catholic Austria to suppress the Reformation. This made the enemies of Zwingli overbearing, and political troubles were added to doctrinal disputes. Protestants were persecuted and some were murdered.

Four cantons took up arms, and it appeared probable that the Reformation would gain a military victory, but before the decisive battle was fought a compromise was arranged. The league with Austria was nullified and the Catho-

lics promised toleration to the Protestants who lived in the Catholic cantons. When the Catholics did not give effect to their promise but continued the old policy of persecution, another civil war broke out, and soon an army of 8000 Catholics invaded the canton of Zurich. The Zwinglians at once raised a small army of 2700, the reformer himself joining the forces, not as a

View in the Alps.

opposite Zwingli (1484–1531).

[101]

combatant but as a chaplain. In 1531 a battle was fought at Kappel in deadly earnest and with great bitterness. Zwingli cared for the wounded and the dying, many of his own relations being among them, including his brother-in-law, stepson, and son-in-law. With hardly an exception, prominent Zurich families had to mourn their dead. About 500 were slain.

Zwingli was among the slain. Wounded in the legs by a spear, and his helmet battered by a stone, he had fallen down. One of the enemy, acting in kindly fashion, offered to call a Catholic priest to hear his dying confession. Unable to speak, Zwingli shook his head. 'Then pray to the Mother of God, and call upon the saints, that God in his grace may accept you', said the foe. Again Zwingli shook his head, an action marking him as a Protestant. More of the enemy then arrived and one of them, reviling Zwingli for holding the reformed faith, struck him with his sword and killed him. His body was next quartered by a hangman who was brought, and according to the law of the Empire, its various parts were mixed with dung and burned, his ashes being scattered to the winds.

Zwingli was only 47 years of age and his death was a cause of intense grief to his followers. Luther was deeply shocked. He believed that the displeasure of God had been shown against the Swiss for resorting to the sword to defend themselves. But before many years had passed the reformed faith had made remarkable progress, not only in the German but also in the French cantons.

Zwingli's successor at Zurich was Henry Bullinger, and under his teaching a Confession of Faith was accepted by all the reformed cantons. It was known as the Helvetic Confession (Helvetia having been the name of Switzerland in the days of ancient Rome) and was signed also by Knox and other Scottish ministers, by the churches of the southern Rhineland, and by the reformed congregations of Poland and Hungary.

25

John Calvin

John Calvin was born in July, 1509, at Noyon in Picardy, France. Occasionally, when he had come to years, he would speak of himself as 'a man from among the common people', but although one his grandfathers was a boatman or possibly a cask-maker, his father, Gerard, had risen in the world and held the post of notary and ecclesiastical registrar. He had married the daughter of an inn-keeper. Four or five children were born to them, John being the second. He distinguished himself at school, and when he was twelve years of age his father, who was in close touch with the local bishop, secured for him an ecclesiastical appointment, so that he became a 'clerk' and received the Roman Catholic tonsure. Obviously he was intended for the priesthood.

In due course the young Calvin went to study classics in the University of Paris, but before long his father quarrelled with the bishop of Noyon and decided that he did not wish his son any longer to prepare for the priesthood. He therefore instructed him to leave Paris and to study law at Orleans. This he did, but in 1531 his father died and his son was now free to choose his own career. He returned to Paris. A little later, however, he went back to Orleans to complete his study of law. In Paris he published his first literary work, a commentary on a book by Seneca, a writer who lived in the days of the old Roman Empire. But by this time he had been deeply influenced by the doctrines of the German reformers; they made a very strong impact on his conscience. We know little about his actual conversion, for, unlike Martin Luther, he rarely mentions himself in his later writings, but this much he says (and almost every word is significant):

My father had intended me for theology from my early childhood ... then, changing his mind, he set me to learning law ... until God at last turned my course in another direction by the secret rein of his providence. By a sudden conversion he tamed to teachableness a mind too stubborn for its years, for I was so strongly devoted to the superstitions of the papacy that nothing less could draw me from such depths of mire.

'A sudden conversion!' But the word translated 'sudden' can also mean 'unexpected', and Calvin may mean that his conversion surprised him even more than it surprised others. But converted he certainly was, and the event has had very great results for Protestant Christianity.

Calvin was a pale-faced young man, with sparkling eyes, sedate and earnest beyond his

Calvin as a young man, *from the painting by Holbein at Castle Aschbach, near Bamberg, West Germany.*

years. In Paris he was so strict and severe in manner that some of his fellow-students dubbed him 'the accusative case'. His happiest hours were spent among his books. His judgment was almost unerring; he was never carried away by extravagances or by wild enthusiasm. He obeyed his intellect rather than his passions. But his heart became filled with love for God and the people of God. Of all the reformers none has conferred greater benefits upon the Church of God than John Calvin, for none of them dug so deeply into the Scriptures by prayerful study, or brought so much fine gold of truth from the mine of God's Word as he.

Calvin now openly took the side of the despised and persecuted Protestants of Paris; he visited them and comforted them as much as possible. His friend Nicholas Cop was elected rector of the University of the city and Calvin seems to have assisted him to prepare his inaugural address in which he attacked the Roman Catholic Church and advocated reform after the mode urged by Luther. When news of this reached the King, Francis I, he required the arrest of the heretics. Cop, being forewarned, fled from Paris, and ultimately found refuge in the Swiss city of Basel which had, years before, been his father's home. As for Calvin, some accounts say that he escaped from the window of his room in a basket, but the evidence for this statement is inconclusive. Others merely tell us that, when his room in Paris was searched, his enemies failed to find him there. After a period of wandering he too found refuge in Basel in 1535. It was a city of comparative freedom, and a place of refuge for many. Erasmus, who died the following year, was living there, as also were Henry Bullinger, William Farel and others. It was a German-speaking city. Calvin did not speak German, but there was enough French spoken to make him feel at home, and then, too, scholars could always resort to the use of Latin.

Two principal occupations occupied Calvin at this time. In the first place he gave assistance to a certain Peter Robert who was working on a translation of the Bible into French. But at the same time he was writing a book ever afterwards known, in its English translation, as *Calvin's Institutes*, a treatise on the Christian religion, though a more exact title would be *Instruction in the Christian Religion*. It was dedicated to the king of France and Calvin hoped that it would convince him that the persecution of those who were receiving the reformed faith was wrong, foolish, and unwarranted. The book was published at Basel in 1535. It was republished, with additional material, from time to time, and eventually became, apart from the Bible itself, the most important book ever printed on the subject of the Christian faith.

After spending a little more than a year in Basel Calvin moved to Strassburg but to reach it was difficult owing to war between Francis I and Charles V. He had to make a long detour to the south and in doing so planned to spend one night in Geneva. News of his arrival reached William Farel, a French reformer who was already at work in the city, and a man fully capable of using strong language when he thought the cause of Christ demanded it! But let Calvin himself explain what happened:

Farel, who burned with an extraordinary zeal to advance the gospel, immediately strained every nerve to detain me. And after he had learned that my heart was set upon devoting myself to private studies, and finding that entreaties were in vain, he went on to say that God would curse my retirement and the peace of study that I sought, if I withdrew and refused him my help when the need for it was so urgent. I was so terror-stricken that I abandoned the journey I had planned; but I was so sensible of my natural shyness and timidity that I would not bind myself to accept any particular office.

It was in this way that young Calvin, aged 27 years, entered upon his first stay in Geneva.

Farel and Calvin were powerful preachers of the Word of God, and the listeners were many. But the two men were not satisfied that the people should become hearers only; they wanted them to become doers of the Word. To bring this about they introduced a strict discipline, too strict for many. Those who resented it—they were called Libertines—practised their assumed liberties more than they practised Christian virtues. Finally they won over the Council of Geneva to their views, and as a consequence Farel and Calvin were soon banished from the city. It almost seemed as if the work of reformation was to end in inglorious failure.

Leaving Geneva, Calvin returned to Strassburg where he became pastor to a French refugee congregation, and did his utmost to organize the church in accordance with the teachings of the New Testament. He compiled a psalm book which included French metrical translations made by Clement Marot and some of his own translation. This began to popularize psalm-singing throughout reformed churches. Then, too, he was engaged in writing commentaries on Scripture, and in contending for the faith at various conferences. He also decided to marry, the lady of his choice being a widow, Idelette de Bure. Later, a son, Jacques, was born to them but he lived only a few days.

Calvin lived for about three years at Strassburg, during which time the Roman Catholic

Church tried to recover control of Geneva. But, in the providence of God, some of Calvin's friends succeeded in obtaining control of the Genevan city Council, and it was decided to invite Calvin to return. He was reluctant to do so, not because his pride had been hurt by his former banishment from the city, but because he doubted whether he was the right man for the work which the situation demanded. Eventually, in 1541, he consented to return. He was received with great joy and set about the task of bringing the civil and religious life of the city under the discipline of God's Word. The instruction of youth was taken up with great energy. At first he preached twice on Sundays and three times during the rest of the week, but from 1549 he preached twice on Sundays and every day in alternate weeks.

Calvin's salary was fixed at 500 florins a year, the sum being a considerable one because it was desirable for him to entertain certain visitors passing through the city. He was also granted an allowance for wheat, wine and clothing; and a house and garden were provided for him. Wine was the common beverage of the times, such things as tea and coffee being quite unknown to Europeans. At best it was frugal living for a man in his position, but Calvin paid little attention to outward display and the 'good things' of life. Upon his return to Geneva, a cloak of broad cloth was given him as a present, of which he was evidently in great need.

Calvin's return to and settlement in Geneva took place in September 1541. It was an event of great importance in the story of the Reformation, for he donned, as it were, the mantle that Luther was soon to lay down, and the influence of his work and his writings quickly spread to all parts of Western Europe. It has been well said that to omit Calvin from the history of Western Civilization 'is to read history with one eye shut'. As the story of the Reformation unfolds further, the truth of this statement will become increasingly clear.

26 John Calvin in Geneva

By the middle of the 16th century John Calvin was the dominant figure of the Protestant Reformation. After Luther's death in 1546 all who had become convinced of the errors of the Roman Catholic Church looked to Calvin for guidance and instruction. The geographical position of Geneva, and the growth of the reformed movement in most parts of Europe, caused the city and its leader to be regarded as a rallying point. This was especially the case with those who fled from persecution. Geneva became a haven of refuge to Protestants whose lives were

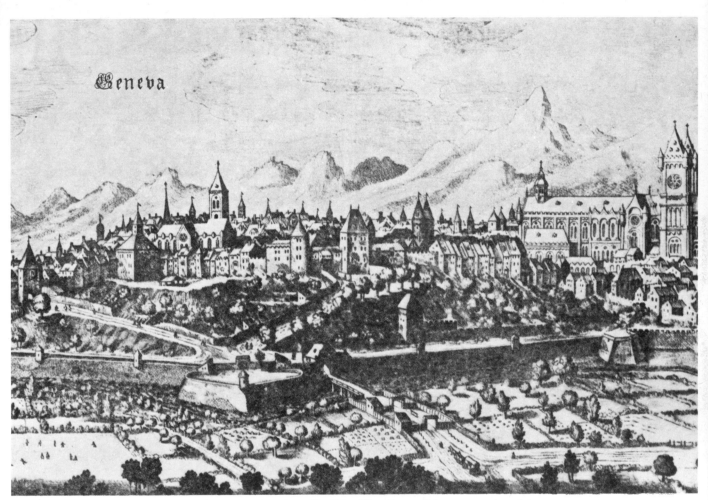

Geneva

endangered; its gates were ever open to provide fugitives with security. One such person was John Knox of Scotland. Young men often went to Geneva to be prepared for the work of the ministry of the gospel in central and western Europe.

It was in Geneva that several of the English and Scottish refugees set about the task of preparing a new translation of the whole Bible into English. The first edition was printed in 1560 and it soon became the favourite version of Protestants in England and Scotland. Of course, Calvin was not directly involved in its production, but as he had very great influence upon those responsible for it, in an indirect way he and his teachings werè related to it, and especially perhaps to the marginal notes which belonged to it. It was a potent influence in

View of Geneva in 17th century. On the right is St. Peter's Cathedral.

promoting the growth of Puritanism in England. Even when the famed Authorized Version of the Bible appeared in 1611, another 30 years passed before the Geneva Bible ceased to be printed.

Never had a European city before Calvin's time been organized so thoroughly for religious purposes as Geneva. The aim was the regulation by the church of the lives of its members, and of the whole life of the community. With great regularity 'almost the whole city came together to hear the Word of God'. Geneva was divided into three parishes; five ministers and three assistant ministers were appointed to conduct services at daybreak, noon, and in the afternoon, on Sundays; and there were services on Monday, Wednesday, and Friday in addition. Seventeen sermons a week in a city of 13,000 people! Calvin himself, as we have mentioned previously, preached regularly in the cathedral. Communion was held quarterly. Attendance at worship was enforced by fines for avoidable absence, and men were appointed to deal with delinquents.

As for the education of youth, all was carefully planned. The very young were taught the catechism and provided with lessons in the church. Then came the school where not only 'the three R's' were taught, but also the Latin and Greek classics, together with logic and even rhetoric. All who were capable of it, were taught the Greek New Testament. Naturally, much attention was paid to the doctrine of Christianity. There was regular instruction in Scripture, much psalm-singing, and diligent attendance at sermons and various lectures.

Beyond the school was the academy or university, the crown of the educational system. 27 lectures were given each week. At its head was the rector who was actually in charge of the entire educational system. There were professors of Latin, Greek and Hebrew, the arts and theology. Prizes were awarded, and diligence and efficiency met with praise.

There is no doubt that, in Calvin's time and for many years afterwards, Geneva produced scores, if not hundreds, of highly educated men.

As for the mass of the citizens, a wide variety of laws regulated their eating and drinking, their buying and their selling, their dress and their morals; but it must be remembered that all such laws were freely made by the governing body of the city, and the greater part of the citizens not only accepted them but welcomed them. Their lives were regulated at every point. Naturally there were discordant elements also. Not all the city's inhabitants wished to 'deny ungodliness and worldly lusts', and to 'live soberly, righteously, and godly' as Scripture and the laws required, and from time to time Calvin was troubled. But he never relaxed his efforts to lead men in the ways of the Lord, and on the whole he met with remarkable success. His character and influence were known to all, and felt by all.

One matter calls for special comment, for Calvin's enemies never forgot to charge a certain matter against him, namely, the death of the heretic Servetus which occurred while Calvin was substantially in control of Geneva, though not a member of its actual governing body, his power and influence being moral and spiritual rather than official. Servetus denied the doctrine of the Trinity and the Roman Inquisition had already condemned him to death by burning. But he escaped from the hands of the Romanists, and unwisely entered Geneva, where he was identified and put on trial for heresy. He became defiant as he tried to defend himself, and even accused Calvin of being a heretic and demanded *his* death. But the whole of Protestant Switzerland was firmly on the side of Calvin and the Genevan Council. The latter ordered that Servetus be burned alive. Calvin asked for a milder form of death for the heretic, but did not gain his point.

Calvin was certainly at fault, not of course in opposing the heresy of Servetus—he exposed it thoroughly—but in accepting the widely-held belief of the age that heretics should be put to death. We are all prone to judge men of former days by the standards of the age in which we ourselves live. In the 16th century, unhappily, it was common practice to sentence men to death for heresy, and that by burning. The Roman Church put countless numbers of Protestants to death, even as the Roman Emperors had done in days of old. They would have put Servetus to death by burning if they could have caught him. And unhappily, in this respect, Calvin was not free from the errors of his times. But let it be emphasized that he did not wish Servetus to be sent to the stake. It has been rightly remarked that 'although in the 16th century thousands of Protestants suffered the same fate at the hands of Roman Catholic persecutors Calvin has been constantly vilified for his part in this single execution'. Perhaps God allows blemishes in his own children, while on earth, in order that men should not idolize them and put them, as it were, on pedestals.

Calvin possessed a very weak and sickly physical frame. His body was also weakened by fasting and study, for he passed days without food and nights without sleep. It would have been a laborious task for a robust man to accomplish what Calvin did; much more was it so for one of frail physique and constant illnesses. But the reformer never shrank from the

Calvin preaching in the Cathedral of St. Peter's, Geneva, in his old age.

opposite The Monument to the
Reformers at Geneva. Figures
from left to right are those of
Farel, Calvin, Beza and Knox.

multitude of his tasks. If he was not preaching he was writing commentaries; if not writing commentaries he was penning letters, for he carried on a vast correspondence; and at every turn he was counselling others, or in other ways promoting the cause of the Kingdom of God. Unhappily, his wife died only nine years after their marriage, and for the rest of his life Calvin lacked the attention that only a wife can supply.

Calvin's greatest immediate influence was exerted through his teaching. Students thronged his lectures. When they returned to their homelands to meet the demands for Protestant witness which Europe provided, they carried in their minds and hearts the great truths of Scripture which Calvin had expounded in their hearing, and spread the light of the gospel to all parts. Most of them proved to be 'workmen who needed not to be ashamed; rightly dividing the word of truth' (2 Timothy 2 : 15).

That the Reformation was a work of God is clearly seen in the men whom God chose to bring it about, each in his time and place. The cornerstone of the building of God's Church is his own Son, who remains immovable and unchangeable, 'Jesus Christ the same, yesterday, today, and for ever'. The upper structure had become dilapidated and the forerunners of the Reformation (Wycliffe, Huss and Savonarola) had begun to tear down parts of it. Then Luther came; he completed the razing of the upper structure and then set up the new structure, solid and strong, resting firmly upon the foundation of God's Word. The completion of the building, however, was left to John Calvin, a master builder. His keen mind enabled him to read in more detail the plans and specifications of the great work, and in accordance with them, he performed his part so well and so accurately

that to this day his work remains an abiding influence in the Christian Church.

There are some who pour scorn on Calvin and his work; and among them are men who speak as if Calvin taught nothing but the doctrine of predestination. But it is not so. Calvin taught 'the whole counsel of God', and even concerning predestination none can truthfully say that what Calvin wrote and preached in any way departed from Scripture. What Scripture taught Calvin believed; and what Calvin believed he proclaimed to all who would listen to him; and from his own day to ours men of discernment have regarded him as perhaps the greatest of all Christian teachers since the time of the apostles.

Two or three years before he died Calvin became even more sickly than usual, if that were possible. His friends advised him to curtail his labours, but to them he replied, 'Do you want the Lord to find me idle?' He had to be carried to meetings which he wished to attend. In March 1564 he was taken to the City Hall to attend a meeting of the Council and he thanked them for what they had done for him. Several weeks later the 'Little Council' of the city visited him on his sick-bed. The end came on the 27th May, his mind remaining clear to the last. He was 54 years of age. Like a candle, he had consumed away so that he might give light to his age. His funeral was simple, and lest his followers in their grief should create the cult of a new saint, he was buried in the common cemetery of the city without a tombstone, so that, as in the case of Moses, 'no man knoweth of his sepulchre unto this day'. His treatises and commentaries are his monuments, and they will continue to be printed and studied as long as there are those who cling to the eternal truths of Scripture, and as long as there is a Church militant on earth.

27

England receives the Light (1)

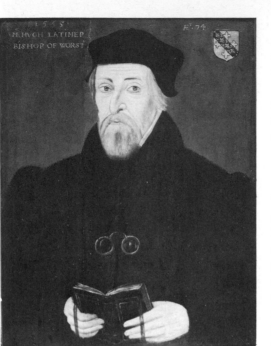

Hugh Latimer by an unknown artist, 1555.

It was inevitable that the influence of the movement begun by Luther on the Continent of Europe should be felt in England, and especially in the University cities of Oxford and Cambridge where the doctrine of the German reformer was earnestly, and doubtless hotly, debated. Indeed the inn where a few Cambridge scholars congregated became known as 'little Germany'. The group included 'little (Thomas) Bilney', Hugh Latimer, Myles Coverdale, Matthew Parker, and in all probability William Tyndale, all of whom rose to fame in Protestant annals.

The English king of the time was Henry VIII who, until his death in 1547, remained a bitter enemy of the reformed faith, even though it has often been claimed that he was responsible for the Reformation in England. But, whatever else he did, he had no love for Protestant doctrine and Protestant worship. In opposition to the teachings of Luther he wrote a treatise for which Pope Leo X rewarded him with the title of Defender of the Faith. To this day British coins remind us of the award, for they are inscribed Fid. Def. or F.D. (Defensor Fidei), and there are still those who look to the British crown to defend the Christian Faith.

Henry had been granted permission by the Pope to marry Catherine of Aragon after the death of his brother Arthur, her previous husband, but as his love for Catherine waned, especially after her failure to give birth to a living son and heir to the king—two sons had died in infancy—he requested another Pope to annul the marriage. To state the matter more exactly, Henry asked the Pope to declare that the papal permission given him to marry Catherine was contrary to the law of God, and that, in consequence, he had not been married to Catherine in any true sense at all. Hence he was free to marry another. Pope Clement VII did not actually refuse Henry's request, but deliberately prolonged negotiations, never intending to reach a decision favourable to the king. The Emperor Charles V, who had presided over Luther's trial at the Diet of Worms in 1521, was Catherine's nephew, and the Pope could not afford to displease him; he was the most powerful monarch of his time. So the English King waited and fumed in vain.

Henry wanted to marry Anne Boleyn, a lady-in-waiting at the court, and finally, in desperation, he broke with the Pope and the Roman Catholic Church. Without Papal approval he secured the appointment as Archbishop of Canterbury of Thomas Cranmer, a man willing to accept Henry's claim that he had never been married to Catherine according to the law of God, and to join Henry and Anne in marriage. The King then declared himself head of the Church in England. He beheaded Thomas More and John Fisher, two principal men opposed to his actions, persuaded Parliament to pass Acts making the new arrangements in Church and State lawful, and dissolved the numerous monasteries. The monasteries were strongholds of the Papacy. By these measures the king brought about the political Reformation.

But, as has been said already, Henry was never a Protestant. He continued to defend the principal teachings of the Roman Catholic Church, required all people in England and Wales to adhere to the Roman creed, and was quite willing to put to death men and women who opposed his will by embracing Protestant doctrine.

In one matter, however, Henry, advised by Cranmer and Thomas Cromwell, his chief minister of state, took a very important decision concerning the Bible. In the year 1538 he required a copy of the Scriptures in an English translation to be placed in every parish church in his kingdom, and the churches were to be left open at all convenient hours of the day so that people might have access to the volume. Two years earlier, the reformer Tyndale, when dying at the stake, had prayed, 'Lord, open the king of England's eyes', and many believed that the giving of the Bible to the people was the fulfilment of this prayer. The title page of what was called the Great Bible of 1539 shows Henry as king giving the Bible to Cranmer and Cromwell, who in their turn present the Bible, Cranmer to the clergy of the land, Cromwell to the people of the land.

In 1533 Anne Boleyn gave birth to a daughter, later Queen Elizabeth I; but the king's affections

Thomas Cranmer, painting of 1546 by Gerlach Flicke.

were already growing cold, and as she had not presented him with the son and heir he wished for, he soon brought false accusations of unfaithfulness against her, and Anne was executed. To the king's great joy his next wife, Jane Seymour, gave birth to a son, Edward, who succeeded his father upon the throne when he was a mere nine years of age. He reigned until 1553, dying at the age of sixteen.

Between 1547 and 1553 the Reformation in England and Wales made very rapid progress. Cranmer, by this time a genuine Protestant, welcomed reformers from the Continent, cooperated with the king's regents in removing images from churches, and replaced the Roman Catholic Missal (Service Book) by the English Prayer Book. Actually two such books were issued, the first in 1549, the second in 1552. The former retained certain Roman usages, and, as Protestant teaching became more firmly established, it gave place to the 1552 Book which also contained 42 Articles of Religion, still printed in the Church of England Prayer Book but reduced to 39.

The death of the youthful Edward VI was a tragedy for the British nation, for in those days, in England as on the Continent of Europe, it was taken for granted that the religion professed and followed by a nation must correspond with that professed by the occupant of the throne. An attempt was made to enthrone the Protestant Lady Jane Grey, but it failed, and Mary, the daughter of Henry VIII and Catherine of Aragon, became queen. She determined to re-establish Roman Catholicism throughout her realm. Shortly she married Philip of Spain, the son of the Emperor Charles V, and the persecution of Protestants commenced. Many leading churchmen fled to the Continent to escape her wrath: some found refuge in Germany, others in Calvin's Geneva.

The story of the persecutions of Mary's reign is told in great detail by John Foxe in his famous *Book of Martyrs*. He spared no pains to collect reliable information from public records and from eye-witnesses about the trial of Protestants before Catholic bishops and others, and he gave graphic accounts of the actual burnings. In all nearly 300 men and women were burnt at the stake. Chief among them were Hugh Latimer, Bishop of Worcester and Gloucester, Nicholas Ridley, Bishop of London, and Thomas Cranmer, Archbishop of Canterbury. The three were burned at Oxford, though Cranmer's burning was about six months later than that of the others. Latimer encouraged his fellow-sufferer with the famous words: 'Be of good comfort, Master Ridley, and play the man. We shall this day light such a candle by God's grace in England as I trust shall never be put out'.

Bishop John Hooper of Gloucester—he had taken Latimer's place in that city—was burned outside his cathedral. A person who visited him shortly before he suffered urged him to consider that life is sweet and death is bitter, and that if he would yield to the queen he might thereafter do much good. He replied:

True it is that death is bitter and life is sweet, but the death to come is more bitter and the life to come is more sweet. Therefore for the desire and love I have to the one, and the terror and fear of the other, I do not so much regard this death, nor esteem this life; but have settled myself through the strength of God's Holy Spirit, patiently to pass through the torments and extremities of the fire now prepared for me, rather than to deny the truth of God's Word.

Another prominent reformer, John Bradford of Manchester, was among the many burned at Smithfield, London. Robert Ferrar, Bishop of St. David's, Wales, was burned at the town of Carmarthen.

Soon after Mary's reign began Archbishop Cranmer was imprisoned in London, but later he was sent to Oxford and sentenced to undergo 'degradation', that is, various ceremonies were gone through to indicate that he no longer held office in the church. For instance, Bonner, Catholic bishop of London, scraped Cranmer's fingers and nails to undo the effects of the anointing which he had received twenty-three years previously when made archbishop. This having been done, however, his enemies suddenly changed their methods. They placed him in pleasant apartments, gave him liberty to walk in the open air, and spoke in such a kind way to him that he was overcome and persuaded to sign a paper renouncing his Protestant beliefs. Yet the queen was not satisfied. She had never forgiven Cranmer for his share in the setting aside of Henry VIII's marriage with her mother, and it was her will that Cranmer, despite his renunciation of his Protestant beliefs, should still be burned.

On the morning of Saturday, 21st March, 1556, 150 faggots of wood were piled in Oxford's Broad Street. A sermon was to be preached to the assembled crowds, but it was a wet morning and the preaching took place in the packed University Church, where a small platform had been erected on which the archbishop stood. After the sermon, he was called upon to speak to the congregation and to inform them that he had returned to 'holy mother Church'. But to the amazement and confusion of his accusers, he

The order and manner of the burning of *Anne Askew, John Lacels, John Adams, Nicholas Belenian,* with certaine of the Councell sitting in Smithfield.

Burning of Protestants (1546) at Smithfield,-Anne Askew, John Lacels, John Adams, Nicholas Belenian, from Foxe's *Book of Martyrs*.

boldly announced that in signing a recantation of his former beliefs his hand had 'offended in writing contrary to his heart'. 'Therefore,' he continued, 'my hand shall first be punished, for if I may come to the fire it shall be first burned. And as for the Pope, I refuse him as Christ's enemy, and Antichrist, and all his false doctrine'.

'Stop the heretic's mouth', the priests shouted. 'He must be out of his mind,' said a chief by-stander. There was no need to hurry Cranmer to the stake. He ran rather than walked there from the Church, and, as he had vowed, he held his right hand steadfastly in the flames, except that once he was seen to stroke his face with it as if to wipe away the flames. 'This unworthy right hand', and 'This hand hath offended', he repeated 'as long as his voice would suffer him'. The iron band which held him to the stake is still to be seen in an Oxford museum.

28

England receives the Light (2)

For three chief reasons we introduce at this point an English Reformation martyr named Anne Askew. Firstly, she was martyred during the reign of Henry VIII, whereas it is sometimes taken for granted that 16th-Century Protestants were put to death for their faith in the reign of Queen Mary Tudor only. But Henry's reign had its sufferers for conscience and for Christ's sake. Secondly, Anne Askew well represents the many women who 'loved not their lives to the death'. For obvious reasons, the history of the Reformation period, as of all periods in the Christian era, is largely devoted to the witness and activities of men. But godly women also played their part and bore their witness. Thirdly, it is helpful, in the 20th century as in all others, to realize how martyrs bore testimony before their judges, and to remember that the Lord gave a special promise to his 'witnesses', as recorded in Luke 21.15: 'I will give you a mouth and wisdom, which all your adversaries shall not be able to gainsay nor resist.'

Anne Askew was the daughter of a Lincolnshire knight and was about 25 years of age when she was burned at the stake, after being tortured upon the rack by none other than the Lord Chancellor of England himself, in order to get her to abandon her 'heresies'. Finally she swooned away and was taken to a house and laid in a bed, 'with as weary and painful bones as ever had patient Job'. During her imprisonment she wrote a poem of twelve verses of which we give three:

Like as the armèd knight
Appointed to the field,
With this world will I fight,
And faith shall be my shield.

Catholic Church. In her own account of the ordeal she numbered the questions put to her:

(1) DARE: Do you believe that the sacrament hanging over the altar is the very body of Christ really?

ANNE: Why was Stephen stoned to death?

DARE: I cannot tell.

ANNE: No more will I answer your vain question.

(Anne meant Dare to understand that Stephen had seen Christ in glory as Son of Man, standing at the right hand of God—Acts 7.56—so that it was not possible for his body to be in a pix above a Roman altar on earth.)

(2) DARE: A woman has testified that you have read how God is not in temples made with hands.

ANNE: So it is said in the 7th and 17th chapters of the Acts of the Apostles as Stephen and Paul spoke.

DARE: How do you take those sentences?

ANNE: I will not throw pearls among swine, for acorns are good enough.

(3) DARE: Why did you say that you would rather read five lines in the Bible than hear five masses?

ANNE: Because the one does greatly edify me, the other nothing at all: as St. Paul says, 'If the trump give an uncertain sound who will prepare himself to the battle?'

(4) DARE: You have said that if an evil priest ministered, it was the devil and not God.

ANNE: I spoke no such thing, but I said that an evil person ministering to me could not hurt my faith; but in spirit I received nevertheless the body and blood of Christ.

The entrance to the Great Hall at Little Sodbury Manor, Gloucestershire, where Tyndale taught the pupils of Sir John Walsh in the early 1520s.

Faith is that weapon strong
Which will not fail at need;
My foes therefore among
Therewith will I proceed.

On Thee my care I cast,
For all their cruel spite
I set not by their haste,
For Thou art my delight.

Anne was a person of ready speech and wit and in no uncertain way she was accustomed to state her convictions. She was taken into one of London's halls for close questioning by Christopher Dare, a theologian of the Roman

(5) DARE: What have you said concerning confession ?

ANNE: That, as St. James saith, every man ought to acknowledge his faults to others, and the one to pray for the other.

(that is, Anne did not hold to the Roman Catholic confessional).

(6) DARE: What have you said of the King's book ? (*The Erudition of a Christian Man*, compiled by various theologians and published by order of Henry VIII).

ANNE: I can say nothing about it for I never saw it.

(7) DARE: Have you the Spirit of God in you ?

ANNE: If I have not I am but a reprobate or cast-away.

(8) DARE: I have sent for a priest to examine you as to the sacrament of the altar.

PRIEST: What do you believe about the sacrament ?

ANNE: I will say nothing (because, said Anne, I perceived him a papist).

(9) DARE: Do you think that private masses help departed souls ?

ANNE: It is great idolatry to believe them of more value than the death that Christ died for us.

Later, Dare handed Anne over to Sir Martin Bowes, Lord Mayor of London, for further questioning:

BOWES: Thou foolish woman, after the words of consecration (i.e. in the service of the mass), is it not the Lord's body ?

ANNE: No, it is but consecrated bread, or sacramental bread.

BOWES: What if a mouse eat it after the consecration ? What will become of the mouse ? What sayest thou, foolish woman ?

ANNE: What shall become of it, say you, my Lord.

BOWES: I say that that mouse is damned.

ANNE: Alack, poor mouse!

Sent back to prison, Anne was visited by a priest instructed by Edmund Bonner, Bishop of London. He questioned her closely about 'the sacrament of the altar', only to receive the emphatic reply, 'What I have said, I have said'. Bonner himself, therefore, decided to talk with her, thinking perhaps that his high office would bring her to a change of mind. Among other questions he asked 'whether private masses benefited souls in purgatory'. Anne replied to him as she had replied to Dare. Bonner answered, 'What sort of an answer is that ?' 'Though it were but mean', she replied, 'yet it is good enough for the question'. A little later she again replied to his arguments, so that 'he flung himself into his chamber in a great fury' (so runs the record). The 'irresistible power' of a bishop had come up against an 'immovable object', namely, the faith of a true Protestant, even though found in a 'weaker vessel'.

The burning of Anne Askew, in company with three others, took place outside St. Bartholomew's Church, Smithfield, London. As depicted in old editions of Foxe's *Book of Martyrs*, on a platform erected alongside the stake sat the Lord Chancellor, the Duke of Norfolk, the Earl of Bedford, the Lord Mayor of London, and other notables. A sermon was preached, pardon being offered to the 'heretics' if only they would recant while yet there was opportunity. Anne, outspoken as ever, com-

mended whatever seemed scriptural in the preacher's words, but when he set the Word of God aside, she corrected him, saying, 'There he misseth and speaketh without the Book'. Next she was given a letter, said to be written by the King himself, also offering her pardon if she would but follow the example of the preacher who had saved himself some time previously by a recantation. 'I came not hither to deny my Lord and Master' was, for Anne, the only reply that would content her conscience. 'Let justice be done', cried the Lord Mayor, and without further delay the fire was kindled. 'Thus were these blessed martyrs', says Foxe, 'compassed with flames of fire as a blessed sacrifice unto God.'

We have described the trial and martyrdom of Anne Askew at some length in order to

preserve the testimony of a remarkable young woman and to illustrate the strong faith of the many who held no office in the Church of their day. The English nation as a whole was profoundly stirred by the burnings; they remained long in the memory, and the more so as a copy of Foxe's Book was placed in all parish churches in the reign of Elizabeth, so that all who could not afford to buy a copy—and it is a very large book—could read it on church premises.

It was not only martyr-fires, however, that turned England into a Protestant nation. Another factor of even greater importance was the translation of the Bible into English and the rapid growth of its circulation. The pioneer in this important work was William Tyndale, a scholar skilled in the Hebrew and Greek languages. It is even said of him that, whichever of seven languages he spoke, the hearer would suppose him to be speaking in his native tongue. After studying at the Universities of Oxford and Cambridge between the years 1510 and 1521, and becoming convinced that most of the clergy knew very little of the Bible, indeed no more than was quoted in their Missal (Mass Book), he resolved to give the nation a Bible that even a ploughboy could understand. But he soon discovered that the Roman Church would never permit an English translation (or in fact any other translation) to be made and printed in England. Consequently he went to Germany, where he hoped to find liberty in one or other of its many small States—it was by no means a united country—and in 1525 he had completed the translating of the New Testament. It was printed with great difficulty, for, although the first printing of the Latin (Vulgate) Bible took place in Germany with the approval of the Church, the translation of Scripture into the

language of the people was opposed as strongly in the Rhineland as in England. Finally Tyndale's books arrived in England hidden in bales of merchandise. The Church committed to the flames every copy it could find. At length, after much effort, it caught and burned Tyndale himself. It was a happening for which he had long prepared. He had taken refuge, in his later years, in a house in Antwerp where English merchants enjoyed certain privileges, but a false friend betrayed him to his foes. For a while he was kept in prison at Vilvorde, 9 miles north of Brussels. It included a winter, and last century in Belgian archives a researcher discovered a letter—the only letter preserved in the reformer's own hand—written to the Governor of the prison. It runs as follows:

. . . I entreat your lordship, and that by the Lord Jesus, that if I am to remain here during the winter, you will request the Procureur to be kind enough to send me from my goods which he has in his possession, a warmer cap, for I suffer extremely from cold in the head, being afflicted with a perpetual catarrh, which is considerably increased in this cell. A warmer coat also, for that which I have is very thin: also a piece of cloth to patch my leggings. My overcoat is worn out, as also are my shirts. He has a woollen shirt of mine, if he will be kind enough to send it. I have also with him leggings of thicker cloth for putting on

above The martyrdom of Tyndale, from Foxe's *Book of Martyrs.*

opposite In order to accomplish the translation of the New Testament, Tyndale went into exile in 1524. Twelve years later he was captured in Antwerp and imprisoned as shown here in the Castle of Vilvorde, nine miles north of Brussels, being executed in October 1536.

above; he also has warmer caps for wearing at night. I wish also his permission to have a lamp in the evening, for it is wearisome to sit alone in the dark.

But above all, I entreat and beseech your clemency to be urgent with the Procureur that he may kindly permit me to have my Hebrew Bible, Hebrew Grammar, and Hebrew Dictionary, that I may spend my time with that study.

And in return, may you obtain your dearest wish, provided always that it be consistent with the salvation of your soul. But if, before the end of the winter, a different decision be reached concerning me, I shall be patient, abiding the will of God to the glory of the grace of my Lord Jesus Christ, whose Spirit, I pray, may ever direct your heart. Amen.

W. TINDALE.

Beneath a surviving portrait of Tyndale, in Hertford College, Oxford, are two lines in Latin. We give them in an English translation:

That light o'er all thy darkness, Rome,
  In triumph might arise,
An exile freely I become,
  Freely a sacrifice.

We have previously mentioned that the placing of an English Bible in all parish churches took place as an answer, though not intended so, to Tyndale's dying prayer. He had hoped to publish the Old Testament in English as well as the New, but the work had to be completed by others. Under God England owes to Tyndale a very great debt of gratitude. He will ever remain one of the worthiest of her sons.

29

Scotland Transformed

It is customary to hold that the man who, above all others, brought the Reformation into Scotland was the intrepid John Knox. Certainly Knox is Scotland's greatest reformer. But two others at least deserve mention even in such a brief history as this. Indeed the account must go back earlier than the 16th century, for Scotland was not without its Lollard martyrs, notably Paul Craw, a native of Bohemia, who was burned at the stake at St. Andrews, Fifeshire in 1433, with a ball of brass in his mouth to prevent him from exhorting the onlookers.

Scotland's first Reformation martyr was Patrick Hamilton whose mother was in the direct line of descent from King James II of the House of Stuart. For a short time he studied at Wittenberg, the city of Martin Luther, and on his return to Scotland he boldly preached Protestant doctrine. As a result, in 1528, James Beaton, the Archbishop of St. Andrews, resolved upon his death. Much power was in Beaton's hands, for the King, James V, was a mere youth of sixteen, and the Archbishop was as powerful in the State as in the Church.

St. Andrews, one of the most historic spots in Scotland. In the middle distance are the ruins of the castle where John Knox began his public ministry in 1545. In the burial ground are the graves of Samuel Rutherford and others of the Covenanting period. In the dungeons of the castle Patrick Hamilton and George Wishart were held before their martyrdom (1527 and 1546).

Hamilton was arrested, confined in a dungeon at St. Andrews Castle by the sea, and then brought to trial. He was charged with numerous heresies, a Dominican friar named Alexander Campbell disputing against him. At the stake the fire was slow in burning and his agonies were prolonged. To Campbell he said, 'Brother, you do not in your heart believe that I am a heretic'. Foxe's *Book of Martyrs* records that he cited the friar to appear before the high

God as Judge of all men, to answer on or before a certain day of the next month whether his accusation was just or not, and adds that 'the said friar died immediately before the said day came'.

Patrick Hamilton's influence in Scotland was great. It is said that 'his reek infected all it blew on'; in other words, many were drawn to the Reformation by his testimony, What are termed 'Patrick's Pleas' (or places)—his points of Reformation doctrine—'became a corner-stone of Protestant theology in Scotland and England'.

But Archbishop Beaton had not learned his lesson. He continued to burn Protestants. Ten years after Hamilton suffered, five were burned on the Castle Hill at Edinburgh, that the people of Scotland's capital city and for miles around might see the blazing pile and take warning. But God raised up fresh witnesses to his truth, the best-known of them in the 1540's being George Wishart, at one time a schoolmaster in Montrose. Persecuted in Scotland for his faith he found refuge in the Bristol area of England where for a short while his courage failed him and he 'burned his faggot', a ceremony devised to show that the participant confessed that he deserved the stake. Soon, however, he found his way to Germany and Switzerland where his faith was strengthened, and after a time he returned to his native land resolved to preach the Gospel to his countrymen. Crowds flocked to hear him and he began to address them in the open air, convinced, as he declared, that Scotland would be illuminated with the light of Christ's gospel 'as clearly as ever was any realm since the days of the apostles'. But another Beaton was now in power—Cardinal David Beaton, nephew of James Beaton—and

he brought Wishart to trial at St. Andrews. The reformer urged that all teaching must be tested by Scripture. For example, during his trial the subject of purgatory was debated. Turning to his accusers, Wishart said, 'If you have any testimony of the Scriptures by which you may prove any such place, show it before this auditory'. But, says Foxe, 'this accuser had not a word to say for himself; he was as dumb as a beetle in that matter'.

As in the case of Hamilton the stake was erected outside St. Andrews Castle, the tower immediately opposite being fitted with tapestry and cushions so that the higher clergy might witness the burning at their ease. Wishart died nobly. Before the flames did their work he announced to the people, 'He who from yonder place beholds me with such pride shall within a few days lie in the same as ignominiously as he is now seen proudly to rest himself.' About three months later the Cardinal met his death. A band of his enemies, overcoming all resistance, burst into his apartments and killed him out of hand. The murder was a breach of God's law. 'Avenge not yourselves' says the Scriptures: 'vengeance is mine, I will repay, saith the Lord'. Yet with the words of a Scottish historian we may well agree: 'Viewed as an event in providence we may recognize in it a just judgment from God on a cruel persecutor; while, at the same time, considered as the deed of man, we condemn the instruments whose passions were overruled for accomplishing it'.

As for the Cardinal, I grant
He was a man we well could want,
  And we'll forget him soon;
And yet I think, the sooth to say,
Although the loon is well away,
  The deed was foully done.

John Knox preaching at St. Andrews on 11th June, 1559. Prominent in the foreground is the Duchess of Argyll and behind her the Catholic prelates, including Archbishop Hamilton. This was the occasion on which it was threatened that Knox would be shot in the pulpit. St. Andrews at this date was still a centre of Catholic power. *From the painting by Sir David Wilkie.*

But we pass on to the life and work of John Knox who gave the Scottish nation a body of Protestant doctrine and a pattern of worship that endured. He was born at Haddington in the early part of the 16th century, studied at Glasgow University, became a firm Protestant, defended Wishart from his enemies, and was owned as in a very real sense the martyr's successor. As persecution developed he decided to seek refuge on the Continent of Europe, but before he could do so he was captured by a French force which landed at St. Andrews to assist the Scottish king. He and others were taken to France and condemned to work on French war galleys, efforts being made to bring them back to the Roman Catholic fold. In his *History of the Reformation in Scotland* Knox recounts how on one occasion a 'glorious painted lady'—an image of Mary—was presented to him to be kissed. 'Trouble me not' said he to the bearer; 'such an idol is accursed and therefore I will not touch it'. 'Thou shalt handle it' said several Frenchmen, at the same time thrusting it violently to his face and putting it between his hands. Knox then took the idol and, spying his opportunity, cast it into the river, at the same

time crying, 'Let her save herself; she is light enough; let her learn to swim'. After this, says Knox's *History* no Scotsman was urged with that idolatry.

Knox's captivity lasted 19 months. 'It was not for nothing', says a historian, 'that the hand which gave to Scotland its liberty should itself for nearly the space of two years have worn fetters'. But for a while, on release by the French, Knox thought it wise to take refuge in England which was moving rapidly into Protestantism under Edward VI. He was appointed one of the king's chaplains, but when Mary came to the throne, he escaped to Germany and Switzerland. In Geneva, where Calvin was chief preacher, he found that which he judged to be 'the most perfect school of Christ that ever was in the earth since the days of the apostles. In other places I confess Christ to be truly preached, but manners and religion so truly reformed, I have not yet seen in any other place'. He spent four happy years in Geneva. Returning to Scotland in 1559 he found the people perplexed and confused. King James V had died 16 years previously, leaving the crown to his daughter Mary who was born only a week before her father's death. Mary's mother, Mary of Guise, took over the control of affairs until her daughter came of age and was still at the head of affairs when Knox returned from Geneva. Mary Queen of Scots herself in the previous year had married the Dauphin, the heir to the French throne, who a few months later became King of France as Francis II. Mary was now Queen of France as well as Queen of Scotland, and very soon the Courts of France and Spain let it be known that they regarded her as Queen of England also, for they refused to recognize Elizabeth as Mary Tudor's rightful successor.

In Scotland certain Protestant barons, who became known as the Lords of the Congregation, endeavoured to make their country adopt the Protestant faith, although the Scottish government was strongly Roman Catholic.

As soon as Knox arrived in Scotland he contended vigorously against idolatry and urged the people to turn to the plain truth of the gospel. Nor were his efforts in vain; his preaching was very powerful, and many embraced the truth of God's Word. One of the visible signs that Scotland now experienced reformation was the destruction of many of the buildings belonging to the Roman Church. Knox cared little or nothing for grand buildings, and especially so when they were used to propagate idolatry, yet he did not urge the wanton destruction of property. Some of his supporters, however, were prone to demonstrate enthusiasm for the Reformation by the destruction of abbeys and monasteries, Knox commenting on their work, that, after all, 'the best way to keep the rooks from returning was to pull down their nests'.

It was under the influence of John Knox that the Presbyterian system of church government was introduced into Scotland. In the English system of church government bishops were very powerful—the word 'bishop' is derived from the Greek word 'episcopos', meaning 'overseer' —but the Presbyterian system is based upon the authority entrusted by the church to elders (Greek 'presbyteros'). In time to come, as we shall see, the two systems came into conflict. At first, however, they existed peaceably side by side; but historically they developed along separate lines.

Another aspect of Reformation work in Scotland was the encouragement of education. An attempt was made to establish a school in every parish for the instruction of youth in true religion, grammar, and the Latin tongue. In the chief towns colleges were set up for the education of the more gifted and capable students. In consequence learning made great progress in the land and Scotland became renowned for its standard of education. One very remarkable example of scholarship is recorded by a 16th-century annalist. A Mr. Row, minister at Perth, boarded the children of nobility and gentry in his house and instructed them more particularly in languages. At table the conversation was all carried on in French, and the chapter of the Bible at family worship was read by the boys in Hebrew, Greek, Latin and French.

Knox's pulpit. Now in the National Museum of Antiquities, Edinburgh.

opposite Statue of John Knox outside St. Giles' Cathedral, Edinburgh.

John Knox's House,
Edinburgh.

But education was only a side-line with Knox whose great concern was to spread the knowledge of Christ and his gospel to all parts of Scotland. He had many adversaries, for he boldly denounced the Mass and other aspects of the doctrine of the Roman Church. 'I have learned', he said, 'plainly and boldly to call wickedness by its own terms, a fig a fig, and a spade a spade'. Concerning the Mass he said, 'One Mass is more fearful to me than if 10,000 armed enemies were landed in any part of the realm'. No wonder, therefore, that his life was endangered!

After the death of her French husband Mary Queen of Scots, no longer Queen of France, returned to Scotland to resume control of the government. The tenets of the Roman Church had taken deep root in her mind and heart, and it was her constant endeavour to prevent the progress of the Protestant faith in Scotland. It was inevitable therefore that she came into direct conflict with Knox. The reformer's opinion of her is striking. 'If there be not in her', he said, 'a proud mind, a crafty wit, an indurate (callous) heart against God and his truth, my judgment faileth me'. This opinion was formed as a result of several interviews which Knox had with the Queen, and of these a highly interesting record remains. On one occasion Mary said to Knox, 'What are *you* in this commonwealth?' 'A subject born within the same', he replied, 'and although I am neither earl, lord or baron in it, yet has God made me a profitable member within the same, and both my vocation and conscience require plainness of me'. On hearing such words it was with difficulty that the Queen recovered her composure.

But Mary had troubles other than those of religion. Her second and third marriages proved disastrous and in 1568 she fled to England to seek the help of Elizabeth. She was not allowed liberty, but was kept in pleasant confinement, and always remained a danger to the English Queen as plots were formed in her favour. Ultimately, after 20 years, Elizabeth signed Mary's death warrant.

Knox died in 1572. Occupied for long years in ceaseless struggle against opposing forces he became as he said, 'weary of the world' and 'thirsting to depart'. He was buried in Edinburgh, the Regent of Scotland speaking over his grave the long remembered words, 'Here lies one who never feared the face of man'.

What was formerly St. Giles' Churchyard, Edinburgh is now part of Parliament Square, and the place of Knox's grave was formerly marked by a stone with the simple inscription, I.K. 1572. The removal of this stone in recent years indicates how little the blessings which the Reformation brought are prized in the Scotland of today.

As in the case of England, religious affairs in 16th-Century France were closely linked with the occupant of the throne. When Lutheran teachings began to enter France the king was Francis I. He was three years younger than Henry VIII of England and in character very similar to him. Like Henry he took pride in patronizing men of letters, though probably he paid little attention to the learned Jacques Lefèvre who has been called 'the father of the French Reformation'. At first Francis I regarded the Reformation as a struggle of mind against a very conservative Church, but he had no real sympathy with Protestant teachings and his outlook was far from spiritual. In 1516 for political reasons he made a Concordat with the Pope, and before long, Frenchmen who leaned towards Luther, and later towards Calvin, knew that their lives were imperilled. In our chapter on Calvin it was mentioned that the Genevan reformer, himself a Frenchman, dedicated his *Institutes* to Francis I in the hope that persecution might be averted. But as Lutheran teachings gained adherents Francis became the more furious and many were burned at the stake. By 1545 thousands had been killed or sent to the

30

The Huguenots of France

Jacques Lefèvre d'Etaples
(1450–1536).

arrows'. He meant, of course, that in Geneva men would be trained to spread Reformation doctrine effectively.

The French king fought back by forbidding pedlars to sell books. Unlettered persons were forbidden to discuss religious matters at home or at work or among neighbours. Printers were regularly visited by government agents. All packages entering France from beyond the frontiers were inspected. Nevertheless Reformation work and witness continued, secretly when necessary, publicly where the king's authority was weak. In 1559 Henry II met his death at a tournament, his temple being pierced by a lance which he failed to avoid.

From about the year 1560 French Protestants were known as Huguenots. Their name and their creed alike came from Geneva, Certain Genevan patriots were known as Eidgenossen, or Confederates, and this name seems to have been transferred to French refugees in that city. From them it spread speedily throughout France. Not that the Huguenots were evenly distributed. Their chief strength lay in the area bounded on the North by the River Loire, and by the Rivers Rhone and Saône on the East, with Normandy and Dauphiné as outposts. Socially they had numerous followers among the lesser nobility, tradesmen, and professional men in the lower middle class. Very few of the great noblemen joined them and similarly the mass of the peasantry remained solidly Catholic. Paris itself, influenced by its famous university— it had 65 colleges—and its great religious houses, remained a papal stronghold.

The chief Huguenot leaders were Louis de Bourbon, Prince of Condé, and Gaspard de Coligny, Admiral of France (though he never commanded on the sea), 'the military hero of the

galleys, and twenty-two towns and villages had virtually been destroyed.

Dying in the same year as Henry VIII— 1547—Francis was succeeded on the throne by his son Henry II who had married Catherine de Medici, an Italian. For ten years she bore her husband no children, but subsequently she had seven, of whom three successively were kings of France. Henry II carried on his father's policy with even more ardour. A special committee of the French Parlement was formed called La Chambre Ardente (the Burning Chamber) from the number of its victims. To escape, not a few fled to Geneva which became thronged with refugees. Young men of courage, trained in Geneva, often returned to France at the risk of their lives to distribute books and tracts. 'Send us wood', Calvin had said to his fellow-countrymen, 'and we will send you back

French Reformation'. Condé was slain in battle in 1569. On the Catholic side, members of the Guise family who were related to the king were the chief leaders, particularly Francis de Guise and Charles, a cardinal of the Roman Church.

The death of Henry II brought his son to the throne as Francis II, a youth of sixteen, who had married Mary Queen of Scots. Before long, however, he died of a disease of the ear, and was replaced by his brother Charles IX, a boy of ten. Catherine de Medici, his mother, then became Regent of France. At the time of her husband Henry II's death she had been left with a family of five children, and was determined to protect their interests against the Guises on the one hand and the Bourbons on the other. The Bourbons had married into the

important House of Navarre, a kingdom on the frontier with Spain, and were represented by their Prince Henry, a friend of Coligny and a Huguenot, though not a man of deep religious convictions.

Shortly after 1560 a period of religious wars, which lasted on and off for thirty years, set in for France. Into the details of these wars we cannot here enter, but we concentrate attention on the lights and shadows of the period. At the centre of action was Catherine de Medici, and although at the beginning she seemed to wish to maintain a balance of power between Protestant and Catholic forces, it soon became clear that her ultimate aim was to crush the Huguenots.

Craftily she hit upon a plan to gain her object. To cement a treaty between the two parties, she proposed that the Catholic Princess Margaret, the sister of king Charles IX, should be given in marriage to Henry de Bourbon, the new Huguenot king of Navarre. All the notables of the land were invited to Paris where the marriage was to take place. Among them was Admiral Coligny. The Huguenots were not aware of the trap that was being set for them.

Before the festivities which followed the wedding were over, there occurred one of the most hideous crimes recorded in history. The date was St. Bartholomew's Day, 24 August, 1572. On the evening of that day Catherine went to her son, the king, and told him that the Huguenots had formed a plot to assassinate the royal family and the leaders of the Catholic party, and that, to prevent the utter ruin of their house and cause, it was absolutely necessary to slay all Protestants within the city walls. Catherine had prepared a document to this effect and she presented it to the king for signature, in order to make it an official document.

Admiral Gaspard de Coligny (from the original in the National Library of France, Paris).
'We must follow Jesus Christ, our Captain, who has marched before us. Men have stripped us of all they could . . . solely through the hatred they bear towards us because it has pleased God to make use of me to aid His Church.'

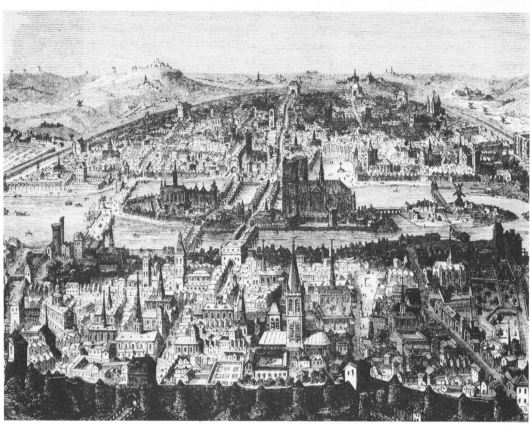

A view of old Paris.

The weak-minded king at first refused to contemplate such a dreadful crime against a section of his subjects, but finally, pressed by his mother, he yielded and exclaimed, 'I consent, but, then, not one of the Huguenots must remain alive in France to reproach me with the deed; and what you do, do quickly'.

The Paris mob was to be given a free hand; only Henry of Navarre, the bridegroom on the occasion, was to be spared. At midnight, August 24th, the castle bell tolled; this was the signal for the horrible butchery to begin. Coligny was one of the first victims. When the hordes appeared and stormed his house, he realized what was about to happen. 'Friends', said he to his companions, 'Flee and save your lives. I for one am ready to die, and I trust myself to God's mercy'. Some of his friends escaped.

Thirsting for blood the crowd faced the calm, dignified Admiral, a young man taking the lead. 'Are you Coligny?' he asked. 'I am he' was the response; 'young man, reverence my grey hairs'. A stab with a sabre was the answer. Mortally wounded, the body was hurled to the pavement in response to the command that came from the courtyard below. While Coligny's dead body lay there, Henry of Guise stooped down, looked at the Admiral, and said, 'I recognize him; it is he himself'. Then, kicking the gentle face, he went out, gaily encouraging his followers. 'Come, soldiers, take courage, we have begun well. Let us go on to find others, for so the king commands'.

The body of the Huguenot leader was treated shamefully. The head was cut off and carried to Catherine and Charles. It was afterwards embalmed and sent to Rome as a present for Pope Gregory XIII. The hands were also cut off and for three days the trunk was dragged about the streets of Paris by a band of brutal youths. For three days and nights the massacre continued within the city. Thousands were put to death. Orders were issued to the cities of France to purge themselves of heretics. In many places this decree was disobeyed, but in others it was carried out, and frightful massacres took place.

Philip II of Spain received the news with undisguised joy, for the massacres agreed with his own line of policy. Queen Elizabeth of England expressed disapproval but decided not to quarrel with France because of her dread of Spain. Pope Gregory XIII was so overjoyed that he commanded a salute to be fired, all the church bells to be rung, and a grand *Te Deum* to be sung. For three nights Rome was illuminated. The Pope also had a medal struck in honour of the victory of the Church. It included an angel carrying a sword and a cross. But, says the famous French statesman Sully, the outrage was followed by twenty-six years of disaster, carnage and horror.

The Massacre of St. Bartholomew: a scene in Paris on the night of 24th August, 1572.
Coligny, Admiral of France (though he was never in naval command) and leader of the Huguenots, had been shot at in the street on the 22nd August. The bullet tore a finger from his right hand and shattered his left elbow. On the 24th he was dragged from his bed, killed and cast from his window into the courtyard below. The illustration seems to attempt to combine both happenings. *From the Mansell Collection.*

31

The French Crown and the Huguenots

Not all the Huguenots were killed in the terrible massacre of St. Bartholomew's Day in Paris. Three out of every four escaped. Their case reminds us of what is declared of Old Testament worthies in the 11th chapter of the Epistle to the Hebrews: 'Through faith (some) escaped the edge of the sword . . . (others) were slain with the sword' (verses 34, 37). Of the pastors of the Huguenots in Paris, only two were killed, although no lives were more eagerly sought after than theirs.

Several pastors had a miraculous escape. In the case of Merlin, chaplain to Coligny, God's providence seemed almost as distinct as in the case of the prophet Elijah. After reluctantly leaving Coligny, at his earnest request, and clambering over the roof of a neighbouring house, he fell through an opening into a garret full of hay. Not daring to show himself, since he did not know whether he would encounter friend or foe, he remained in this retreat for three days, his only food being an egg which a hen laid daily within his reach. Finally he got clear away.

Charles IX reigned only a short time after the Massacre. He died in 1574 at the age of 24, a victim of remorse and periodic insanity. When thus attacked, the horrors of the terrible night tortured his excited imagination. Catherine, his mother, remained callous and unrepentant. She was the Jezebel of her day, the counsellor of others to do wickedly. She died in 1589 'forsaken and abhorred' by Catholic and Protestant alike. None lamented her dying.

Charles had been succeeded by his brother Henry whom his mother, by gold and intrigue, had earlier managed to get elected to the throne of Poland. He too died in 1589, but the real ruler of France during his reign had been Catherine. Henry met his death by assassination.

Henry of Navarre followed Henry III as Henry IV, the Huguenot husband of Catherine's daughter Margaret. With him better days seemed to dawn for the Protestants. But the Catholics would not consent to give their allegiance to such a king, and war continued. Henry won battles and besieged Paris itself, forcing some of its citizens, as some believe, to eat the flesh of their own children through lack of food. Finally a Spanish army from the Netherlands relieved the city. Henry then offered to recognize Catholicism as the state religion while he remain Protestant. This offer was refused; it pleased neither party. Ultimately Henry persuaded himself that 'Paris was worth a mass'; in other words he decided to own the Catholic Church as 'the true Church' and to yield obedience to its claims and to its Pope, his reasons being as follows: (1) He had failed to win France by force of arms; (2) The Huguenots were but a small minority of the nation; (3) the great majority of Romanists would never accept a Huguenot as king or leave him secure upon the throne; (4) Spanish soldiers in Spain itself and in the Netherlands were poised to invade the kingdom.

But the main reason for Henry's 'conversion' was his lack of true religious conviction. He was gallant, brave, generous, and patriotic, but his creed could be changed to suit political requirements. He was no Mr. Valiant-for-the-Truth. The Huguenots could truly say, 'Put not your trust in princes'.

With the king's 'conversion' the Romanists seemed to have emerged as victors from the long civil war, and if the king had insisted (as in the settlement in Germany) that all his subjects must conform to Rome, it would have been a dark outlook for the Huguenots. But in the famous Edict of Nantes (1598), a settlement was proclaimed which secured certain definite rights for the Huguenots, and gave securities that those rights would be respected.

There was to be liberty of conscience throughout France, and a liberty of worship for the Huguenots in certain 'specified places'. Huguenots were to enjoy the normal civil rights of Frenchmen, and were to be free to open schools and print books in the 'specified places'. They were to pay tithes, a portion of which would be returned to them by the king for the support of their ministers.

Obviously this was a very important religious settlement, and during the reign of Henry IV it held firm. But the king's life ended in 1610; he was assassinated by a fanatic employed by the Jesuits, his implacable foes.

The Jesuits were a Catholic order founded in 1534 by Ignatius Loyola, a Spaniard, their chief aim being the complete extermination of Protestantism. They called their Order the Society of Jesus. Responsible only to the Pope and exempted from all other jurisdiction, they bound themselves by oath to unconditional obedience to the Pope. Country, friends, personal interest, even private opinion and conscience were nothing; the rules of the Order were everything to them. They specialized in providing a high standard of education for the sons of the nobility, and by this means their influence was enormous. They penetrated into all the relationships of life and obtained possession of secret information that would further their aims. The most notorious principle of the Society of Jesus was, 'The end justifies the means'. Hence they would engage in murder if they judged that the Catholic Church would

benefit by it. Ravaillac, the murderer of Henry IV, was undoubtedly a tool in their hands.

After 1598 the Catholics were determined to have the Edict of Nantes declared null and void, and throughout the 17th century they laboured to have it so. A great French statesman, Cardinal Richelieu, came to their aid. Richelieu was a political rather than a religious persecutor. He held that the Huguenots were virtually 'a state within a state' and to him this was unacceptable. He therefore waged war against them and in 1629 compelled them to accept the Peace of Alais which confirmed them in their liberty of worship and their civil rights, but took from them all other rights. Henceforward the Huguenots ceased to be a formidable political party; they soon became satisfied with their religious liberty, gave full allegiance to the monarchy, and became famed for their frugality, manual skill, and high standard of morality. The statesman Colbert, later in the century, described them as the thriftiest, most hard-working, and most intelligent of the King's subjects.

In the second half of the 17th century France was ruled by Louis XIV, the grandson of Henry IV. He was a mere child when he came to the throne and for almost twenty years the land was ruled by Cardinal Mazarin. But when Louis came of age, and regarded himself as an absolute monarch—did he not say 'The state: I am the state!'—it became his ambition to require all Frenchmen to belong to the Roman Catholic Church, and this necessitated the complete Revocation of the Edict of Nantes of 1598. Louis said: 'My grandfather loved the Huguenots and did not fear them; my father feared them and did not love them; I neither love nor fear them'. He also said that if the extirpation of Protestantism in France 'required

TEMPLE DE LYON NOMMÉ PARADIS

that with one of his hands he should, as it were, cut off the other, he would submit to it'.

The king began in an indirect way the dreadful task he had set himself. He forbade the Huguenots to bury their dead except at night; not more than twelve were to meet together for a marriage or a baptism; in their schools nothing but reading and writing was to be taught. Next he tried to bribe the poorer Huguenots with money and to exclude those in a higher social position from government posts, from the legal and other professions, and even from the trades by which many of them earned their living. Pastors were forbidden to preach. Shortly the Dragonnades commenced. They were a system of billeting dragoons, the worst disciplined of troops, on Protestant families. A cartoon of the period shows a Protestant signing his conversion-paper on a drum-head labelled 'An evangelical appeal', while an armed dragoon threatens him with a musket loaded with a crucifix. As might have been expected, Huguenots fled from the land in large numbers. But Louis forbade emigration and sent to the galleys those caught in the act.

The final blow came in 1685 when Louis revoked the Edict of Nantes. Protestant worship was suppressed. All Protestant churches were to be demolished. Huguenot children were to be brought up as Roman Catholics. Despite all the king's efforts to prevent emigration, many thousands made good their escape. Three thousand a week escaped to Switzerland. Thousands more found refuge in Holland and England. Two hundred preachers became pastors in the churches of Holland and for twelve years the fugitives were exempted from paying the Dutch taxes. In Prussia the Great Elector gave 20,000 Huguenots free land near Berlin. Probably over 300,000 got away from France. They included the most skilful of French craftsmen, and their settlement in countries adjacent to France greatly benefited the industries of those countries. Louis XIV paid a very heavy price for national Catholic orthodoxy. With less excuse and in a more enlightened age he committed the same blunder as Philip II of Spain; he 'ruined his country in the name of religion'.

32

The Netherlands receives the Truth

The name Netherlands (low lands) reminds us that a part of the lands now known as Holland and Belgium are below the level of the sea. Centuries ago the waters of the North Sea frequently submerged them and the Dutch and Flemings had literally to snatch territory from the waves and to retain it by building extensive dykes along their sea-coast. Naturally a life of so many hardships, continual struggle, and never-ending watchfulness had a great influence in shaping the character of the Dutch people. It made them deliberate, painstaking, accurate, diligent, and persistent.

Moreover it made the Dutch a deeply religious people, for their battle against the elements made them conscious of their dependence upon the One who sets the sea its bounds, and who told Job that he set 'bars and doors' to the waters, and said to them, 'Hitherto shalt thou come, but no further, and here shall thy proud waves be stayed' (Job 38 : 10–11). A territory obtained under such great difficulties was prized very highly, and time and time again in their history the people of Holland have shown remarkable resolution and patriotism.

At the opening of the 16th century the Low Countries contained a crowded and busy population of three million souls. The ancient marshes had been transformed into carefully tilled fields and pastures. The walled cities numbered between two and three hundred. Trade came in from all parts, by sea and by river. As for religion, in the Netherlands, as in all other parts of western Europe, the Roman Church held sway. But the Renaissance was influential there, too. Erasmus, the greatest of Renaissance scholars, was a native of Rotterdam.

Like other countries of the west, the Netherlands had its forerunners of the Reformation. One group was known as The Brethren of the Common Life, their first leader being Gerard Groote (1340–84), a contemporary of the Englishman, John Wycliffe, and a native of Deventer. The Brethren remained in the Roman Church although they aimed at its reform. Being moderate in their agitation, they were tolerated, but through them God was preparing the soil in which the seeds of the Reformation would later sprout and thrive. Bread cast upon the waters may not be seen until after many days.

The Netherlands was one of the widely-scattered possessions of the Emperor Charles V. The prosperity of its agriculture, its fisheries and its trade was pleasing to him, for thereby his revenue was much increased. He possessed more power in the Netherlands than in Germany, even though he was not normally resident there. When the Protestant faith and doctrine reached the land—it came down the Rhine from Germany—it was received with great favour by the people. Luther's writings found ready acceptance, and later the impact of Calvin's teachings was felt also. In fact Calvinistic doctrine was received with even greater favour than Lutheranism, for it seemed to suit the genius and character of the Dutch people, and to fit in with their aspirations after liberty from oppression.

It was not long before Charles V began to show his hatred for Protestantism. His lack of success in dealing with the Protestant princes of Germany made him the more eager to show his power in Holland. The Inquisition, often called the Spanish Inquisition, was introduced. It was one of the main instruments of the Counter-Reformation, the movement begun by Popes and Cardinals and others to overthrow Protestantism. Protestants were questioned about their beliefs, often under torture and

Delegates at the Synod of Dort meeting in a large recreation hall in Dort, The Netherlands.

threat, and those who would not conform to the requirements of the Pope and Church were dealt with unmercifully. They perished at the stake or upon the scaffold, and were strangled or even buried alive. These persecutions began about 1523 and continued with more or less severity until Charles V abdicated in 1555. Yet at the end of this period the Reformed doctrine, notwithstanding all the Emperor's cruelties, was far more widely spread and deeply rooted in the Netherlands than when he entered upon its extirpation by fire and sword.

When it was reported to Luther how many of the servants of God had endured martyrdom cheerfully, he wrote to the Christian believers in Holland, Brabant and Flanders, pointing out to them their privilege, that not only were they blessed to hear and to accept eternal truth, but moreover, that some of them had been deemed worthy to die for the cause of the Lord Jesus, for 'precious shall their blood be in his sight'.

It has been estimated that, during Charles' reign, more than 5,000 people suffered death on a charge of heresy. Yet the Emperor failed to realize that the blood of the martyrs was the seed of the church, and that the more he persecuted Protestants the more they multiplied and grew, as did the Hebrews at the hands of a persecuting Pharaoh (Exodus 1 : 12). At the age of 55, the Emperor, disappointed and care-worn, stepped down from the throne. He had set his heart on spending his closing years in monastic seclusion in Spain, and this he did until his death in 1558. His principal hobby seems to have been the making and collecting of clocks. The story is told that, after vainly endeavouring to make some of his clocks run and chime in unison, he passed the remark: 'How foolish I have been to think I could make all men believe alike about religion, when I cannot make two clocks keep the same time'. He is also reported as having said that his failure to burn Luther at the time of the Diet of Worms was his greatest regret.

Charles V was succeeded by his son Philip II of Spain, whom we have already mentioned as the husband of Queen Mary Tudor of England (in all he was married four times). It was he who sent the Spanish Armada against England in 1588. For the last 40 years of his life he never left Spain; he spent most of his time at his desk, reading and writing endless despatches and reports, boasting that 'with a bit of paper he ruled over two hemispheres'.

If Charles had chastised the Dutch with whips, Philip planned to chastise them with scorpions. Saying that he would not reign over heretics, he prepared to carry his father's policy to its fatal conclusions. At first, however, persecution died down. Philip had left his half-sister, Margaret of Parma, as Regent in the Netherlands. She was not a willing persecutor and she virtually promised the Dutch not to use the Inquisition as long as Philip's attention was not called to their land by outbreaks of disorder.

An important Dutchman of those days was Guy de Bray who wrote the thirty-seven articles of the Belgic or Netherlands Confession of Faith which was highly esteemed in the Reformation Churches. He was a well-educated man, but not a preacher, much less a famous theologian. By trade he was a painter. This Confession set forth what the Reformed Churches believed concerning the Bible, God, man, the way of salvation, the church, and government. In later life De Bray took refuge in France. He was accompanied by his friend Peregrin de la Grange. But they found that

France had its dangers as well as the Netherlands, for they were captured and imprisoned. Heavily chained they lay in a dungeon. Once a noble lady visited them and sympathetically exclaimed, 'Poor men, I do not understand how you can stand this any longer'. But De Bray answered her,

Madam, our sleep in this dungeon is more restful than the sleep of many a ruler upon his soft bed. Now we suffer for the Name of our Lord, but one day we shall reign with him. The crown of eternal life is awaiting us above. The noise of these fetters is music in our ears; it is the prelude of the harping of God's angels.

In 1567 the two men received the martyr's crown.

The opposition to Philip II's policy of persecution in the Netherlands was led by William of Orange, usually known as William the Silent. A German by birth, he had inherited family estates in the small independent principality of Orange, not far from the famous town of Avignon in southern France, on the condition of being brought up as a Roman Catholic. As a youth he entered the service of Charles V, and it was upon his arm that the Emperor leant, a broken man, at the ceremony of abdication. William was gentle and affable in his behaviour and was well-received by all classes of people in the Netherlands. Although called 'the Silent', this feature only applied on one special occasion when he felt it wise to hold his peace; normally he was skilled and fluent in conversation.

In 1566 Philip II required Margaret of Parma to enforce his policy of persecution. All his subjects were to accept the decrees of the Council of Trent (1545–63) which codified the beliefs and practices of the Roman Church. All who refused to do as Philip required were to be delivered into the hands of the Inquisition. Officials who hesitated to act upon these instructions were to be replaced by 'men of more heart and zeal'. 'Now', said William, 'we shall see the beginning of a fine tragedy'.

By this time William had become a Lutheran —after another six years he became a Calvinist— and it was as a Lutheran by conviction that he took up arms against the Duke of Alva who, as governor of the Netherlands, controlled the strong Catholic army. Alva had a high military reputation, and boasted: 'I have tamed men of iron, and shall I not now be able to tame men of butter?' To begin with, he set up the Council of Blood, an arbitrary and tyrannical court. One of its members is reported, when roused from naps in court, to have cried out automatically, 'To the gallows! to the gallows'. Thousands were put to death, thousands had their goods confiscated by the state, thousands fled to England, Germany, and elsewhere. Alva promised Philip a 'stream of wealth, fathoms deep, from the Netherlands'.

Not a few Dutchmen determined to resist Spain on the sea, and a force known as the 'Gueux de Mer' (Sea Beggars) was formed. They seized Brille, near Rotterdam, and held it against all odds. Other sea-coast towns similarly defied the Spanish armies, the Dutch in some cases opening the dykes, and admitting the sea, in self-defence. The defence of Haarlem is a case in point. It cost Alva's son 12,000 men to reduce a garrison of 4,000. At Leyden the breaching of the dykes enabled the Sea Beggars to come to the town's relief, while the Spaniards retreated in dismay. Historians are agreed that Alva's tyranny and ferocity almost surpass belief. He was, says one, 'the incarnation of fiendish cruelty', and yet his policy, in all but

The interior of the Grote Kerk, Haarlem (from the painting by Berkheuer, 1673). The Reformation brought large numbers of the Dutch population under the sound of the Word of God.

its failure, was a policy after Philip's own heart. The Spanish troops were often successful in land fights, for they were experienced fighters and well armed, but they were no match for the Sea Beggars wherever a ship could float.

In 1580 Philip promised 25,000 crowns in gold and other rewards to the man who captured William the Silent dead or alive. For four years the reward remained unclaimed, but in 1584 the Dutch leader was assassinated, his foes being assisted by the free access which William gave to his person. He is famed in history as 'the founder of the Dutch Republic'. His family motto was 'Je maintiendrai' ('I will support') and he was long remembered for his helpfulness to others, and for steadfastness of character. When he died, runs the ancient record, 'the little children cried in the streets'.

Finally Holland obtained its freedom from the yoke of Spain and the Pope. In 1609 a Twelve Years' Truce between Spain and the Netherlands was agreed upon, and this virtually meant the recognition by Spain of the republic, although the official recognition did not come until the Treaty of Westphalia in 1648.

Very important religious events took place in Holland in the early part of the 17th century. They had to do with the doctrine of salvation taught in the Scriptures. Jacobus (James) Arminius, a Professor of Theology in Leyden University, the great training-ground of the Dutch clergy, denied a number of the teachings of Calvin, and asserted that, while God had made salvation possible through Jesus Christ the Saviour, he had left it to the sinner to decide whether he would or would not accept salvation. This implied of course, that it was possible for Christ to have died in vain. Professor Gomar (whose followers were known as Gomarists or Calvinists, as distinct from the Arminians), a colleague of Arminius in the University, held to the biblical truth of election and predestination, and taught that the salvation of any person was the result of the sheer grace of God's sovereign will and activity. In 1609 Arminius died, but his followers pressed their claims and the controversy became so fierce that in 1619 the Synod of Dort (Dordrecht) was convened by the Calvinists to declare and formulate the true doctrine. It was attended by selected representatives from the Netherlands, England, Scotland, Germany and Switzerland. The teachings of the Arminians were condemned, the Belgic Confession and the Heidelberg Catechism were upheld, and in 93 Canons the chief points of the doctrine of the Reformed Churches were made clear. Three-hundred Arminians were shortly expelled from office in the Netherlands and many of them went into exile. But after 1630 they were allowed to return.

To this day the findings of the Synod of Dort are held in great esteem by the Calvinistic Churches of all lands.

Prague.

33

The Thirty Years' War in Germany (1618–48)

It will be remembered that the struggles between Roman Catholics and Protestants in the 16th Century resulted in wars which greatly troubled France, Germany and the Netherlands. But another religious war was yet to be fought. It took place in Central Europe in the mid-17th Century and was the worst war of them all, 'the most appalling demonstration of the consequences of war to be found in history'. In Bohemia only 6,000 villages escaped destruction out of 35,000, and three-quarters of the population disappeared. The total population of what was called The Empire—formerly called the Holy Roman Empire—was reduced by almost two-thirds.

War casualties, famine, pestilence, and emigration accounted for this. In many areas agriculture was completely ruined; wolves came in where sheep had formerly grazed; forests began to replace fields. Walled towns were unhealthily crowded with refugees from the countryside; industry and trade suffered eclipse. Schools and Universities were closed down. Women and children and non-combatants suffered greatly.

Why all this? The plain answer is that the 'religious settlement' in Germany, effected by the Peace of Augsburg in 1555 was not really a 'settlement' at all. It applied to Roman Catholics and Lutherans only and left the ruler of each State—and Germany was a mass of States, mostly small—to decide the religion of his State. Hence Lutherans living in a State where the ruler was Catholic were denied religious liberty; similarly Catholics suffered in a Lutheran state. Furthermore, a Lutheran prince might be followed by a Catholic prince, in which event the entire State was required to change its religion, as for example in the Palatinate, where successive Electors compelled their subjects to change their religion three times in twenty-five years. And again, in the half century after 1555 many Germans became Calvinists but they were not given mention in the Peace of Augsburg and therefore had no liberty of worship in any State. There were also many disputes about land, which was also reckoned to be either Catholic or Protestant, but into such matters we need not enter. All these troubles were bound to come to a head sooner or later. And so we move on to the year 1618, by which time two militant Leagues had been formed, the Evangelical or Calvinist Union and the Roman Catholic or Holy League.

The ensuing troubles began in Bohemia, the country of the Czechs and of John Huss, where the Reformed doctrines had taken a powerful hold on the affections and convictions of the people, nine-tenths of whom had embraced the Reformation. Ferdinand II was their king; he was also Emperor in Germany and a most zealous Catholic. 'Rather', said he, 'would I be cut in pieces than allow the Church of Rome to be despised'. He persecuted the Bohemian Protestants with rigour and cruelty. But the Bohemians carried their protests to the capital, Prague, and after much heated argument they threw Ferdinand's deputies out of the windows of the council building, a sign of disapproval not uncommon in Czech history. Some have called it de-fenestration (from the Latin words 'de', from, and 'fenestra', window).

A general revolt now began. Soon the Bohemians renounced their allegiance to Ferdinand and chose for their king Frederick, Elector Palatine, in the southern Rhineland. But Frederick was no match for the Emperor when the trial of strength took place on the battlefield. The battle of the White Mountain (near Prague) decided the fate of Bohemia, the Elector became a fugitive not only from Bohemia but from his own territories also, and Ferdinand established his authority more firmly than before. A savage persecution followed. Three out of four Czechs disappeared and the fourth was enslaved to some alien to whom the Emperor sold or gave his property. Bohemia as a state vanished from the map for 200 years. As for Frederick, henceforth called 'The Winter King' because of the brevity of his reign, he took refuge in Holland with his wife Elizabeth, daughter of King James I of England.

Soon the conflict between Catholics and Protestants moved from the south to the north of Germany. At this point of time Christian IV, king of Denmark came to the aid of the Protestant cause. The Emperor's forces were led by a very able soldier named Tilly; a second army recruited by the Emperor was led by an even greater commander, Albert of Wallenstein. In the outcome Christian IV was defeated by Tilly. He fled to his islands while the Catholic army occupied most of the Danish mainland. In 1629 the Treaty of Lübeck ended this stage of the war. Austria was now overjoyed; the Emperor at Vienna was in his glory; his cause seemed to be triumphant, and the Protestant hopes seemed doomed to disappointment.

But in this dark hour of calamity the dismayed Protestants suddenly saw light ahead, for to their aid came one who turned the fortunes of battle and laid the foundations of the final peace settlement. He was Gustavus Adolphus, King of Sweden, born in the year 1594. It is claimed that he spoke German, Dutch, French, Italian and Swedish, and understood Spanish, English, Polish and Russian. He also possessed some knowledge of Latin and Greek. Most important of all, he was an evangelical Christian who read his Bible regularly and was deeply concerned to help the Protestant cause.

In June, 1630, Gustavus Adolphus crossed the Baltic Sea and landed on German soil with a well-trained army numbering 18,000 men. Opposing him was a very much greater army commanded by Tilly, already the victor in thirty desperate battles. Ferdinand and his court held the Swedes in contempt and, remembering the overthrow of 'the Winter King' and of Christian IV, said: 'Another of these snow kings has come against us. He too will melt in our southern sun'.

For a time the Protestants of Germany hesitated to join Gustavus, for they were greatly disheartened, and before the Swedish forces could show their prowess Tilly had besieged and

Gustavus Adolphus, King of Sweden: he died in battle in 1632.

almost destroyed the great city of Magdeburg, one of the few places which had welcomed Sweden's intervention in the war. Nearly the whole population of 30,000 was massacred, only about 4,000 surviving. When the slaughter began, and no escape was possible, the children were formed in procession and marched across the market-place singing Luther's hymn:

Lord, keep us steadfast in thy Word,
Curb Pope and Turk who by the sword
Would wrest the kingdom from thy Son,
And set at naught all he hath done.

Enraged by the singing, Tilly, like a second Herod, ordered all the children to be slain. The city's buildings were set on fire, and in a few hours nothing but the cathedral and some homes of the poorest of the people remained of what had been one of the finest cities in Germany. So dreadful is war!

Tilly wrote to the Emperor, 'Never was such a victory since the storming of Troy or of Jerusalem. I am sorry you and the ladies of the court were not there to enjoy the spectacle'.

From that time, however, the Emperor's success began to decline. The sack of Magdeburg roused the Protestants from their inactivity; it united them as the Massacre of St. Bartholomew in France had united the Huguenots. They rallied and marched under the standard of Gustavus, and soon their prospects began to improve. The Emperor had ordered the disarmament of Saxony and this state threw in its lot with the Swedes, whose king marched south and challenged the army of Tilly. The battle of Breitenfeld followed. Tilly, who was himself severely wounded, met with a crushing defeat; 10,000 of his men were taken prisoner. He had sufficiently recovered, however, by the following year to fight Gustavus again, this time near the River Lech. Not only was he defeated again, but on this occasion he received his death-wound.

It almost seemed as if the Swedish king could now have marched against Vienna, but the Emperor humbly asked the aid of Wallenstein, with whom he had previously quarrelled. Wallenstein consented to help on condition that he was made the virtual dictator of Germany both militarily and politically. The test of strength between the opposing armies soon came. They met at Lützen on the 6th November, 1632. On the morning of that day, after the blessing of the Lord had been invoked, the whole Swedish army sang Luther's great hymn, 'A mighty fortress is our God' and also Gustavus' own battle-hymn, 'Fear not, O little flock, the foe'. Then the King and his army kneeled down and again offered prayer. A dense fog which covered the field of battle lifted about ten o'clock. The king then addressed his troops, gave the watchword, 'God with us', cried 'Forward' and led them personally against the foe. But there came the moment, in the tumult of battle, with the fog again descending, when the king found himself isolated from his men. He fell wounded. One of the enemy, seeing his plight, asked him who he was, and he replied: 'I am the king of Sweden: and this day I seal with my blood the liberty and religion of the German nation!' Hearing such words, a soldier shot him through the head. When the Swedes heard of this blow to their cause they fought with even greater valour, caused the Emperor's troops to quit the field of battle, recovered the king's body, and mourned for him even in victory. Later the corpse was laid to rest in a Stockholm Church.

The war continued for another eighteen years. Wallenstein and the Emperor soon found themselves at cross-purposes once more, and in 1634 the general was murdered in his tent by an Irish soldier of fortune. Later the French joined in the war, for Cardinal Richelieu believed that it could be manipulated to the advantage of the French Bourbon House against the Austrian House of Hapsburg. But finally, all parties wearied of the struggle, and in 1648 the Peace of Westphalia was signed. Widespread territorial changes occurred. Calvinists received equal rights with Lutherans and Roman Catholics. The Emperor abandoned his plan to force Catholicism upon Germany. No principle of religious toleration was formulated, but this proved to be the last of the great wars of religion. Protestantism had won the right to exist in Central Europe. But it was long before Germany recovered from its wounds.

34

English Puritanism, chiefly under Elizabeth

Having looked at events in France, Germany and the Netherlands during much of the 17th Century, we must look at the progress of the Christian Church in England and Scotland during the same period, but in doing so we must take a glance backwards into the reign of Queen Elizabeth, for it was during her reign that the Puritan movement really began. It soon became an aggressive force within the Church of England.

The Elizabethan Church settlement, by which in England and Wales a return was made to Protestantism, was brought about by two Acts of Parliament (1559). A new Act of Supremacy declared the Queen to be Supreme *Governor* of the Church of England—Henry VIII had formerly proclaimed himself to be Supreme *Head*—and a new Act of Uniformity re-introduced the Second Prayer Book of Edward VI's reign with a few omissions and additions. To use any other form of public prayer was declared a punishable offence. Non-attendance at church on Sundays and holy days carried a fine of one shilling for each offence—a very substantial part of a labourer's weekly wage! In 1563 the 42 Articles of Religion, as accepted in 1552, were approved by the Church, though reduced to 39, and from the year 1571 they were imposed as a test of orthodoxy upon the clergy. At about the same time a Book of Homilies (sermons) was also re-introduced in an attempt to ensure that the clergy preached the doctrine of Scripture and had good models of sermons for their guidance.

The nation at large accepted these changes, but opposition to some, if not all of them, and to other aspects of the Church settlement, came from two quarters. On the one hand, men and women who remained Roman Catholic objected to them in their totality; on the other hand the Protestants who believed that the Reformation of the Church was not yet complete—they soon came to be termed Puritans—pressed for further change.

The first dispute in which the Puritans were involved concerned vestments, a word used to describe the dress prescribed by the Church for its clergy. To some of them the dress was 'the livery of Antichrist' and was to be regarded in the same way as 'meat offered to idols'. The Queen herself was disposed to adopt a policy of severity to all who opposed her wishes, and as for the Puritans 'she would root them out, and the favourers thereof'. Some of the Puritans suspected her of leanings towards Rome, for during her sister Mary's reign she had gone to mass. Later she had said privately that she acknowledged 'the real presence'—as did Romanists—in the Lord's Supper, and had sometimes prayed to the Virgin Mary. But there were no such tendencies developing after 1570 when Pope Pius V had issued a bull excommunicating Elizabeth and declaring her no longer Queen of England. Actually the bull put the Queen's life in peril.

A further subject of dispute between Puritans and the Queen concerned 'prophesyings', a word used to describe unofficial religious meetings for the study of the Scriptures and for preaching. To the Queen they represented the beginning of an attempt to introduce a further reformation of the Church, and in 1577 she required Edmund Grindal, Archbishop of Canterbury, to suppress all such meetings and to punish those responsible for holding them. But to her amazement Grindal refused to do so, for he saw no harm in them, whereupon she suspended him from office, although she allowed him to keep his title of Archbishop. Five years passed before the royal anger died away. By that time Grindal was almost blind, and a few months later he died.

The Queen's rigorous policy was continued by

Whitgift, Grindal's successor at Canterbury. By this time many of the Puritans inclined towards the presbyterian form of church government, their chief representative being Thomas Cartwright who had held high office in Cambridge University. But he had been the victim of persecution and for a time had found refuge on the Continent of Europe. He refused the offer of James VI of Scotland to be made Professor of Theology in the University of St. Andrews. Ultimately, however, he found that the climate of Antwerp, where he had settled, was injuring his health, and he returned to England. He died in 1603, his views on church government continuing to have considerable influence long after that date.

One further aspect of Puritan activity at this time deserves mention, however briefly. In 1587 a series of seven Tracts were published in England. They were called the Martin Marprelate Tracts. In somewhat coarse, but at times humorous language, they held up the bishops and clergy of the Church of England to ridicule and reproach. After long and diligent search the government discovered where the Tracts were printed, and punished the culprits, but to this day the identity of 'Martin', the writer of the Tracts, remains obscure.

During Elizabeth's reign the main Puritan party was content to remain within the Established Church in the hope that it would be further reformed. But a section of the party, represented by Henry Barrow, John Greenwood and others, became known as Separatists because they held that all true believers should cut themselves adrift from the Church of England. They met with severe persecution at the hands of both Church and State.

The outstanding political event in the reign of Elizabeth was the defeat of the Spanish Armada in 1588. It has ever remained also one of the highlights of naval, not to say religious, history. Philip II of Spain, formerly married to Elizabeth's half-sister Mary Tudor, was bent on the overthrow of English Protestantism. As the chief political leader of the Counter-Reformation it was his ambition to assist Rome to stamp out Protestantism in every part of Europe. In the case of England he made deep-laid preparations for action when the time was ripe, but he was held back by the claims of Mary Queen of Scots to the English crown. He had no desire to enthrone Mary, but her death at Elizabeth's hands in 1587 set him free to move and without further delay he began to organize his attack. His plan for a direct sea-borne invasion was abandoned on the ground of expense. Instead it was planned to win command of the English Channel so that a Spanish army could be transported to England from the Netherlands to strengthen the army carried from Spain in the 130 ships which made up the Armada. On the 19th July, 1588, it was sighted off the Lizard, proceeding towards Dover in crescent formation. Ten days later it arrived off Calais. English fireships were carried by the wind among the Spanish ships, which weighed anchor and made for the North Sea in considerable confusion. A running battle followed until the English sea-captains had used up all their ammunition. Meanwhile the weather had deteriorated and the Armada made for home by sailing northwards into 'the Norway Channel', in order to round the north of Scotland and skirt the western coast of Ireland. Storm after storm blew up. Never had such a large fleet of warships been in such distress. 'I sent you', said Philip later to his admiral, 'to fight against men, not with the winds'. Not a few galleons that got as far as Ireland met with disaster on her coasts. Says Professor Garrett Mattingly, 'They came in without charts or pilots, often without anchors, in ships so crippled as to be barely seaworthy and with crews so weakened by privation and disease they could barely work them'. But quite a number managed finally to limp home, their crews doubtless meditating on what Mattingly terms their 'impossible mission'.

'God blew with His winds and they were scattered' was inscribed on Elizabeth's commemorative medal, while Philip devoutly wrote to his bishops, 'We are bound to give praise to God for all things which He is pleased to do. . . . In the storms through which the Armada sailed it might have suffered a worse fate, and that its ill-fortune was no greater must be credited to the prayers for its good success, so devoutly and continuously offered'. Philip began the building of a second invasion fleet, but within a year his death occurred. Fanatical, bigoted, gloomy, he had persecuted Protestants through the Inquisition with relentless cruelty, believing nevertheless that in so doing he was rendering service to God. England could well give thanks that she had escaped his hand.

A new era began in England in 1603 when Queen Elizabeth I died, and James I, the son of Mary Queen of Scots by Lord Darnley, her second husband, came to the throne. He had been brought up as a Presbyterian, but when he came to England he heartily embraced the church principles of the Anglicans, and gladly received the homage of the bishops and archbishops.

James soon discovered, however, that not a few of the English clergy desired more reform within the Church than 16th-Century changes had brought about. In fact, before he reached London he was presented with a petition supposedly signed by a thousand clergymen and hence called The Millenary Petition. It asked for the removal from the Church of what certain ministers of the Puritan party called 'the rags of popery', that is to say, Romish practices which remained after the Reformation. The king, though not pleased with the Petition, accordingly called a Conference in 1604. It met in Hampton Court, the London palace surrendered to King Henry VIII by Wolsey at the time when his fall from power began.

Bishops and Puritans entered into debate on disputed matters, the King acting as chairman. But one of the Puritans happened to use the term 'Synod' and this, because it savoured of Presbyterianism, caused his Majesty to break out into a violent temper. 'If', said he, 'you aim at a Scottish Presbytery, it agrees as well with a monarchy as God and the devil! No bishop, no king'. By this he meant that if presbyters replaced bishops, he himself would soon be driven off the throne.

The Conference soon broke up, and before long 300 clergymen were deprived by the bishops of their livings in the Church of England. But one result of the Conference was decidedly good. The king had suggested a new translation of the Bible. His hope was that this might take the place of the popular Geneva Bible as the version used by the people. As already stated, the Geneva Bible had been produced by those who left the country during Mary Tudor's reign (1553–1558), and it contained marginal notes which James considered decidedly 'unpleasant' and opposed to the interests of monarchy. Arrangements for the new translation went ahead and in 1611 the Authorized Version was published. It gradually replaced the Geneva Version in public esteem and is recognized as the best version ever produced in the English

language. Learned and unlearned alike found delight in its pages and many of its idioms and phrases have become part and parcel of the English tongue.

The Authorized Version was supplied with two Addresses—one to the King, and another, very much longer, to the Readers. In the former, Queen Elizabeth I is spoken of as 'that bright Occidental [western] Star', and James is termed 'most dread Sovereign', France being included as a part of his kingdom. In reality the bishops flatter the king. At the same time they complain against 'popish persons who desire to keep the people in ignorance and darkness by denying them the Scriptures in their own language'. On the other hand they speak against the Puritans as 'self-conceited brethren who run their own ways and give liking unto nothing but what is framed by themselves and hammered on their anvil'. So all who use Bibles containing this Address can read for themselves what the bishops of those days thought about Puritans and Roman Catholics!

A further result of the Hampton Court Conference was that a number of those whose consciences would not allow them to worship in English parish churches decided to emigrate. These were the Separatists already mentioned. Some of them went to Holland but after a time they decided to make a home for themselves in North America where some of their fellow-countrymen were already settled. We shall mention them again in a later chapter.

35

English Puritanism under the Early Stuarts

During the first half of the 17th Century the Puritan party made steady, indeed rapid, progress in England. It was assisted by the fact that it could count on the support of dozens, if not scores of members of the House of Commons. In the city of Cambridge it prospered greatly, for there, in Elizabeth's reign, Sir Walter Mildmay, who held high office under the Queen, had founded Emmanuel College. The Queen is reported to have said to him: 'Sir Walter, I hear you have erected a Puritan foundation'. 'No, Madam,' he replied, 'far be it from me to countenance anything contrary to your established laws; but I have set an acorn, which when it becomes an oak, God alone knows what will be the fruit thereof.' Thomas Fuller, Church historian, writing in 1655, commented, 'Sure I am at this day, it hath overshadowed all the University, more than a moiety [half] of all the present masters of colleges being bred therein'.

Probably the most influential of all Cambridge Puritans was William Perkins (1558–1602), though he belonged to Christ's College, not to

of Paul Baynes of Cambridge, and his own ministry was patterned upon it. At the age of forty he was appointed preacher at Gray's Inn, a famous school of law in London, where his sermons made a deep and lasting impression. When he was forty-nine he became Master of St. Catherine's Hall, Cambridge, while retaining his London post. In Cambridge crowds of University men flocked to his sermons. It was said of him:

Of this blest man, let this just praise be given,
Heaven was in him before he was in heaven.

His influence remains to the present day, for his best writings are still in print, and known world-wide.

One other name in this early Puritan period must not be left unmentioned. Thomas Goodwin (1600–79) belongs to both Cambridge and Oxford. At the age of nineteen he rode from

William Perkins, (1558–1602).

Emmanuel College, and died before three years of the 17th century had run their full course. His conversion to Christ was dramatic. As one day he walked the streets of Cambridge, he overheard a woman warning her fretful child to 'beware of drunken Perkins'. The expression reached him as an arrow shot from the bow of Almighty God, and before many months had passed 'drunken Perkins' had become an exemplary and a highly influential believer. His strongly Calvinistic sermons attracted crowds of academic hearers, and some of his writings were translated into half a dozen European languages. He has been described as 'the Calvin of England'.

Richard Sibbes (1577–1635), the son of a Suffolk wheelwright, is another of the early Cambridge Puritans who achieved lasting fame. In his early manhood he attended the preaching

Thomas Goodwin, (1600–1679).

Cambridge on horseback 35 miles to listen to the preaching of the Puritan John Rogers of Dedham, Essex. It so happened that Rogers was rebuking his congregation for their neglect of the Word of God and that, as he warmed to his theme, he boldly personated the Lord in order to render his reproofs the more impressive. But the event is best described in the words of the Puritan John Howe:

Well, I have trusted you so long with my Bible: you have slighted it; it lies in such and such houses all covered with dust and cobwebs. You care not to look into it. Do you use my Bible so? Then you shall have my Bible no longer'. Next he takes up the Bible from its cushion, and seemed as if he were going away with it, and carrying it from them; but immediately he turns again, and personates the people to God, falls down on his knees, cries and pleads most earnestly, 'Lord, whatsoever Thou dost to us, take not Thy Bible from us; kill our children, burn our houses, destroy our goods; only spare us Thy Bible, only take not away Thy Bible'. And then he personates God again to the people: 'Say you so? Well, I will try you a little longer; and here is my Bible for you, I will see how you will use it, whether you will love it more, whether you will value it more, whether you will observe it more, whether you will practise it more, and live more according to it'. But by these actions he put all the congregation into so strange a posture that a stranger who was present had never seen the like before. The place was a mere Bochim (Judges 2 : 1-5), the people generally (as it were) deluged with their own tears.

As for Thomas Goodwin, he told me that he himself, when he got out (of the meeting place) and was to take horse again to be gone, was fain to hang a quarter of an hour upon the neck of his horse weeping, before he had power to mount, so strange an impression was there upon him, and generally upon the people, upon having been thus expostulated with for their neglect of the Bible.

Later in the century, Goodwin, who was of the Independent persuasion, was appointed President of Magdalen College, Oxford, and he became one of the most influential of the Puritans. His writings (in 12 volumes) were reprinted during Queen Victoria's reign.

Puritans by the score could be mentioned if space permitted. Their influence upon England was profound, though many considered their Christian witness far too strict and narrow. In not a few cases their writings have been republished, so that in another sense than that intended in the Book of Revelation 14.13 'their works do follow them'. And those works still bear fruit in Christian lives.

James I was followed by his son, King Charles I, who married Henrietta Maria, a Roman Catholic princess of France, and thereby incurred the keen displeasure of Parliament which was strongly Protestant and becoming increasingly Puritan in its sympathies. Charles quarrelled with Parliament continually during the first five years of his reign, and not only on matters political. On one occasion the members of the Commons spoke openly against Arminian doctrine in the Church. In 1629 the king decided to rule without calling Parliament and for eleven years (1629–40) he did so.

During the period of Charles' absolute government he was advised by two men in particular—William Laud, who became Archbishop of Canterbury, and Thomas Wentworth, Earl of Strafford. We are here concerned with the former of these men, for it was he who directed the king's religious policies. One part of Laud's policy was to persecute Puritan clergy and to require them to conform to *his* ideas about worship. Men who defied him were taken before either the Court of High Commission or the Star Chamber. A common form of punishment was the branding an offender's cheeks with the letters S.L. (Seditious Libeller) or S.S. (Sower of Sedition), though one Puritan claimed that 'S.L.' meant the 'Stigmata of Laud'. Heavy fines were also imposed and in some cases the ears of offenders were cut off. William Prynne, a lawyer who suffered in this way, at a later date drew up the charges which resulted in Laud's execution at the hands of Parliament in 1645.

But Laud was not content to rule the *English* Church alone with rigour, he determined to impose his religious principles upon Presbyterian Scotland. In 1637 it was decreed that the Church of England Prayer Book should be read in Scottish Churches, including St. Giles, Edinburgh. The opposition was strong, even fierce. The story has often been told of how a certain Jenny Geddes, at the moment when the Prayer Book was being read, rose up in anger from the stool on which she sat, threw the stool at the Dean's head, and called out with all the strength she could muster, 'Will ye read that book in my lug (ear)?' The uproar was great and soon Scotland rose in revolt. People flocked to sign the National Covenant upholding Presbyterianism. The Scottish Church, they said, must not be ruled by bishops.

Emmanuel College, Cambridge.

Two wars followed without much delay. They are called The Bishops' Wars (1639–40). The king soon found that it was impossible to coerce Scotland into obedience. He was short of money also, and found it difficult to raise troops. Accordingly he felt compelled to recall Parliament. Two Parliaments met in quick succession —the Short and the Long Parliaments. The latter arrested Laud and Wentworth, charged the king with tyranny, and declared that the will of Parliament must prevail. Contrary to all precedent the king went to the House of Commons in person to arrest five of his chief opponents, but he found that 'the birds had flown'. By 1642 the rift between king and Parliament had become so wide that war was in sight. The inevitable happened; the sword must decide.

Into the events of the Civil War, or rather two Civil Wars (1642–8) we cannot here enter. They ended with the victory of the Parliament's New Model Army and the execution of Charles I in 1649. But political and military developments were accompanied by religious changes of great importance.

Parliament and the king met in battle in 1642 and in consequence John Pym, Parliamentary leader and a Puritan, decided that an ally for Parliament must be found. Overtures were made to Scotland, and in 1643 a League and Covenant brought a Scots Army into the war. The contracting parties pledged themselves to undertake 'the reformation of religion in the kingdoms of England and Ireland in doctrine, worship, discipline, and government, according to the Word of God and the example of the best reformed churches'. In addition it was agreed that 'popery and prelacy (government of the church by bishops) should be extirpated'. The two parties also undertook to 'bring the churches of God in the three kingdoms to the nearest conjunction and uniformity in religion' (including confession of faith, form of church government, directory for worship, and catechising) that was possible. The English Parliament accepted these conditions and agreed to convene an Assembly of English and Scottish ministers who would combine to bring about the desired changes.

The meeting place of the Assembly was a large room attached to Westminster Abbey, London; hence it is known as the Westminster Assembly. It drew up a famous Confession of Faith, also Larger and Shorter Catechisms. Some of the greatest Puritan ministers belonged to the Assembly, for example, Thomas Goodwin of Oxford University. Samuel Rutherford, famous for his Letters, was one who represented Scotland. Richard Baxter, a Puritan of later days, goes so far as to claim that 'since the days of the apostles (there has never been) a Synod of more excellent divines, taking one thing with another, than this Synod and the Synod of Dort were'.

In the English-speaking Churches the Westminster Confession has exercised great influence, and not only among Presbyterians. Much of its language was written into the Savoy Declaration of 1658 (Independent or Congregationalist), and the Baptist Confession of 1689, for on the essentials of salvation these Churches, and the Presbyterian Church, were at one. American Confessions of Faith also owe a great debt to the Westminster Assembly. As for the Larger and Shorter Catechisms, these too have had great influence, especially in the Scottish Churches. For many generations the Shorter Catechism was 'the real Creed of Scotland as far as the mass

The signing of the Scottish National Covenant in Greyfriars Churchyard, Edinburgh, on 28th February, 1638. Some wrote 'until death' after their signature; some 'did draw their own blood and use it in place of ink'. *From a painting by William Hole RSA.*

of the people was concerned', and comment has often been passed on its striking opening lines, as for example by Thomas Carlyle: 'The older I grow—and I now stand upon the brink of eternity—the more comes back to me the first sentence in the Catechism which I learned when a child, and the fuller and deeper its meaning becomes: What is the chief end of man? To glorify God and to enjoy him for ever'.

But the Parliament's New Model Army

contained many men who believed that Presbyterianism was about to be forced upon them. Many of them were of Independent persuasion; they believed that each local church was separately responsible to the Lord Jesus Christ. Furthermore, the Parliament and the Army fell apart, pursuing rather different policies, and it was the Army which finally triumphed. As for the Scots, they came to terms with the king for, after being captured, he made certain promises in favour of Presbyterianism and thus secured their help. The Scots army then had to be defeated before the New Model Army could enforce its will upon the land.

Among the Independents at this time was a group known as Fifth Monarchy Men. In the Book of Daniel, chapter two, four world kingdoms are mentioned, followed by a fifth kingdom, which they interpreted as that of the Lord Jesus Christ, which overcomes and takes the place of all others. This group of men, mostly members of the New Model Army, believed that Christ's kingdom was about to be set up and that they were to be the instruments in its appearing. Before long they learned the unscripturalness of their expectations.

The outcome of the wars was the setting up of the Commonwealth, with Oliver Cromwell,

A meeting of the Westminster Assembly. *From a 19th-century painting by J. R. Herbert R.A.*

'the great Independent', as Protector. It represented the triumph of political Puritanism, but despite the best of intentions the members of the Commonwealth Parliaments (and they were drawn from all parts of the British Isles) never solved the problems which faced them. Cromwell and his Parliaments did not well agree. As Protector he quarrelled with them, even after a hundred duly elected members had been turned back at the door. At the same time the people at large believed that they were being made subject to a military dictatorship.

In religious matters the public reading of the Book of Common Prayer was forbidden by law, but not infrequently it was tolerated, if performed in quiet unobtrusive fashion. Anglican ministers were often deprived of their position, and in their place ministers were appointed who were approved, by a body of men called 'Triers', as sound in doctrine and neither vicious nor profane in manner of life. The 'Triers' were leading men of Presbyterian, Independent or Baptist conviction. The Council of State declared that 'none be compelled to conform to the public religion by penalties or otherwise, but that endeavours be used to win them by sound doctrine, and the example of a good conversation'. But liberty of religion was not 'extended to Popery or Prelacy, or to such as under a profession of Christianity hold forth and practise licentiousness'.

In sum, provided that the Prayer Book was not used, all forms of Protestant worship could be practised openly. Cromwell himself was essentially of a tolerant spirit. It has often been pointed out to his honour, that for the first time for almost 400 years Jews were now allowed to enter England and to meet for synagogue worship.

Statue of Oliver Cromwell outside the Houses of Parliament, London.

A notable appointment made by Cromwell was that of John Owen, the greatest of Puritan theologians and an Independent, to the office of Vice-Chancellor of Oxford University, the Protector himself being Chancellor at the time. Never had the University known such an industrious Vice-Chancellor, or one more learned in Holy Scripture! His many treatises are still available to readers after the passing of 300 years.

When Cromwell died in 1658 and his son Richard became Protector—he was a mere shadow of his father—it was not long before the Stuart monarchy in the person of Charles II was restored to the throne. Puritan rule in Church and State suddenly ended and the fair hopes that had been built up during twenty years of struggle were denied their fruition.

It was also at this time that the Society of Friends, commonly known as Quakers (on account of their bodily reactions during worship) came into being. The Society was founded by George Fox, the son of a Leicestershire weaver, and held that true worship was essentially inward (as indeed it is) and was not to be linked with anything external, such as a body of ministers, baptism, or even the Lord's Supper. The Society professed no clear-cut creed and claimed that the silent converse of the soul is as acceptable in worship to God as the utterance of prayer and praise. The early Friends seemed to hold the fundamentals of the Christian faith, but as they never held to a creed it was not difficult for men to accuse them of departure from the faith.

They adopted great simplicity of dress and addressed others by their Christian names. 'Thee' and 'thou' also belonged to their everyday speech. To a considerable extent they relied on 'the inner light' of the Holy Spirit as a rule of life, and this tended to a neglect of divine guidance through the Scriptures. In later years they formed settlements in the West Indies and North America. The Colony of Pennsylvania was established by the Quaker William Penn in 1681. He wished to give it the name of Sylvania, but King Charles II insisted on the prefix Penn, for he thought highly of Penn's father, Admiral William Penn. So Pennsylvania it became.

The Restoration of the Stuart line of kings took place in the year 1660, Charles II guaranteeing liberty of conscience to all his subjects. But Scripture warns men not to put their trust in princes, and it was not long before the persecution of Puritan ministers began. Bishops, with seats in the House of Lords, again obtained power. The code of laws which legalized and regulated persecution is called by historians The Clarendon Code after the politician in power at the time. One of its measures was an Act of Uniformity (1662) which required all clergy to give 'their unfeigned consent and assent' to everything in the Book of Common Prayer. Not far short of 2,000 clergy were unable to do this with a good conscience and they were driven from their livings into Nonconformity, often called Dissent. A Conventicle Act of 1664 forbade religious meetings in which the Prayer Book was not used. The penalties for breaking the Act were very severe. The Five Mile Act (1665) forbade ejected clergymen to come within five miles of a city or corporate town; this was designed to deprive most of them of the power to earn a livelihood for themselves.

One of the best known sufferers for conscience' sake in Charles II's reign was John Bunyan. He was not a clergyman of the Church of England but a tinker or brazier of Bedford whom God had called to preach the gospel. Local magistrates sentenced him to imprisonment unless he told them that he would give them his promise not to preach, but this he refused to do. He declared that he would remain in prison till the moss grew on his eyelids rather than fail to do what God had commanded him to do. 'Do you not love your wife and children, then?' said the magistrates. 'Indeed I do', he replied with warmth, 'very dearly, but in comparison with Jesus Christ I do not love them at all'. He remained in Bedford

36

English Puritanism under the Later Stuarts

John Bunyan, 1628–1688. *Painting of 1684 by Thomas Sadler.*

gaol a total of twelve years, earning his living, as far as possible, by making leather boot laces.

Bunyan, though a man of very little formal education, but gifted with great originality and insight, wrote, in all, 68 books, the most famous —and 'famous' is almost too weak a word to use about it—being *The Pilgrim's Progress*, the best allegory ever written. It tells how Graceless, a dweller in the City of Destruction, became a Christian and went on pilgrimage to the Celestial City. Next to the Bible itself it is probably the best known of all Christian books. It has been translated into many languages and has a worldwide appeal. Bunyan is also the author of the world's second-best religious allegory; its title is *The Holy War*. It describes the capture of the City of Mansoul by Emmanuel, Son of El Shaddai (the Almighty), and the attempt of Diabolus (the Devil) to recapture it.

Grace Abounding to the Chief of Sinners, one of the best and greatest autobiographies in the English language is another of Bunyan's works. It describes in vivid language and great detail his conviction of sin, his struggles against unbelief, his entrance into the meaning and the comfort of Holy Scripture, and much more that belongs to the realm of Christian experience. It also deals with his call to the Christian ministry, when he preached what he 'smartingly did feel'. It is not too much to claim that, spiritually speaking, Bunyan's writings render him the greatest and most influential of the Puritans.

Books by Puritans appeared in great numbers throughout the 17th Century. William Gurnall of Lavenham (Suffolk) produced *The Christian in Complete Armour*, a work often reprinted. Richard Baxter of Kidderminster (Worcestershire) wrote *The Saints' Everlasting Rest*. Joseph Caryl, a London preacher, produced a very large and famous *Commentary on the Book of Job*. John Owen—already mentioned—wrote volumes on most Christian themes, and also a lengthy *Commentary on the Epistle to the Hebrews*. As the Puritan period drew to its close Matthew Henry began a *Commentary on the Bible* which still ranks as one of the most useful ever written. Much of it was preached in sermon form in the city of Chester during the years 1687 to 1712.

But we must return to events linking the Church with kings and political events. Charles II died in 1685. Although the law of the land made him 'Supreme Governor' of the Church of England, he lived and died a Roman Catholic, a matter he concealed from the nation at large until his life was far advanced. It was during his reign that the Scottish Covenanters suffered fearful persecution. Their claim was that King Jesus was the only rightful Head of the Church of God

and that they could not submit to the intervention of the country's monarch in matters of Church and conscience. Charles had not been long on the throne before he required the Scottish Parliament to declare that he was head of the Church as well as head of the State, and that he had decided to impose the Episcopal system—government of the church by bishops—upon Scotland. At once there was trouble. Appeal was made to the National Covenant of earlier days (which, about ten years earlier, Charles had himself professed to accept) by which multitudes pledged themselves to resist to the death all interference of the king in the affairs of the Church. Charles, however, was now willing to enforce obedience to his decrees by force of arms, and for 25 years a life-and-death struggle between King and Covenanters went on. The royal troops engaged in all kinds of cruelties, but without avail. The Covenanter Movement was, as it were, hydra-headed. The hottest period of perse-

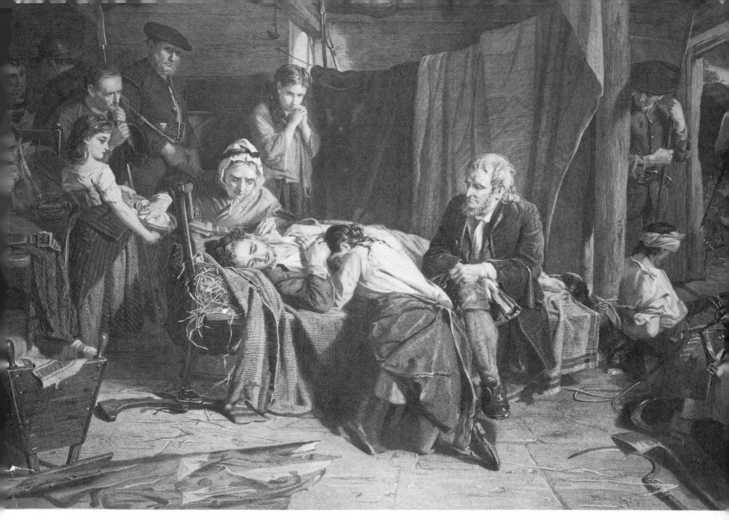

cution was during 1684–5; it was termed 'The Killing Times'. Not until 1688 did deliverance come to the persecuted. Two of the best known members of the Covenanting body were the first and last of its martyrs; James Guthrie and James Renwick. 'They loved not their lives to the death' (Rev. 12 : 11).

Charles II died in 1685 and was succeeded on the throne by his brother, James II, who had never hidden the fact that he was a Roman Catholic and that it was his desire to restore Romanism in both England and Scotland. He was in league, as his brother also had been, with Louis XIV of France who, it will be remembered, was the persecutor of the Huguenots. The year when James ascended the English throne was also the year when Louis revoked the Edict of Nantes and caused thousands of Huguenots to take to flight from their homeland.

James applied his religious policy craftily. He

A not unfamiliar scene in Scottish homes during the persecution suffered by Christians in the reigns of Charles II and James II.

Halt passenger, take heed what you do see,
This tomb doth shew, for what some men did die.

Here lies interr'd the dust of those who stood
'Gainst perjury, resisting unto blood;
Adhering to the Covenants, and laws
Establishing the same; which was the cause
Their lives were sacrific'd unto the lust
Of Prelatists abjur'd. Though here their dust
Lies mixt with murderers, and other crew,
Whom justice justly did to death pursue:

But as for them, no cause was to be found
Worthy of death, but only they were found,
Constant and stedfast, zealous, witnessing,
For the Prerogatives of CHRIST their KING.
Which Truths were seal'd by famous Guthrie's head,
And all along to Mr. Renwick's blood.
They did endure the wrath of enemies,
Reproaches, torments, deaths and injuries.
But yet they're those who from such troubles came,
And now triumph in glory with the LAMB.

From May 27th 1661 that the most noble Marquis
of Argyle was beheaded, to the 17th of Feb'ry 1688
that Mr. James Renwick suffered; were one way
or other Murdered and Destroyed for the same Cause, about
Eighteen thousand, of whom were execute at Edinburgh, about an
hundred of Noblemen, Gentlemen, Ministers and Others; noble
Martyrs for JESUS CHRIST. The most of them lie here.

For a particular account of the cause, and manner of their Sufferings, see
the Cloud of Witnesses, Crookshank's and Defoe's Histories.

issued Declarations of Indulgence, giving liberty of worship to those who did not conform to the requirements of the Church of England. They therefore covered both Protestant non-conformists and Roman Catholics. All clergy were required to read such a Declaration in their churches on an appointed day. Seven bishops, including Sancroft, Archbishop of Canterbury, refused to obey and were sent to the Tower of London. To the nation's joy they were soon acquitted. This was a severe blow to the king.

Could James continue on his way? Could he act contrary to the law? Could he bring back England to the authority and power of the Pope? The crisis came when his second wife presented him with a son, called by the general public 'The Pretender' because it was alleged that the babe had been smuggled into the palace and called the king's son, though not born to him by his lawful wife. But there was no truth in this story.

By his first wife James had two daughters, brought up by their mother as Protestants, and one of them was expected to follow James upon the throne. But James' second marriage, followed by the birth of a son, meant that a Roman Catholic king would follow James. Certain politicians took quick action. They turned their eyes to Holland, and to William of Orange, a descendant of William the Silent, and Europe's Protestant champion in wars against Louis XIV. Moreover William had a double link with the English royal House; his mother was a daughter of Charles I and his wife was the elder daughter of James II. The invitation to William was accepted as gladly as it was given. He landed at Torbay, Devonshire, with a Dutch army, on November 5th, 1688, and James II shortly fled to France as an exile. England and Scotland were thus saved from Romanism.

An Act of 1689 gave religious toleration to all Protestants on easy terms; and the throne became and remained Protestant. For the safeguarding of both Church and State the Bill of Rights of 1689 declared that papists, then and for all future time, were to be incapable of succeeding to the English throne. The Scottish Parliament acted similarly. Roman Catholics, although no longer persecuted, did not receive official liberty of worship until a century later.

James, the Pretender, and his son Charles, known as The Young Pretender, were supported by the Jacobites (Latin Jacobus=James), who made bids for the throne by force of arms in 1715 and 1745, but their efforts ended in failure. And when the House of Hanover assumed the English throne in 1714, by invitation under the Act of Settlement of 1701, necessarily the requirements of the Bill of Rights still held good. The anomaly of a Roman Catholic king as the Head of a Protestant Church has never been repeated.

As the 17th Century was about to close an interesting development took place in respect of the propagation of the gospel at home and abroad. In 1698 the Society for Promoting Christian Knowledge (the S.P.C.K.) was formed. Its pioneer was Dr. Thomas Bray, a Church of England clergyman who had laboured hard to strengthen the Church by the provision of libraries of religious books in many English parishes. He had also visited Maryland in North America 'for the propagation of true religion in (England's) foreign plantations'. It was soon felt, however, that the new Society was not well fitted for overseas work, and in 1701 a second Society, the Society for the Propagation of the Gospel in Foreign Parts (S.P.G.) was formed. In the long period of its existence it has done much to establish branches of the Church of England in most parts of the world.

opposite Memorial stone in Greyfriars Churchyard, Edinburgh. It commemorates the Covenanters and their sufferings from 1661 to 1688. The figure 'eighteen thousand' is a mistake and ought to be considerably lower.

37

The Faith in North America during the 17th Century (1)

In one form or another the Christian faith was first planted in North America in the late 16th Century. The Spaniards and Portuguese had introduced Roman Catholicism into South and Central America during the first half of the century, and after a time the Spaniards took possession of Florida also, and then voyaged as far north as Chesapeake Bay. In 1565 they made a permanent settlement at St. Augustine in Florida. Shortly afterwards they slaughtered French colonists who had settled at the mouth of the St. John's River.

In 1583 Sir Humphrey Gilbert, a native of Devonshire and step-brother to Sir Walter Raleigh, founded the first British colony in North America. It was located at St. John's, Newfoundland. 'The carriage of God's Word into those very mighty and vast countries' was stated to be one of the express objects of the expedition. Two years later Sir Richard Grenville, a Cornishman and a cousin of Raleigh, landed settlers on the coast of Virginia. The enterprise was financed by Raleigh who spent about £40,000 in all upon it. But the men sent out from England were ill-suited to the requirements of the scheme and it came to nothing. A more successful attempt was made in 1607, although by that time Raleigh was a prisoner in the Tower of London. It is of interest to note that in his will he bequeathed £100 for the Christianization of the natives of Virginia, the 'first missionary legacy', it is claimed, 'which the English church has on record'.

The Grenville expedition of 1585 included a zealous Christian named Thomas Harriot who achieved distinction in later years as a mathematician and scientist. He had been Raleigh's mathematical tutor, and accompanied Grenville as a surveyor of land. He is here mentioned, however, because he made good endeavours to reach out to the Indians of North America with the gospel. An account of Virginia which he produced after his return to England throws light on his work:

Many times, and in every towne where I came, according as I was able, I made declaration of the contents of the Bible: that therein was set foorth the true onely God and his mightie works; that therein was contained the true doctrine of salvation through Christ; with many particularities of miracles and chiefe points of religion, as I was able then to utter and thought fit for the time.

Harriot adds that an Indian chief, 'so grievously sick that he was like to die', sent for some of the newly-arrived Christians and asked them to intercede with God for his life, or, if death awaited him, that he might be with God in Paradise'.

One result of the colonization of Virginia in 1607 was the conversion to Christianity of Pocahontas or Matoaka, the daughter of Powhattan, an Indian chief. She is said to have saved the life of John Smyth, one of the most prominent of the settlers, when her father was about to kill him. She yielded herself readily to Christian teaching, professed faith in the Saviour, took the name of Rebecca, and married a colonist named John Rolfe. As his wife she came to England in 1616, but the English climate seems to have proved too severe for her, and after a year she died at Gravesend. She was the first Red Indian to cross the Atlantic to England, and was a person of considerable public interest.

Meanwhile the French, having been disappointed in their venture on the St. John's River, had shown interest in the area watered by the River St. Lawrence. Their explorer, Jacques Cartier, long before, had explored at least as far inland as Montreal, and the French crown had declared its interest in 'the discovery, settlement, and conversion of the Indians'. In 1608 Champlain arrived and planted the first French settlement at Quebec with the result that Roman Catholicism became established there. Before the century ended La Salle had explored the area of the Great Lakes and the entire length of the River Mississippi. France—and the Roman Church—then laid claim to the two great waterways of the continent and the whole of its great central valley.

Two other European powers also showed interest in America. In 1626 Dutch settlers established the New Netherlands, the chief settlement being named New Amsterdam, later renamed by the English New York. A group of Swedes established New Sweden at the mouth of the Delaware River in 1639. But the Swedes soon dropped out of the race for colonies; in 1655 the Dutch dispossessed them. In their turn the Dutch were dispossessed by the English during the Anglo-Dutch war of 1665–7. By the end of the century, therefore, the English possessed the entire eastern seaboard from Maine in the north to the northern border of Florida, except for the area later called Georgia.

It is interesting to note that the pattern of religion in the English American colonies corresponded to the pattern of religious divisions in the mother country. Those divisions were, in general, as follows:

(1) members of the Church of England who, either by conviction, expediency or indifference, were content with the Reformation Settlement of 1559.

(2) members of the Church of England who wanted the Church to engage in the reform of its liturgy and practices; in other words, the Puritans.

(3) Separatists who regarded the Church of England as 'Babylon', hence their flight from it.

(4) Roman Catholics.

We have already seen how the colony of Virginia began. From the outset the Church of England worship there followed the pattern of the homeland, and without delay the system of parishes and parish churches was introduced.

The colony of Maryland, dating from 1632, was founded by Lord Baltimore, a Roman Catholic. Arriving in Virginia he discovered that it was necessary to take the two Protestant oaths of allegiance and supremacy. This he would not do, but he secured from the king the grant of a part of Virginia that had not been occupied, and he named it Maryland after Charles I's queen Henrietta Maria. All new settlers were welcomed but Catholicism was favoured.

Much more renowned was the settlement of New England by the Pilgrim Fathers, commencing in 1620. This settlement represented Separatism at its truest and best. Few there are who are unwilling to acknowledge that the 'sailing of the Pilgrim Fathers', and all that it entailed of sufferings accepted as the result of convictions of conscience, was as honourable an undertaking as the annals of history can supply.

The story really begins in 1606 when Separatists from Gainsborough in Lincolnshire broke the law of England by emigrating, without government permission, to Amsterdam, where they could exercise liberty of conscience in matters religious. Their pastor was John Smyth. A little later a similar party, located at Scrooby in Nottinghamshire, also tried to sail to Holland from the port of Boston (Lincolnshire) but met with not unexpected difficulties. In fact its members were imprisoned for a time. But by 1608 they had made their get-away. Almost simultaneously another party of Separatists succeeded in getting to Leyden where they lived by manufacturing woollen goods. But after eleven years of exile various considerations brought about their departure. William Bradford, one of the chief of their number, and later to become Governor Bradford of Plymouth Colony, supplies us with all but the last of the following:

(1) *Grim poverty.* Eminent scholars were working as porters. Some of the exiles lived on twopence a day.

(2) *The fear of war with Spain.* A 12-year truce between Spain and the Dutch was about to end, and who could say that old enmities

might not lead to an outbreak of fighting in which the English exiles might unwillingly become involved?

(3) *Fear for their children.* In their youth some of them were in danger of being influenced by unwelcome Dutch customs, for example, the profanation of the Lord's Day. The temptations of city life also had attractions for some of them.

(4) *The desire to advance the gospel.* Bradford tells us that this was 'not the least' of the reasons for leaving Holland. He speaks of 'a great hope and inward zeal of laying some good foundation, or at least to make some way thereunto, for the propagating and advancing the gospel of the kingdom of Christ in those remote parts of the world; yea, though they should be but even as stepping-stones unto others for the performing of so great a work'.

(5) *Allegiance to the British crown.* The exiles remained Englishmen at heart. They had no desire to forfeit their nationality or to renounce their lawful obligations to King James I.

And so it came about that the exiles, who were so soon to become pilgrims, took leave of the country in which for about twelve years they had found a place of refuge. Their pastor, John Robinson, who remained in Holland, falling down on his knees, blessed them. 'And they all with watrie cheeks, mutual imbrasses, and many tears tooke their leave one of another'. 'The lot was cast into the lap' but 'the whole disposing thereof was of the Lord' (Proverbs 16 : 33).

'Where lies the land to which the ship would go? Far, far ahead, is all her seamen know'.

(Arthur Hugh Clough)

By 1619 the resolve of the pilgrims to cross the Atlantic had been taken. The Virginia Company promised them access to the new colony. Two ships were chartered in England to convey them to their new home. In August, 1620, they set sail from Southampton. But the Speedwell, the smaller of the two ships, sprang a leak, and as hurried repairs proved unsatisfactory 18 of her 30 passengers returned to London while the remaining 12 were transferred to the overcrowded *Mayflower*[1] which already carried 90 pilgrims—men, women and children. Probably,

[1] It is highly probable that parts of the *Mayflower* are still to be seen in England, for the vessel appears to have been broken up when no longer seaworthy, some of its timbers being built into a barn at Jordans, Buckinghamshire (Jordans is in the heart of 'the Milton and Penn country'—the Penn who has given his name to Pennsylvania, U.S.A.). The discovery was made by Dr. Rendel Harris who describes it in full detail in a booklet entitled 'The finding of the "Mayflower" ', published in 1920. He also supplies photographs of 'a part of the keel or stem-bands', 'the cracked beam of the ship', and so on.

38

The Faith in North America during the 17th Century (2)

with the crew, the entire ship's company must have numbered about 140 persons. Judged by modern standards the accommodation was miserably poor; the *Mayflower* was as closely packed as the slave ships which in the following century plied between the African coast and America. Privacy for individual pilgrims was impossible. Ventilation below decks was bad, even in fair weather. In bad weather, when the hatches were battened down—and here we quote the words of an English poet laureate, John Masefield, himself a seafaring man—the pilgrims 'could only lie and groan and pray in stink and misery, while the water from ill-caulked seams dripped on them from above'.

After a voyage lasting two months the *Mayflower* reached Cape Cod in the area afterwards called New England. They had hoped to settle much further to the south, in Virginia, but the ship's crew refused to convey them there and insisted that they must go ashore where they had struck land. It required immense courage to do so. It was mid-November and winter was approaching. The coast appeared bleak and uninviting. The natives might prove unfriendly. The resources of the pilgrims were small. Timber houses would have to be erected speedily. Food supplies were bound to be scanty for months if not years ahead. But the challenges were met. It was impossible to turn back. Within six months nearly half of the company had died. But with God's help the survivors accomplished the impossible, and in the next twenty years they were joined by multitudes of other Puritans, probably about 20,000 in all.

What sought they thus afar ?
  Bright jewels of the mine ?
The wealth of seas, the spoils of war ?
  They sought a faith's pure shrine !

Aye, call it holy ground,
  The soil where first they trod:
They have left unstained what there they found—
  Freedom to worship God !

(Felicia Hemans)

The words of John Masefield are significant. He writes:

Emigration nowadays is seldom an act of religious protest . . . a generation fond of pleasure, disinclined towards serious thought, and shrinking from hardship, even if it may be swiftly reached, will find it difficult to imagine the temper, courage, and manliness of the emigrants who made the first Christian settlement of New England. For a man to give up all things and fare forth into savagery, in order to escape from the responsibilities of life, in order, that is, to serve the devil, 'whose feet are bound by civilization', is common. Giving up all things in order to serve God is a sternness for which prosperity has unfitted us.

An important step forward was taken in 1629 when the Massachusetts Bay Company was formed to assist Puritan emigration to America and to ensure that the control of the new 'plantation', that is, the New England colony, should be located in America and not in England. To celebrate the occasion a fleet of six ships carrying 400 Puritans and all needful supplies, together with 'a plentiful provision of godly ministers' set sail for New England. Cotton Mather, the historian of these events—he wrote *Magnalia Christi Americana* (the great and wonderful things of Christ in America) in 1702—describes an incident which accompanied their sailing:

When they came to the Land's End, Mr. Higginson (a clergyman of the Church of England), calling up his children and other passengers to the stern of the ship to take their last sight of England, said, 'We will not say, as the Separatists were wont to say at their leaving of

Harvard in 1726.
Founded in 1636 close to
Boston, Massachusetts, its first
president was the Puritan
leader Thomas Shepard.

England, Farewell, Babylon! farewell, Rome! but we will say, Farewell, dear England! farewell, the church of God in England, and all the Christian friends there! We do not go to New England as Separatists from the Church of England, though we cannot but separate from the corruptions of it; but we go to practise the positive part of church reformation and propagate the gospel in America'.

A very important development took place in 1636 when Harvard College, in Cambridge, Massachusetts, was established. 'The oldest institution of learning in the United States', it takes its name from an Englishman, John Harvard (1607–38), born in London, and educated at England's Cambridge University. He did not arrive in North America until 1637, but in the previous year a plan had been formed to open a 'schoale or colledge' for the purpose of educating 'the English and Indian youth in knowledge and godliness'. Harvard died of consumption in 1638, and as he had no child he left half of his estate—he was a comparatively wealthy man—and also his library of 320 volumes, to the proposed college, which was accordingly named after him. The spot where it was erected was named Cambridge because many of the colonists, like Harvard himself, had been educated in the English University of that name. The College played an important part in the religious development of New England.

In 1649 a mere remnant of the English House of Commons—it was called The Rump—passed an ordinance for the founding of a Corporation for the Propagation of the Gospel in New England, and arranged for a collection to be made for it throughout England and Wales. A part of the money contributed was sent to support the work of a minister of the gospel of whom mention must now be made.

John Eliot, born in the year 1604, had come under the influence of a clergyman named Thomas Hooker who kept a grammar school in Essex and later became pastor of the First Church at Cambridge, Massachusetts. Eliot emigrated to New England in 1631 and was soon appointed as 'teacher' of the church at Roxbury. With the help of others he was responsible for the publishing of the first book printed in New England in 1640. It was a metrical version of the Psalms and has always been known as 'The Bay Psalm Book'.

Shortly Eliot made a great effort to preach the gospel to the Indians. He learned their language, or at least one of their languages, for there was considerable variation among the tribes, and with great labour he translated the whole of the Scripture into it. It was published in Cambridge, New England, in 1664. A copy of it was sent to England for presentation to King Charles II, and of it a leading Puritan said: 'Such a work and fruit of a plantation was never before presented to a king'. Cotton Mather wrote: 'Behold, ye Americans, the greatest honour that ever ye were partakers of—the Bible, the only Bible that ever was printed in all America from the foundation of the world'. One of the longest words in this Indian Bible is found in Mark 1.40: we give it a line to itself:
Wutappesittukqussunnoohwehtunkquoh.
Its meaning is, 'kneeling down to him'. The word for 'loves' in the same language contains 24 letters, that for 'question' 41 letters!

Before he died with the words 'Welcome, joy' upon his lips, Eliot saw 1100 Indian Christians as members in six churches, one under John Hiacomes, the first Indian minister, stationed at Martha's Vineyard, and one, his own successor at Natick; his name was Takawompbait. At Harvard there was a small college to train Indian pastors and teachers.

Eliot lived to the age of 86, his whole life being filled with labour for Christ. His first biographer remarked that 'Toile' is the anagram of his name. Preaching, writing, translating, testifying to the Lord Jesus Christ and his gospel of grace, occupied his days. A leading author described him as 'one of the most extraordinary men of my country'. God buries his workmen, as he buried Moses, but he carries on his work.

Throughout the 17th Century there was a direct connection between troubles in England and the Continent of Europe on the one hand, and religious settlements in America on the other. As we have noticed, it was the persecution of English Puritans under James I that led to the settlement of New England. During the reign of his son and successor, Charles I, the persecutions for which William Laud, Archbishop of Canterbury, was responsible, had similar consequences.

Later in the century some English Quakers moved to America. Founded, as we have seen, by George Fox who, despite his eccentricities, 'combined with profound religious conviction a high degree of tact and common sense and the faculty of organization', this persecuted sect increased rapidly in numbers. It obtained a notable addition to its ranks when, in 1667, William Penn became a convert. He possessed wealth and influence and looked to America as a place of refuge for his persecuted friends. By his efforts the State of Pennsylvania was founded in 1682. From its beginnings it granted complete religious toleration to all, and early concluded a treaty of peace with an Indian tribe.

Besides Englishmen there was a steady stream of immigrants to America from Germany, Holland, and Scandinavia. A company of Mennonites, a Protestant sect taking its name from Menno Simons and dating its origin in Zurich,

John Eliot, first missionary to the Indians in New England. A portrait painted when he was 55.

from 1525, founded Germantown which now forms a suburb of Philadelphia. From the Rhenish Palatinate came a crowd of refugees driven from their homeland by the armies of Louis XIV in 1688. So numerous were they that the term 'Palatine' was soon to be applied to all fugitives from Germany, from whatever region. Then, too, the Revocation of the Edict of Nantes in 1685 by the same French monarch resulted in a number of Huguenot refugees turning to America as their new home.

In these various ways the population of the American colonies was a medley of peoples. Benjamin Franklin later estimated that Pennsylvania, for example, consisted of one third Quakers, one third Germans and one third 'miscellaneous', the last-mentioned including a large group of Welshmen to whom William Penn had promised 40,000 acres of land where they could retain their own language and institutions.

Thus is came about that the 17th Century was for the Protestant churches of western Europe a time of remarkable territorial expansion. Vast areas, only thinly peopled, were occupied, and in some small measure the knowledge of the Lord began to cover the earth as the waters cover the sea. But greater things lay in the womb of the future.

39

The Pietists: Spener, Francke, Zinzendorf

As we have seen in an earlier chapter, the Thirty Years' War in Germany led to a great increase in the measure of religious liberty, and to a considerable extent Christianity flourished there in the years following the war. The truth was earnestly confessed and practised by many. But soon Luther's words were verified: 'The Word of God is seldom retained in its purity in any one place beyond the period of twenty or at best forty years. The people become accustomed to it, grow cold in their Christian love, and regard God's gift of grace with indifference'.

Spiritual life in many places fell to a low level, and many who still retained the outward form of the true faith lacked genuine heartfelt repentance. Sad it is that the attractions of the world, and the example of worldly friends, sometimes prove too strong for the followers of Jesus Christ! It has often been the case that, after a time of blessing, a generation rises that leaves the narrow path and joins the throng on the broad way that leads away from God. When this happens, God, who never forgets his Church, sends forth his servants who, like the prophets of old time, warn backsliding Christians and admonish them to repent and turn again to the Lord.

One of these men was Philipp Jakob Spener (1635–1705). He and his adherents were called Pietists, a word (derived from Latin: pietas) akin to the English word 'pious'. But, as used in Germany, it was intended to brand the pious people as fanatics. Spener was deeply moved by the distress of the Church, and as instruction in Scripture was sadly neglected, he began to gather young people around him. He prayed with them and to them he explained the Bible, and the Christian way of life. God blessed his efforts and many became eager to learn true Christianity. In 1670 Spener began to deliver lectures on biblical subjects in Frankfurt. Other pastors followed his example, and the number of Pietists increased rapidly. In 1695 a university was founded at Halle, and it was not long before it became the centre of Pietism. In this way a living faith was revived where dead orthodoxy had existed.

Pietism was not mysticism, for the latter was liable to cause its adherents to withdraw from the mainstream of life in the world, and to become detached from what Scripture terms 'good works for necessary uses'. The Pietists were keen to perform works of humility and practical usefulness.

When about fifty years old Spener left Frankfurt for Dresden where he became the chief preacher in the court of Elector Johann George III. The courtiers ridiculed and mocked him to such a degree, however, that ultimately he left Dresden and accepted a call to labour in Berlin. Here too he suffered many hardships until his death in 1705. It had not been his task to lead earnest believers out of the Lutheran Church, but to make them more spiritually minded and more useful to their fellow men while they remained Church members.

Not all the Pietists, however, possessed the simple faith and holy zeal of Spener. Religious pride, a boasting in their piety akin to that of the Pharisees of the New Testament, soon showed itself among them. Others taught erroneous doctrines, and still others were 'righteous overmuch'. They made the 'narrow path' narrower than the Lord made it. Some of them even prohibited the taking of a walk, and even frowned upon laughter.

Another noteworthy Pietist was August Hermann Francke, a pupil and then an intimate friend of Spener. He laboured in Leipzig, Hamburg, and Erfurt, where his piety provoked persecution. In 1692 he became pastor and professor at Halle, and it was at Halle that he then served the Lord until his death thirty-five years later. He was a most diligent pastor, a man full of faith and good works. The poor were often to be found at his door, where they were never denied some form of assistance. When Francke found that they were usually quite ignorant of the things of the Spirit of God, he gathered them into his house and began to instruct them. He was also very much concerned to teach ignorant children, but to do so he needed a school. To obtain the means for this he invited contributions from friends able to bear the expense, and from those who visited his house. One day he found eight silver coins in the box in which donations were placed, and this made him so enthusiastic that he exclaimed, 'Now I shall open the school!' A student whom he invited to become the teacher began the work and the Lord blessed it greatly. A room in the parsonage served as schoolroom, so that, at first, it was not necessary to erect or to hire a building. When the great benefits of the school were seen, not only the poor but also the well-to-do asked that their children be admitted.

Francke's greatest work, however, was the

Count Zinzendorf.

erection and maintenance of an Orphanage. It was a monument of faith, for Francke did not have the means to establish such an institution. But he went forward in faith, for it was founded and entirely supported by free-will offerings. Once, when the treasury was empty, and the treasurer came to him saying, 'All the money has been paid out; there is nothing left', Francke, fully confident of divine help, answered: 'This is a sign that the Lord will help us'. And so it proved.

Before Francke died 2507 children were being helped and instructed each year. They were taught by 175 instructors. Both John Wesley and George Whitefield were encouraged to begin orphanage work by Francke's example. In the case of Whitefield, it was Charles Wesley who first suggested to him the founding of an Orphan House in Georgia, but Francke's example undoubtedly spurred him on; John Wesley visited the Halle Orphanage in 1738 and was greatly impressed by what he saw.

When Francke planned the Orphanage some of his critics urged that it was too large to be maintained by voluntary subscriptions; but he replied to them: 'I know how large a house I require in order to regulate the work in a proper manner. But know this, that when God has once built this house, he will still be as rich and as able as he was before to provide for the poor that will reside in it.'

Another leading Christian of those days was Nicholaus Ludwig, Count von Zinzendorf. His mother lost her husband soon after the Count was born, and in her Bible, where she recorded the birth, she wrote: 'May the Father of mercies rule the heart of this child, so that he may walk honestly and uprightly. May sin never rule over him, and may his feet be steadfast in the Word;

then he will be happy for time and eternity'. The Church of God owes very much to godly mothers! At the age of ten Nicholaus was sent to the school of Pastor Francke where his spiritual life was richly nourished. Shortly he wished to study theology, but his guardian—his mother had married again—persuaded him to study law. This led to service in the State but it was not much to his taste. Then something unforeseen happened; a new factor began to operate in his life.

We have given attention earlier to John Huss, and to the Moravian Brethren, the followers of Huss. During the life-time of Zinzendorf they were severely persecuted, and some of them asked for shelter on the estate in Saxony which Zinzendorf had purchased from his grandmother. He readily granted their request. One of them, Christian David, a carpenter, struck an axe into a tree to begin the building of the first house, and as he did so he quoted the words: 'Blessed are they that dwell in thy house; they will be still praising thee'. (Psa. 84 : 4). In all, more than 300 refugees settled on the estate. They called their settlement Herrnhut, meaning 'the Lord's protection'. This became the principal Moravian centre, sheltering Lutherans, Calvinists and Hussites. Zinzendorf loved them as brethren in Christ and wished them to live together as members of the same body. But this was not an easy matter.

In 1727 the first 'New Moravian Church' was organized. Emigration from Herrnhut frequently took place, and soon congregations of 'Herrnhutters' were found in Holland, England, Denmark and North America. Zinzendorf himself became a preacher among them. In 1741 he made a voyage to America to visit the Lutheran Church in Philadelphia. He wanted to unite the Lutheran and the Reformed Churches in his scheme of Church union, but it came to nothing and after two years he returned to Europe.

The Moravian Church took great interest in missionary enterprise, and in 1732 the first of its missionaries set sail for the Isle of St. Thomas in the West Indies. Others were sent to Greenland, Lapland, Ceylon, Algiers, Labrador, and to various parts of Africa, Asia and Australia. We mention William Carey in a later chapter. On his way to the memorable meeting which founded the Baptist Missionary Society—it was held in a back parlour in Kettering, Northamptonshire—he threw down before his fellow ministers the 'Periodical Accounts' of missions of the Moravian Church. 'See what these Moravians have done!' he exclaimed. 'Cannot we follow their example and in obedience to our divine Master go into the world and preach the gospel to the heathen?' It was a characteristic of the Moravian Church that every member was expected to do his or her share in such a work, at home or abroad.

Count Zinzendorf, a man blessed and made a blessing, died in 1760. In the churches of the west he is best remembered today for his hymn, translated into English by John Wesley:

Jesus, thy blood and righteousness
My beauty are, my glorious dress;
'Midst flaming worlds, in these arrayed,
With joy shall I lift up my head.

Oh, let the dead now hear thy voice!
Now bid thy banished ones rejoice!
Their beauty this, their glorious dress,
Jesus, the Lord our righteousness.

40

The Faith in North America during the 18th Century

In this chapter we turn our attention to the growth of the Church in North America during the 18th Century. Already we have seen how, during the preceding century, large numbers of settlers crossed the Atlantic Ocean from Britain and the Continent of Europe. During the 18th Century, however, another Continent came into prominence. The infamous slave trade between Africa and America had commenced as early as the Elizabethan period. John Hawkins, in 1562, had kidnapped negroes on the coast of Sierra Leone, crossed the ocean to the West Indies, and there traded them to the Spanish planters in exchange for hides, ginger, sugar and pearls which could be sold profitably in England.

Early in the 17th Century the slave trade reached out to the southern colonies of North America, with their rice and tobacco plantations. A Dutch ship with fourteen negroes for sale arrived at Jamestown, Virginia, in 1619. From that time the dismal 'traffic in human flesh' continued to increase, despite protest and attempted prohibition, for southern planters wished to buy slaves for manual work in a climate too hot for the labour of Europeans. Cotton Mather in his *Essays to do Good* wrote of the iniquity of slavery in such strong terms that the American Tract Society, when reprinting his book in a later day, thought it necessary to delete many of the offending sentences.

After the granting by Spain to England of a monopoly of the Spanish slave trade in 1713—the agreement was called The Asiento—large numbers of slaves were shipped to the colonies, many New Englanders eagerly seizing upon the profit to be made in this way. Towards the middle of the century John Newton—the hymn-writer, preacher, and letter-writer of later years —was engaged in the traffic, and even after his conversion he did not at once turn from it.

There were therefore three types of person in North America—the original inhabitants known as Red Indians, very widely scattered, and divided into a large number of different tribes; the negroes who developed their own particular brand of the English language; and the white population which, in the southern colonies, was predominantly attached to the Church of England, but which, in the New England area

showed a perplexing variety of Christian profession. Here were Lutherans, Calvinists, Mennonites, Presbyterians, Independents, Quakers, Roman Catholics, and such lesser bodies as New Born, Dunkers, New Lights, Covenanters, Brownists, Seceders, and Mountain Men.

Merely nominal Christians among the southern planters found it impossible to believe that their slaves had souls which needed salvation. One mistress of slaves is reported to have said to an Anglican minister, 'Is it possible that any of my slaves could go to heaven? and must I see them there?' Not a few entertained the idea that if slaves received Christian baptism they would be automatically freed from bondage; hence Christianity was not for them.

An outstanding worker among American negroes was Elias Neau, a Frenchman who, for his Protestant faith, had suffered three years' imprisonment and seven years in the galleys. When at length he was released he became a trader in New York, a town which then contained about 1000 slaves. Until his death in 1722 he laboured hard for their enlightenment and conversion. It deserves mention that, to counter the belief that baptism would set slaves free from their masters, he persuaded his supporters with political influence to get passed an Act of Assembly confirming the rights of masters over their slaves after baptism.

Christian witness to the Indians was peculiarly difficult, for the tribes spoke a variety of languages, all hard to learn, and hardly any reduced to writing despite the progress made in the days of John Eliot. Gospel preachers had therefore to depend upon the help of interpreters. Had there been a hundred John Eliots, widely dispersed, they would not have been enough to meet the demands of the work. Furthermore, the

opposite William Penn the Quaker, after inheriting land in North America, founded the State of Pennsylvania. He made a treaty with the Indians of the region in 1781, as here shown.

A view of New York in the 18th century.

Indian tribes were nomadic; they did not usually stay long in one place, and this prevented systematic teaching. They moved their wigwams as they pursued wild animals, and were often difficult to locate. Obviously there was a pressing need for ministers of the gospel to adapt their methods to the requirements of the various localities in which they worked, and to the different types of persons to whom God sent them.

A worthy successor to Eliot in Indian work was David Brainerd (1718–47). He was suddenly converted to God while taking a walk. At the age of 24 he was licensed to preach and was appointed by The Society in Scotland for Propagating Christian Knowledge (founded in 1709) to work among Indians. At first he met with little apparent success. He then decided to live among Indians at Crossweeksung, near Newark, New Jersey. Here he had the joy of reaping a harvest, for he was able to baptize 78 Indians in the belief that they had experienced true conversion. But Brainerd was soon worn out by his labours—his health was always precarious—and after barely four years in the work he died. Despite the brevity of his service he is accounted one of the Church's greatest missionaries. One writer even claims that his zeal and devotion to the Lord have not been surpassed since the days of the apostles. Certainly the records of his life—and his *Diary* is a most remarkable document—have inspired many to exert themselves in similar labour, among them Henry Martyn who served God in India and Persia.

Mention must be made of the founding of the colony of Georgia in 1733. It was 'as one born out of due time'. Faith and hope, it has been said, led to the founding of most of the other colonies, but in the case of Georgia the motive was love. General James Oglethorpe, the pioneer worker, wanted to open a place of refuge for all victims of injustice and for sufferers from religious

William Tennent's Log College at Neshaminy Creek, north of Philadelphia.

LOG COLLEGE

Here was located 1736-46 William Tennent's "College" for training Presbyterian ministers. From it came a notable list of religious and educational leaders. Its graduates helped found Princeton University, 1746.

PENNSYLVANIA HISTORICAL AND MUSEUM COMMISSION

Present-day road sign at Neshaminy Creek.

opposite Jonathan Edwards (1703–58).

church at Neshaminy, 20 miles north of Philadelphia. His fame rests mainly on the fact that he built a 'Log College' where men were educated and trained for the work of gospel ministry. In it his own sons were educated, Gilbert, the eldest and most distinguished of them, exercising a very fruitful ministry in New Brunswick.

The 18th Century was but three years old when a notable event occurred in the State of Connecticut—the birth of a boy named Jonathan Edwards, who became a star of the first magnitude in the annals of the Church of God. He was greatly gifted intellectually, and wrote learned philosophical treatises on such subjects as the human will. Towards the end of his life he was appointed President of Princeton College, New Jersey. But he had held office for a mere five weeks when his untimely death occurred (1758), the result of an inoculation against small-pox, one of the scourges of the time. More than one edition of Edwards' writings has been reprinted in recent years. In the world of scholarship he enjoyed great repute. But as a preacher, too, he was noted; many of his sermons are said to have been 'overwhelming', particularly one entitled 'Sinners in the Hands of an Angry God'.

It was while Jonathan Edwards was a pastor at Northampton (Massachusetts) that what is usually called The Great Awakening began. Its beginnings were in the years 1734 and 1735; then it died down for a while, but recommenced in 1740–41. In the second of these two periods it was linked with the preaching of George Whitefield of whom we shall say more later; but in both periods it was a clear evidence of the power of the Holy Spirit to revive God's work 'in the midst of the years'.

After the 1734–5 revival Edwards wrote an account of events linked with it under the title,

persecution. Among the clergy who ministered to the spiritual needs of the settlers were John and Charles Wesley—John Wesley in particular, because Charles Wesley's time was chiefly devoted to secretarial work for Oglethorpe—and after a brief interval, George Whitefield. The last-named built an orphan house in the colony and maintained it by collections taken up during his many preaching tours.

Another name also deserves mention. In 1718 William Tennent, Snr., a clergyman from Ireland, landed at Philadelphia with his four sons. They are representative of the 'immense volume and strength of the Scottish-Irish immigration' of the period. Tennent belonged to the Episcopal Church of Ireland, but soon after his arrival in America he joined the Presbyterian Church of Pennsylvania and became pastor of a

A Narrative of Surprising Conversions. It begins with mention of his grandfather, Solomon Stoddard, who was minister of Northampton for almost 60 years. Edwards became his assistant about two years before he died. The following is a part of Edwards' own account of the general state of the young people of the area about the year 1734:

It seemed to be a time of extraordinary dullness in religion. Licentiousness for some years prevailed among the youth of the town; they were many of them very much addicted to night-walking [keeping late hours] and frequenting the tavern, and lewd practices, wherein some, by their example, exceedingly corrupted others. It was their manner very frequently to get together, in conventions of both sexes for mirth and jollity, which they called frolics; and they would often spend the greater part of the night in them, without regard to any order in the families they belonged to; and indeed family government did too much fail in the town. It was become very customary with many of our young people to be indecent in their carriage at meeting [i.e. unseemly behaviour in church] which doubtless would not have prevailed in such a degree, had it not been that my grandfather, through his great age, was not so able to observe them.

Next Edwards describes how many young persons became increasingly serious about the things of God. Some became concerned to avoid Arminian doctrine, some to understand the truth of 'justification by faith alone', some to know beyond a doubt 'the true and only way of salvation'. Edwards continues:

It was in the latter part of December [1734] that the Spirit of God began extraordinarily to set in, and wonderfully to work amongst us; and very suddenly, one after another, five or six persons were to all appearances savingly converted . . .

106. The main street in
Northampton, New England,
in 1838.

To one young woman with whom I had conversation, it appeared to me that God had given her a new heart, truly broken and sanctified. I could not doubt it. The news of it seemed to be almost like a flash of lightning upon the hearts of young people all over the town, and upon many others . . .

The one thing in their view was to get the kingdom of heaven, and everyone appeared pressing into it. What persons' minds were intent upon was to escape for their lives, and to fly from the wrath to come. There was scarcely a single person in the town, young or old, left unconcerned about the great things of the eternal world. Meetings were greatly thronged. The work of conversion increased more and more. Souls did as it were come by flocks to Jesus Christ.

Many who came to town, on one occasion or other, had their consciences smitten and awakened. There were many instances of persons who came on visits or on business, who had not been long here before they partook of that shower of divine blessing which God rained down here, and went home rejoicing, till at length the same work began evidently to appear and prevail in several other towns in the country.

Edwards' *Narrative* gives many details of the Awakening. It shows us the nature of the Lord's work among men, and supplies comments on 'revival' which are instructive, sober and wise.

Our next two chapters will also include

mention of that 'on-going work'. They trace the course of the Methodist Movement which began in Britain about 1735 and continued with remarkable results to the end of the century and beyond. Although it commenced in another land, it followed almost immediately, as will be noted, after the events mentioned in *A Narrative of Surprising Conversions*. In it we shall see how God used the testimony of the first Methodists, and of George Whitefield in particular, to revive his work. In many parts of North America there were surprising results. Whitefield paid seven visits to his overseas 'parish'. During the last of them he died in harness, and left all that was mortal of him in Newburyport, Massachusetts. To him the American Colonies of those days owed an immense debt, for he brought to them 'the fulness of the blessing of the gospel of Christ.'

The Edwards Memorial Church, Northampton, Massachusetts.

41

Methodism and the Wesleys (1)

In this chapter we shall be largely concerned with the Methodist Movement beginning about the year 1735, but first we shall glance at the earlier years of the century. They were marked by the introduction of hymn-singing into English churches. From the Reformation until the 18th Century it was the custom to sing Psalms translated metrically by Sternhold and Hopkins. This belonged to the Puritan tradition and derived from John Calvin. The Sternhold and

Hopkins version was bound up in the same covers as the Bibles in private use, so that many regarded them as virtually on a level with Holy Writ. So their use tended to die hard. But Isaac Watts insisted that in confining songs of praise to the Book of Psalms, the worshipper was behaving as if Christ had never been born, had never died, and had never been raised from the dead and 'received up into glory'. He argued that in his day Christian praise lacked a New Testament content and he did his utmost to supply the lack. 'To him, more than to any other man, is due the triumph of the hymn in Christian worship', says a modern scholar. Gradually the arguments of Watts prevailed. The Methodist Movement assisted the change, for in the person of Charles Wesley hymnody found its second greatest contributor. Once the fashion became established, many lesser men and several women contributed verses. In 1779 appeared the Olney hymns written by John Newton and William Cowper. The first Methodist *Psalms and Hymns* appeared as early as 1737, when John Wesley, its compiler, was a 'Missioner in Georgia'. He published a much more substantial hymn-book in the same year as the Olney Hymns appeared. The exclusive use of the metrical Psalms died hard; indeed, it is still retained in certain Scottish Churches, but gradually most Protestant churches welcomed the innovation and most modern hymn-books now contain a wealth of hymns, original and in translation, from many lands and centuries.

Another aspect of Christian activity in the earlier part of the 18th Century was the promotion of Christian education by means of Academies. 'Academies' has a wide application, but here we refer only to such of them as trained Dissenters or Non-conformists for the Christian ministry. Conformists, that is to say, members of the Church of England, were usually educated at either Oxford or Cambridge, the only two universities in England at this time. But both universities applied an Anglican test which Dissenters could not endure. Isaac Watts, for example, attended an Academy in what is now north London.

One of the most famous of the Academies was founded by Philip Doddridge of Northampton in 1730. Several Christian workers of note were trained in it, one of the best known being Risdon Darracott who later settled as pastor in Wellington, Shropshire, and became known as 'the Star of the West'. Doddridge also wrote popular hymns, but probably his greatest work was the writing of *The Rise and Progress of Religion in the Soul* (which was blessed to the conversion of some notable men, and was later translated into a great variety of languages, including Tamil and Syriac). Both Watts and Doddridge were Independents (Congregationalists). The chief Baptist minister of the period was John Gill, a man of immense learning, who ministered in London from 1719 until his death in 1771. He and Doddridge both produced biblical commentaries.

By and large, however, the first part of the 18th Century was a period of spiritual decay. Despite the existence in sundry places of 'live' ministries, there was truth in the saying, 'Puritanism was dead'. In the Church of England bishops and parish clergy alike were often given up to worldliness. Sports, politics, entertainments, held their chief interest. Ease rather than labour characterized them. Much of the preaching of the period was remote from gospel truth, and it almost seemed as if true religion would die out altogether. It has been

said, probably with a large measure of truth, that the Established Church was little better than 'a useful branch of the Civil Service', maintaining loyalty to the government and the crown, but showing a minimum of care for the welfare of men's souls.

As for the people at large, drunkenness, immorality, cruel and pernicious sports, unbelief, and complete indifference to the divine message, were their most obvious features. A vague belief

The Holy Club, Oxford, which included among its members John Wesley (addressing the group), Charles Wesley, George Whitefield (immediately left of John Wesley).

in God, accompanied by an almost complete ignorance of the way of salvation, replaced the 'belief to the saving of the soul' which was characteristic of Puritanism.

Revival began in the University of Oxford where, in 1729, several students formed a Society nicknamed The Holy Club by their irreligious fellows. Their purpose was to promote the growth of personal piety. They studied the Bible—hence some called them 'Bible moths'—with much diligence, and engaged in various 'good works'—helping the poor, visiting the sick and those in the local prison, utilizing every hour of the day, and even every fleeting minute, to the benefit either of themselves or of others. Hence another name applied to them was that of 'Methodist', those who practised living according to a fixed plan.

For several years, however, members of the Holy Club failed to understand the sheer grace of the gospel. They tended to hold the view that salvation depended, at least in part, on their own efforts to lead a consistently holy life, and to this extent they desired to contribute something to their soul's salvation. They failed to understand that from first to last salvation is the work of God alone; that 'By grace are ye saved, through faith, and that not of yourselves, it is the gift of God; not of works lest any man should boast' (Eph. 2:8–9). But God was leading them on 'from faith to faith, as it is written. The just shall live by faith' (Rom. 1 : 17).

The Methodist leaders of 1729 were John Wesley and his younger brother Charles, sons of the Anglican minister at Epworth in Lincoln-shire, their mother Susannah being even better known than the father, for she, as much as he, laboured to rear them in 'the nurture and admonition of the Lord', and to supervise their early education. John Wesley was ordained in the Church of England and became a classical tutor in Oxford and a Fellow of its Lincoln College. He had already passed thirty years of age before there was any indication that his career was to be that of an itinerant minister of the gospel rather than one of cushioned ease in university circles. But when God's Spirit works in a man's heart and conscience, his outward life as well as that which is inward may be turned upside down.

It was so with John Wesley. In 1734 he decided that he was called of God to engage in missionary work in the newly-founded American colony of Georgia. But his stay there was comparatively short. In one way or another, but chiefly through the influence of Moravian Christians met on board ship, he was forced to the alarming conclusion that he himself was not truly converted to God. He, a university fellow and tutor, he, an ordained clergyman of the Church of England, he, the product of a Christian home, was as yet ignorant of saving truth and destitute of conversion experience. 'I left my native country', he wrote early in 1738, 'to teach the Georgia Indians the nature of Christianity. But what have I learnt myself in the meantime? What I the least of all suspected, that I who went to America to *convert* others was *never converted* to God myself'.

The revelation led Wesley to reflect on the long years spent at Oxford, and he summed them up in the following words: 'I diligently strove against sin, I omitted no sort of self-denial which I thought lawful. I omitted no occasion of doing good; but could not find that all this gave me any assurance of acceptance with God'. But enlightenment gradually came to him. He wrote:

On shipboard it pleased God of his free mercy to give me 26 of the Moravian brothers for companions, who endeavoured to show me 'a more excellent way'. But I understood it not at first. I was too learned to be wise, so that it seemed foolishness unto me. And I continued preaching, and following after, and trusting in, that righteousness wherein no flesh can be justified.

It was not until Wesley arrived in London after returning from Georgia that the full light of the gospel dawned upon his soul. The occasion is famous in Christian history. He attended a Moravian meeting-house in London where a man read to the company from Martin Luther's Preface to Paul's Epistle to the Romans, in which the German reformer teaches what faith is, and stresses that by faith, and faith alone, a sinner is justified in the sight of God. But we can state the change that came to Wesley in his own words:

I felt my heart strangely warmed. I felt I did trust in Christ, Christ alone, for salvation; and an assurance was given me that he had taken away my sins, even mine, and saved me from the law of sin and death; and I then testified openly to all there what I now first felt in my heart.

The date was the 24th May, 1738, when Wesley was almost 35 years of age.

Charles Wesley, also in London at that time, had entered into the light and joy of salvation only three days earlier. He became the great hymn-writer of Methodism, and we quote from the so-called 'conversion hymn' which he wrote on the occasion:

> *Where shall my wondering soul begin ?*
> *How shall I all to heaven aspire ?*
> *A slave redeemed from death and sin,*
> *A brand plucked from eternal fire,*
> *How shall I equal triumphs raise,*
> *Or sing my great Deliverer's praise ?*

John Wesley (1703–91).

O how shall I the goodness tell,
  Father, which thou to me hast showed?
That I, a child of wrath and hell,
  I should be called a child of God,
Should know, should feel my sins forgiven,
Blest with this antepast[1] of heaven!

Some time later Charles Wesley wrote a second hymn which also bears upon his conversion experience; it runs in part as follows:

And can it be that I should gain
  An interest in the Saviour's blood?
Died he for me who caused his pain,
  For me who him to death pursued?
Amazing love! how can it be
That thou, my God, shouldst die for me!

Long my imprisoned spirit lay
  Fast bound in sin and nature's night:
Thine eye diffused a quickening ray,

[1] antepast = foretaste.

I woke, the dungeon flamed with light;
My chains fell off, my heart was free,
I rose, went forth, and followed thee.

Strangely, John Wesley in recording his experience on the 24th May, omits mention of a late visit on that same day to the house in Little Britain, London, where his brother Charles was lodged, but it is mentioned in the Journal which Charles then kept. Of the evening of the 24th he writes:

At eight I prayed by myself for love . . . Towards ten my brother was brought in triumph by a troop of our friends, and declared, 'I believe'. We sang the hymn (i.e. the first quoted above) with great joy, and parted with prayer.

In all Charles Wesley wrote about 7,000 hymns, including some of the most famous in the English language. They constitute his chief title to fame and have exercised enormous influence throughout the English-speaking world.

42

Methodism and the Wesleys (2)

We have given considerable space to the conversion of the Wesleys because the character of their branch of the Methodist Movement was largely determined by the experiences of the two brothers. No person became a Methodist without a conversion experience born of the convicting work of the Spirit of God. Regeneration by the Spirit's initial work, sanctification by the Spirit's continued work, forgiveness through the atoning work of Christ on Calvary, justification by faith in Christ—these, and related doctrines, were preached in England and Wales, Scotland

and Ireland, North America, and wherever Methodist preachers penetrated.

John Wesley's ministry of preaching is phenomenal by any standards. For half a century he became a wanderer, but a wanderer with a divine commission. He regarded the entire world as his parish. Almost all the clergy closed their pulpits to him, so that for a number of years he preached out-of-doors. Rising about four in the morning, he often preached his first sermon of the new day at five, and usually two or three more sermons before the day ended. He gave most of his

Wesley Preaching at Bristol before the Mayor and Corporation of the city.

attention, not to England's many small villages, but to the chief centres of population, and especially to strategic centres such as Bristol and Newcastle-on-Tyne. Among miners, ironworkers, spinners and weavers, fishermen, and in general the poorer sections of the population, he met with much success. In all he travelled about 250,000 miles, and preached on 40,000 occasions. The converts, and sometimes Wesley himself, suffered persecution, but they met this without flinching and lived down the opposition. A modern Methodist has said of him: 'The truest vision of him one can see is as the man on horseback, the reins loose, the saddle-bags full of books, the little man reading or writing, but always marching on from town to town . . . to conquest and to victory'.

Not only preaching but a considerable amount of literary work occupied Wesley's days. He was a man of fine scholarship who found great pleasure in editing grammars (in five languages) and the works of certain classical authors. He wrote commentaries on Scripture, and prepared a library of 50 volumes of extracts from Christian authors, so that his followers might have abundance of good reading matter. He even wrote a work entitled *Primitive Physic* to let Methodists know how to maintain good health, or recover it when they had lost it.

Perhaps Wesley's greatest literary work was his *Journal*, a record of his day-to-day activities which is of much interest and value. The following is an extract from it, taken almost at random (the date: April, 1744):

Mon. 2—I preached at five [i.e. early morning] and rode on towards Launceston (Cornwall). The hills were covered with snow, as in the depth of winter. About two we came to Trewint, wet and weary enough,

having been battered by the rain and hail for some hours. I preached in the evening, to many more than the house would contain, on the happiness of him whose sins are forgiven. In the morning (a granite mason) undertook to pilot me over the great moor, all the paths being covered with snow which in many places was driven together too deep for horse or man to pass. The hail followed us for the first seven miles; we then had a fair though exceedingly sharp day. I preached at Gwennap in the evening to a plain, simple-hearted people; and God comforted us by each other.

Wed. 4—About eleven we reached St. Ives . . . As soon as we went out we were saluted, as usual, with a huzza and a few stones or pieces of dirt. But in the evening none opened his mouth while I proclaimed, 'I will love thee, O Lord, my strength . . . I will call upon the Lord, who is worthy to be praised; so shall I be saved from my enemies'.

Methodism, though carried on with no intention of separating from the Church of England, met with a very cool or even hostile reception from bishops and clergy, with notable exceptions. It was organized by John Wesley very carefully in 'classes' and even in 'circuits' with their own Methodist preachers and exhorters. It was in certain ways a church within a church; and ultimately, for the sake of the movement's expansion, Wesley felt compelled to assume powers which belonged only to Anglican bishops, chiefly in respect of the ordination of preachers. Yet as long as he lived he and his followers remained within the Established Church. The break with the Church came in 1795, four years after his death at the age of 87.

We have earlier said that Wesley spent a little

time in Georgia, America, in the 1730's. A year after his return to England, on a walk from London to Oxford, he read Jonathan Edwards' *Narrative of Surprising Conversions* (published in England by Isaac Watts and John Guyse) and recorded in his *Journal:* 'Surely this is the Lord's doing and it is marvellous in our eyes'. Yet for long years America's contacts with English Methodists were brought about through George Whitefield, another member of Oxford's Holy Club, not through John Wesley. Perhaps Wesley's Arminian theology helps to account for this. Whitefield's Calvinistic theology, as we shall see, made a much stronger appeal to Americans, especially in New England.

In 1767, however, a certain Philip Embury who in his native Ireland had been one of Wesley's 'local preachers', formed a 'class meeting' in his house in New York, and from that time Methodist Societies multiplied and spread to Pennsylvania and Maryland. After two years Wesley sent two of his preachers to organize the movement. Their success was such that, by 1772, Francis Asbury had been commissioned by Wesley to administer and superintend American Methodism.

Asbury, who had been reared in a Methodist home not far from Birmingham in the English Midlands, was well qualified for the work. He was a man born to command. Wesley, who never visited America after 1737, trusted him implicitly, and in his hands the work prospered.

The War of American Independence (1776–83) brought the Methodist Church into a period of trial. The Americans became republicans whereas John Wesley was a firm monarchist. 'We are not republicans and do not intend to be' was his dictum. But Asbury was able to surmount all difficulties, as he continued to superintend 'The Methodist Episcopal Church of the United States of America'. Whereas Boston (Massachusetts) had been the centre of the Independent churches, New York of the Episcopal Church (Church of England), and Philadelphia of the Presbyterian churches, Baltimore in Maryland now became the headquarters of American Methodism. Asbury made his home there.

In 1784 Wesley sent Dr. Thomas Coke to be Asbury's colleague in an expanding work. It was Coke who persuaded Asbury to adopt the title 'bishop' in place of 'superintendent' for the two of them. This angered Wesley and he said: 'Men may call me a knave, or a fool, a rascal, a scoundrel, and I am content. But they shall never by my consent call *me* bishop.' Yet 'bishop' remained the American title.

Coke travelled widely. Sometimes he was in England, often elsewhere, by reason of the fact that in 1789 he became the director of the Methodist missionary enterprise. This post was given to him despite the offence he gave to his English brethren by sending to George Washington, America's first President, an Address of Congratulation from 'the bishops of the Methodist Episcopal Church'. He died while on a voyage to India in 1814. Two years later Asbury died.

It has often been said that Methodism saved England from revolution and this may well have been so. One of the greatest revolutions of modern times came to France in 1789, and its effects were felt far and wide. There were many fears that it might engulf England in revolution also. But Methodism, springing out of the Church of England, taught obedience to 'the powers that be', and Methodists were the most loyal of all citizens to the British crown. They prayed regularly for the king and his government and were altogether opposed to the unchristian programme of French revolutionists except insofar as that programme aimed at amending social wrongs.

If Methodism served to prevent revolution in the State, it also helped to revive true religion within the Church of England, and during the latter part of the 18th Century the impact of Methodism was felt strongly by many who had no desire to leave the Established Church. They became known as the Evangelicals, and we shall mention them in a later chapter.

43

Methodism and George Whitefield

Leuconomus (beneath well-sounding Greek
I slur a name a poet must not speak),
Stood pilloried on infamy's high stage,
And bore the pelting scorn of half an age,
The very butt of slander, and the blot
For every dart that malice ever shot.
The man that mentioned him *at once dismissed*
All mercy from his lips and sneered and hissed.

In these lines the poet William Cowper introduces us to George Whitefield ('Leuconomus' is Greek for 'white field') and describes the world's reception of one of the greatest preachers of the gospel of all time. 'Infamy', 'pelting scorn', 'butt of slander', 'malice', 'sneered and hissed' depict the reaction of the fashionable world, the world of the drunkard and of the sport-lover, and even the world of the superficially religious, to the message of the gospel preacher, and remind us of the warning spoken to his disciples by the Lord himself: 'If they have called the master of the house Beelzebub, how much more shall they call them of his household ?' (Matt. 10 : 25).

But before we give attention to the work done by Whitefield, we take a look, as with the Wesleys, at the conversion experience upon which that work was based. We possess as full an account of it as of that of the Wesleys, for all three men kept Journals covering the period. In Whitefield's we learn that he, as an undergraduate at Oxford, was introduced by Charles Wesley to the Holy Club. His father having died, his mother and, later, his eldest brother, continued to keep the Bell Inn at Gloucester, but it became possible for George to enter Pembroke College in the University city, and while there he became a Methodist.

For a time, however, like the two Wesleys, he remained ignorant of the part that the grace of God and a God-given faith play in a conversion experience. His conviction of sin was deep and thorough, his exercises of soul at times overpowering; occasionally they hindered him from pursuing his studies, and almost broke down his bodily and mental health. Fasting and other ascetic practices were no remedy. Night and day 'the spirit of bondage' lay upon him. The 'buffetings of Satan' seemed innumerable. But at long last the day of deliverance dawned and, as the sufferer said, 'The days of my mourning ended!'

In his *Journal* Whitefield wrote: 'God was pleased to remove the heavy load, to enable me to lay hold of his dear Son by a living faith, and by giving me the Spirit of adoption to seal me even to the day of everlasting redemption. With what joy—joy unspeakable—was my soul filled?' In later life, as he remembered the glad occasion, he wrote: 'I know the place! It may be superstitious, but whenever I go to Oxford I cannot help running to that place where Jesus Christ first revealed himself to me and gave me the new birth.' The great event occurred in the Spring of 1735 when Whitefield was 20 years of age. It preceded the conversion experience of the Wesleys by about three years. In 1736 came Whitefield's ordination for the ministry at the hands of the Bishop of Gloucester, and the preaching of his first sermon in the same city. 'Some few mocked, but most for the present seemed struck, and I have since heard that a complaint has been made to the Bishop that I drove fifteen mad.' The Bishop expressed the hope that 'the madness might not be forgotten before next Sunday'.

A marvellous career of preaching in all parts of the British Isles and the thirteen American Colonies followed. It lasted 35 years, at first in co-operation with the Wesleys, but later on separate lines. Whitefield's theology from the commencement of his work was Calvinistic, whereas that of the Wesleys resembled the teachings of Arminius, and it was this that led to a breach between them. On the personal level they remained 'brothers in Christ', but in respect of their labours for the Lord they found it better to work apart.

It was Whitefield who led the way in open air preaching against which John Wesley had strong

George Whitefield (1714–70)

Whitefield preaching at
Moorfields, London,
despite much opposition.

initial prejudices. There were two chief reasons for the adoption of a practice severely discouraged by the Church authorities, although mentioned frequently in the New Testament. Firstly, the crowds that flocked to hear the new type of preaching were often so vast that no building was large enough to hold them; secondly, most of the clergy of the Church of England were opposed to what they termed the new 'enthusiasm', and closed their churches to the Methodists. In their view no spiritual good could come to a man outside the walls of a church building. But once again, as in times we have formerly mentioned, the more the opposition grew the more were souls added to the Lord. Whitefield appears to have carried around with him a small movable pulpit to supply needed elevation (although he selected rising ground wherever this would be helpful) and with the aid of an extraordinarily strong and melodious voice he preached the law and the gospel with striking success.

Bristol and London were Whitefield's chief centres in England. Of the preaching to neglected miners at Kingswood, near Bristol, we find the following account in the preacher's Journal:

At four I hastened to Kingswood. There were about 10,000 people to hear me. The trees and hedges were full. All was hush when I began; the sun shone bright and God enabled me to preach for an hour with great power, and so loudly that all, I was told, could hear me. The fire is kindled in the country and, I know, all the devils in hell shall not be able to quench it.

One of the preachers biographers writes of this preaching:

Having no righteousness of their own to renounce, they (the miners) were glad to hear of a Jesus who was the friend of publicans, and came not to call the righteous, but sinners to repentance.

The first discovery of their being affected was to see the white gutters made by their tears which plentifully fell down their black cheeks as they came out of their coal pits. Hundreds and hundreds of them were soon brought under deep convictions, which, as the event proved, happily ended in a sound and thorough conversion.

Whitefield also became deeply involved in the work of a Scottish revival which was centred at Cambuslang, near Glasgow, in 1742. His preaching appealed powerfully to his Scottish hearers, most of whom welcomed his Calvinistic theology. But certain difficulties were encountered when Whitefield moved among congregations which had seceded from the Church of Scotland several years previously. It was their desire that Whitefield's ministry should be confined to their churches, and they objected to his preaching in any parish church which opened its doors to him, and even to his preaching in the open air. But great blessing resulted from what has been termed 'one of the most remarkable revivals of modern times'.

In Wales Whitefield found a kindred spirit in Howel Harris, the Welshman who led a movement similar to the Methodist movement in England. The movement in Wales did not originate with Whitefield, but he was happy to co-operate with its leaders. Harris, in fact, frequently assisted at Whitefield's Tabernacle in London when the English preacher was absent on his far-extended evangelistic tours. Of course, the Welsh Methodist movement was carried on in the Welsh language for the most part. Another leading Welsh minister of the period was Daniel Rowland of Llangeitho, Cardiganshire, a man whom many Welshmen claimed to be one of the greatest preachers since the days of the apostles. William Williams of Pantycelyn, Carmarthenshire, wrote numerous hymns to accompany the preaching, and 'sang Wales into Methodism'. He was the Charles Wesley of Wales. In North Wales Thomas Charles of Bala was the pioneer Calvinistic Methodist, though he belonged to a later generation.

Whitefield paid seven visits to the American Colonies. His first visit was to the newly-established colony of Georgia in 1736, and it was Georgia that retained his affections to the last, for he established the orphan house there, mentioned in the chapter on The Pietists. Its maintenance was a continual burden to him, and for this reason he took up collections during his preaching tours. New England and 'the Middle Colonies' were visited from time to time, and a demonstration was thereby given that orthodox doctrine, and evangelistic zeal and outreach, were not incompatibles. All American pastors were

The First Calvinistic
Methodist Conference
convened in Wales in January,
1743. From left to right:– John
Cennick, Joseph Humphreys,
John Powell, William
Williams, George Whitefield,
Daniel Rowland and Howel
Harris.

given a vivid illustration of aggressive Christianity.

One American farmer, at work in his fields and hearing that Whitefield was to preach a dozen or so miles away at noon, threw down his tools, together with his wife mounted his horse—sometimes he ran alongside to relieve the animal of the double burden—and arrived at the appointed spot to find an immense crowd assembled:

left The Entrance to Daniel Rowland's Church at Llangeitho.

right Daniel Rowlands.

He [the preacher] looked almost angelical, a young slim slender youth. He looked as if he was clothed with authority from the great God. A sweet solemnity sat upon his brow. My hearing him preach gave me a heart wound, and by God's blessing my old foundation was broken up, and I saw that my righteousness would not save me.

Whitefield himself would have desired no better result on that occasion, for in his preaching he ever reminded himself that men cannot be saved before they become conscious that they are lost.

But gospel preaching always provokes opposition, and not only among the worldly-wise; and Whitefield had to bear his share of public abuse and scorn in America as in Britain. The poet Whittier depicts the American scene in the following lines, to be found in 'The Preacher':

Lo ! by the Merrimac Whitefield stands
In the temple that never was made by hands—
Curtains of azure, and crystal wall,
And dome of the sunshine over all !—

A homeless pilgrim, with dubious name
Blown about on the winds of fame;
Now as an angel of blessing classed,
And now as a mad enthusiast.

. . .

Possessed by the one dread thought that lent
Its goad to his fiery temperament,

Selina, Countess of Huntingdon.

Up and down the world he went,
A John the Baptist crying—Repent!

But as the world and the Church well knew, the preacher's message was not limited to the call to repent; he preached Christ crucified, Christ risen from the dead, Christ exalted to God's right hand, as the sum and substance of the gospel.

In the work in England, Whitefield was ably supported by a titled lady, Selina, Countess of Huntingdon, who held firmly to the preacher's Calvinistic doctrine. She attended upon Methodist preaching and used her wealth and her considerable influence in the interests of the kingdom of God. Chapels were built by her for the use of Methodist preachers and congre-gations, and these in later days were known as The Countess of Huntingdon's Connexion. She also founded a College at Trefecca in South Wales for the training of ministers. It is recorded that on one occasion a bishop was complaining to King George III that students and ministers of the Countess had created a sensation in his diocese. 'Make bishops of them; make bishops of them' said the king. 'That might be done' was the reply, 'but we cannot make a bishop of Lady Huntingdon'. 'She puts you all to shame,' remarked the queen. 'I wish there was a Lady Huntingdon in every diocese of the kingdom' was the king's final comment.

We cannot doubt that Whitefield was greatly assisted in his work as an evangelist by his wonderful natural gifts, especially that of superb eloquence. He stands in the front rank of all orators of the English-speaking world, and this gift was wholly dedicated to the ministry of the gospel. It was said of him that he could make men weep by the way he pronounced the word 'Mesopotamia' in the pulpit. The greatest actor of the age declared that he would give £100 to be able to say 'Oh!' as Whitefield said it. Every-where crowds hung upon Whitefield's lips. But eloquence in itself is powerless to bring men into newness of life, and Whitefield was ever con-scious of the need for the ministry of the Spirit of God to accompany his own preaching of the gospel. His splendid gifts were matched by the grace of humility.

Whitefield was blessed, too, with a catholic spirit. All in whom he discerned the converting and sanctifying work of the Spirit of God were embraced in his heart's affections. His love for all true children of God surmounted denomin-ational barriers; his resolve to preach the gospel to every creature under heaven determined his relationship to all the children of men. In season and out of season he adorned the doctrine that he so eloquently proclaimed.

Whitefield died in 1770 at the age of 55, and was buried in Newbury Port, New England. For some time before the end he felt that his life's work was drawing to a close. 'Lord Jesus,' he said, 'I am weary in the work, but not of it. If I have not yet finished my course, let me go and speak for thee once more in the fields, seal the truth, and come home and die.' His request was granted. The last of his field sermons occupied two hours. In it he cried out in a tone of thunder, 'Works! works! a man to get to heaven by works! I would as soon think of climbing to the moon on a rope of sand! How willingly would I live for ever to preach Christ, but I die to be with him'. During the following night, a severe attack of asthma set free the spirit from the worn-out physical frame. So lived and died the greatest evangelist of the modern age. If ever an Englishman lived to the glory of God, it was George Whitefield.

William Williams of Pantycelyn, the chief of Welsh hymn-writers. His best known English hymn is 'Guide me, O Thou Great Jehovah'.

44

Revived Missionary Activity

The fact is indisputable that revivals of true Christianity issue in missionary effort. In the absence of revival and of a healthy Church life missionary interest and effort alike languish. Some may be inclined to dispute the claim, however, by asking in what way the preaching of the gospel to the heathen was the result of the 16th-Century Reformation. The answer is that the Reformation itself was a great missionary effort, the mission field being Central and Western Europe, areas which, although not heathen, were grossly ignorant of the gospel of the grace of God. Not until mediæval darkness had been dispelled could the true light shine out to other parts of the world.

Linked with the growth of Puritanism in the 17th Century was the conviction that the Father in heaven had given the whole world to his Son as his inheritance and the uttermost parts of the earth for his possession (Psalm 2 : 8). Evidences began to multiply that the Puritans were taking this scripture to heart. 'The Pilgrim Fathers were the first Puritan missionaries' writes one historian of Christian missions. It is certainly true to say that the voyagers in the *Mayflower* were not only seeking freedom of worship but were ambitious to reach their Indian neighbours with the gospel. Robert Cushman, one of their number, was set apart 'to promote the conversion of the Indians'. He appealed to England on their behalf in 1621.

It is significant that when the Pilgrims were followed by others who formed the Massachusetts Bay Company in 1629, the Company seal showed the figure of an Indian saying to the men of England, 'Come over and help us'. Oliver Cromwell, despite all his burdens and problems in home affairs, had a keen interest in missionary work, the more so because the Red Indians were the first heathens to become British subjects.

But missionary interest was not confined to the English-speaking world. As early as 1550 Gustavus Vasa, King of Sweden, sent a missionary to Lapland. Calvin hoped to promote gospel work in Brazil. In 1620 the King of Denmark urged the chaplains of Danish settlements in India to preach the gospel to the Hindus. Gustavus Adolphus of Thirty Years' War fame had plans for missions which his godly chancellor Oxenstierna tried to carry out after the king's death in 1732. For example, he sent John Campanius to work among the Red Indians along America's Delaware River. He also had Luther's small Catechism translated into the Indians' language.

In 1721 Hans Egede, a Norwegian pastor, went to the Eskimos, but the results were not startling. Later, when Count Zinzendorf (of whom we have spoken earlier) was visiting the Norwegian court, attending a king's coronation, he met two Eskimos whom Egede had baptized. The result was the sending of Moravian missionaries to Greenland to assist Egede who continued to labour until his death in 1756.

Towards the end of the 18th Century there was a stirring of missionary interest among Baptist ministers in Northamptonshire, England. Their interest was, in part, caused by a book written by Jonathan Edwards of Northampton, New England. The outcome was that twelve of these ministers founded the Particular (Calvinistic) Baptist (Missionary) Society, and to finance it they contributed the initial sum of £13 2s. 6d. which was all they could afford. William Carey,

William Carey (1761–1834) and his Brahman Pundit.

one of their number, had already published a small pamphlet urging Christians to use all the means at their disposal in missionary effort.

Not all ministers of the gospel were in favour of missionary activity. The story has often been told, perhaps with some embellishment, that the elder John Ryland at a Ministers' Fraternal at which Carey, Andrew Fuller and other mission-ary-minded men were present, rebuked Carey for his zeal: 'Young man, sit down, sit down. You're an enthusiast. When God pleases to convert the heathen he will do it without your aid or mine.' Obviously to Ryland, while the conversion of the heathen was earnestly to be prayed for, to attempt it seemed like a profane outstretching of the hand to help the ark of God.

Henry Martyn (1781–1812), missionary to India and Persia.

immense industry both in the work of translating the Scriptures into various Indian languages, and in preaching. There was much to discourage but nothing could diminish their zeal. Carey's own particular flair was for languages. Before leaving England for India he had acquired a tolerably good knowledge of Latin, Hebrew and Greek— a remarkable achievement for a cobbler! In India he succeeded in circulating about 200,000 Bibles, or portions of the Bible, in about forty languages or dialects, besides many tracts and Christian books. For many years he was Oriental Professor at Fort-William College, Calcutta. His knowledge of Eastern languages was truly remarkable.

Another English missionary who worked in India was Henry Martyn, at one time Senior Wrangler[1] (in Mathematics) at Cambridge University. Yet as he grasped the honours of the award, he tells us, 'I was surprised to find that I had grasped a shadow'. After serving for a short time as curate to the famous Charles Simeon of Cambridge he believed that God was calling him to gospel service in India, and he sailed there in 1806. Like Carey he was highly-skilled in language work and much of his time was spent in translating the Bible into Hindustani, and later into Persian. But his health was never good, and he died at the early age of 31. Yet his career was a stimulus to many and continues to be so.

Adoniram Judson, a native of Massachusetts, was one of the most devoted of 19th-Century missionaries from the American Churches. At the age of 24 he and his wife sailed for India with the support of the American Board of Missions (Congregational). During the voyage, however, they adopted Baptist views, were baptized on arrival at Calcutta, and thereby cut themselves

It was Carey who became the first of the new Society's missionaries. His motto was, 'Expect great things from God; attempt great things for God', which is precisely what he himself practised. He arrived in Calcutta, India, in 1793 and died in India in 1834, having been there without a break for the whole of that period. His chief co-workers were John Marshman and William Ward. They were unable to live in Calcutta because of opposition to missionary work by the British East India Company, and had to settle at Serampore, 14 miles inland, under Danish protection. Here they showed

[1] Senior Wrangler (at Cambridge): first among students who graduated with first-class honours.

off from American financial support until, at a later date, they were adopted by the American Baptist Missionary Union.

It is as a missionary to Burma that Judson is remembered. He mastered the Burmese language without undue difficulty, but six years passed before he baptized the first convert. From 1824–26 England was at war with Burma and the Judsons suffered almost incredible hardships. He was imprisoned under most degrading conditions and at times was bound with as many as five pairs of fetters. The records of his sufferings from fever, heat, hunger, and imprisonment have passed into missionary history. One might say that his physical survival was a miracle. His work finally met with success and he has become known as 'the apostle of Burma'.

In the middle of the 19th Century 'the Dark Continent' of Africa began to be opened up. David Livingstone of Scotland was one of the pioneers. He crossed Africa from East to West, made many discoveries in the area of the Zambesi River, wrote his *Missionary Travels* (1857), and even hoped to solve the mystery of the source (or sources) of the River Nile. But it eluded him. He married Mary Moffat, the daughter of Robert Moffat, a pioneer missionary in South Africa.

The Moffats began, in 1820, a work which continued for 50 years. They had been preceded by a Dutchman named John van der Kemp, for whom it has been claimed that 'he laid the foundation for the Christianization of South Africa'. Moffat followed in his steps because, by the peace treaty which ended the Napoleonic Wars, Britain was confirmed in the possession of 'the Cape Province' which had been taken from the Dutch during the wars. As a missionary he worked with the London Missionary Society which had been founded in 1795 as the result of the Bengal Mission of William Carey. It fell to David Bogue, Presbyterian minister of Gosport (near Portsmouth), to organize the work of this Mission which was one of the most important of its type.

The 19th Century saw also the beginning of efforts to reach out to the islands of the Pacific with the gospel. The voyages of exploration of Captain James Cook, the settlement of New South Wales (Australia) as a convict station, and later the acquisition by England of New Zealand, all contributed to Christian interest in the South Seas.

But the inhabitants of the Pacific Isles were noted for their cannibalism and this naturally occasioned intense horror in Christian minds. When John Paton of Scotland informed his Glasgow friends that he purposed to become a missionary in the New Hebrides, 'one dear old Christian gentleman', he says, 'sought to deter me, his crowning argument being "The cannibals! you will be eaten by the cannibals!"'. The risks were indeed great. John Williams, one of the early pioneers in Polynesia, as the area was called, was clubbed to death by the natives. But John Paton's life was preserved. His labours, described by his own pen, are of intense interest. After long, patient and dangerous toil he had the immense joy of seeing some whose hands had been stained by fearful sins brought to repentance and faith in Christ, so that they were able to sit with him at the Lord's table. His joy was almost too great to be borne.

John Paton was preceded in the New Hebrides by another Scotsman, John Geddie, who had emigrated to Nova Scotia in his youth and was sent out as a missionary by the Presbyterian Church of that area. 'When he landed in Aneiteum (New Hebrides) there were no

An old photograph of one of the first Methodist churches in New South Wales, Australia, a building now removed to Vision Valley, Arcadia, Sydney. The first Methodist minister in Australia was Samuel Leigh (1815). Evangelical influence in the colony had arrived with the Anglican chaplain, Richard Johnson, who sailed with the first fleet in 1787 and opened the first church building (in Sydney) in 1793. The first Nonconformist preachers in Australia were eleven missionaries in 1798 who had escaped from the persecution which had ended the initial attempt of the London Missionary Society to evangelize Tahiti. Thereafter Australia was to have close ties with missionary endeavour in the South Pacific.

Christians, and when he left in 1872 there were no heathens.' Such are the wonders of grace!

Mention must be made of China, the Celestial Empire, as it called itself. For many centuries it had been closed to Christian influence. The way in which England began to force the Chinese authorities to open their ports to her trade is a sad story indeed. The date was 1839–42. Indian merchants were trying to force opium into China and England assisted them with her 'gunboat diplomacy'! Victory in war was followed by England's acquisition of Hong Kong. There was a second Chinese War in 1858, the result being that westerners were the more easily able to enter China. Among those who entered China as missionaries was William Chalmers Burns of

Scotland whose labours extended from 1846 to 1868.

Burns was not the first British missionary to enter China, for Robert Morrison of Northumberland had found earlier entrance and had accomplished a remarkable work as the pioneer of Protestant missions. He had become the chief European expert in the difficult Chinese language, both spoken and written, and with the help of one or two others he had translated the entire Bible into Chinese by 1819. The East India Company had given him financial help, surprisingly so in view of its general opposition to missions, but in this case it had found Morrison's linguistic work of great benefit to trade relations with the Chinese. It had, in fact, met the expense, amounting to

£12,000, of printing Morrison's *Chinese Dictionary*, the first that met the needs of Europeans. Morrison was diligent in the work of the gospel but seven years passed after his entry into China before he was able to baptize the first convert.

The best-known English missionary to China in the second half of the 19th Century was Hudson Taylor, a Yorkshireman who founded the China Inland Mission. Earlier missionaries had been substantially confined to China's coastal lands, but Hudson Taylor wanted to reach the vast interior. He met with considerable success. But the mission did not escape the hand of the persecutor. In the late 1890's the Boxer risings took place. The Boxers, a secret society whose Chinese name means 'fist of harmony', were opposed to all 'foreign devils', and a considerable number of Christian workers were driven from the land. One missionary who belonged to an Anglican mission at work in the interior, recorded his experiences in a book entitled *A Thousand Miles of Miracle in China*. He and his family escaped with their lives, but many missionaries made the supreme sacrifice.

Missionary work in Mohammedan lands has always proved particularly difficult because of the intense hostility of the followers of Mohammed to the Person and the atoning work of Christ. Converts in such lands have invariably been few in number, and won with great labour and difficulty.

The 19th Century saw several efforts to reach Israel also with the gospel. The Church of Scotland sent a team of ministerial explorers to Palestine in 1839 and on their return they made a report which gives us a fascinating account of the Holy Land and its peoples at that time. But the Land was then under Turkish rule and missionary progress was retarded. Dr W. M.

James Hudson Taylor (1832–1905), missionary to China, and Founder in 1865 of the China Inland Mission.

Thomson, an American missionary who spent 25 years in Syria and Palestine in the second half of the century has left the Church a most interesting record entitled *The Land and the Book*.

The greatly improved travel facilities of the 20th Century, and the development of inventions and techniques which our forefathers would have supposed impossible, have contributed to change the pattern of modern missionary work, but the apostle's questions are still wholly relevant to the matter: 'How shall they hear without a preacher? and how shall they preach except they be sent? as it is written, How beautiful are the feet of them that preach the gospel of peace, and bring glad tidings of good things!' (Romans 10 : 14-15).

45

The Faith in the 19th-Century Church: North America (1)

The Declaration of Independence celebrated in Boston, 1776. In the background is the State House built in 1713. Much of the resistance to arbitrary government which lay behind the War of Independence stemmed from the same principles with which the Puritans had earlier opposed the absolutism of the Stuart Kings and consequently the majority of Christians in the thirteen colonies took the 'American' side in the War. From a mural by Charles Hoffbauer, copyrighted by the New England Life Insurance Company, 1943, renewed 1971.

In an earlier chapter an account was given of the Great Awakening in the days of Jonathan Edwards and George Whitefield. Its beneficial effects were felt for a considerable period, for it increased the Church numerically and was a stimulus even after its initial impact had died away. It is worthy of note that in certain areas its beginnings were not the result of the work of outstanding men. In 1740, in the county of Hanover, Virginia, the stirring of soul and conscience began chiefly through the reading by a wealthy planter of a few pages of the Scotsman Thomas Boston's *Four-fold State*. About the

same time a Mr Morris was converted by reading Luther's *Commentary on Galatians*. A meeting-house was erected and known as Morris's Reading Room. The work of preaching began, it appears, soon after these events.

Linked with this work was Samuel Davies whose preaching was accompanied by a flood of blessing. He had a deep interest in the spiritual state of the negroes of New England, and taught them psalms versified by Isaac Watts. In these they took great delight. In 1759 Samuel Davies succeeded Jonathan Edwards as President of Princeton College, but two years later he died at the age of 36. He is chiefly remembered by one of the hymns which he wrote, its title being 'The glories of God in pardoning sinners : Micah 7.18'. One of its verses runs as follows:

Great God of wonders ! all thy ways
 Are matchless, God-like and divine;
But the fair glories of thy grace
 More God-like and unrivalled shine;
Who is a pardoning God like thee ?
 Or who has grace so rich and free ?

It is one of the finest hymns ever bequeathed to the Christian Church.

A little over 10 years after Davies' death a local revival occurred at Princeton College, and its results were felt in after years throughout the United States. Twenty-nine men graduated in 1773; three of these became Governors of States, and 23 became ministers of the gospel; four of the latter also became presidents of colleges.

During the years 1776–83 came the War of American Independence, as a result of which the 13 colonies cut themselves off from Britain, shaped their own republican political institutions, and formed the determination to develop their own culture and further to expand their immense territories. To a much greater extent than before they looked upon themselves as 'a new world', related by ties of kindred with the old world of Europe, but now free to work out their own future, unhindered by the nations of the old world.

In the sphere of foreign policy this attitude resulted in the Monroe Doctrine of 1823, occasioned as it was by the danger that European Powers belonging to the so-called Holy Alliance might intervene in the political affairs of South America. The United States gave warning that European Powers must not interfere politically

Francis Asbury (1745–1816), Methodist Leader in America.

or militarily in her affairs, while on her part she would observe the same rule in respect of other nations. But the policy of aloofness did not apply in the sphere of religion. Even so, religious developments in North America were somewhat isolated from those of churches in Britain and Western Europe.

Wars rarely bring good to the Church of God. They tend to undermine public morals and to lower standards of private behaviour. They also tend to encourage disregard of the Lord's Day. The War of American Independence was no exception to the general rule. It is not a matter of surprise, therefore, that the spiritual life of the American Churches was in a state of decline towards the close of the 18th Century. The seeking first of God's kingdom and righteousness was giving way to the seeking after earthly good. Benjamin Franklin's influence had been unspiritual, Thomas Jefferson's Deism, which involved

Archibald Alexander
(1772–1851), a witness of the
revival in Virginia and first
professor of theology at
Princeton Theological
Seminary, 1812. His book *The
Log College* remains the best
account of the leaders of the
earlier Great Awakening in the
Middle Colonies.

the denial of a direct revelation from God, was
opposed to the gospel, and the blatant denial
of Christianity by Tom Paine, whose influence
was considerable, contributed to produce an age
of scepticism and unbelief. To the eye of faith the
outlook seemed dark.

A remarkable change had come over Princeton
College. In 1782 only two among the students
confessed themselves Christians. Suddenly and
startlingly, however, a ray of light brightened the
dark horizon; not, however, in Princeton, but
in the Hampden–Sydney College in the State
of Virginia. Again, the reading of a book,
Joseph Alleine's *Alarm to the Unconverted*, was
linked with an awakening. Students were converted, prayer meetings flourished, and an
awakening spread throughout a wide area.

By the grace of God the revival at Hampden–
Sydney College in the late 1780's was the prelude
to a second period of more general revival. As the

19th Century opened, in the State of Kentucky
what came to be known as 'camp meetings' were
held by Presbyterian preachers, aided by
Methodists and Baptists. In some places between
20,000 and 30,000 persons assembled together,
and meetings continued for six or seven days, in
fact until food supplies failed.

Dr Archibald Alexander, a Presbyterian in
high repute and not given to exaggeration, was
deeply impressed by what he could learn of this
revival. In his report he quotes approvingly the
words of one of his correspondents:

The revival in Kentucky was peculiarly adapted
to the circumstances into which it came. Infidelity
was triumphant and religion was on the point of
expiring. This revival . . . has confounded infidelity and brought numbers beyond calculation
under serious impressions.

As for New England, revivals began in several
places, and in the opening decades of the new
century an almost unbroken series of awakenings
was witnessed. It is recorded that, between the
years 1798 and 1803, 'not less than 150 churches
in New England were favoured with the special
effusions of the Holy Spirit, and thousands of
souls, in the judgment of charity, were translated
from the kingdom of Satan into the kingdom of
God's dear Son'. Yale College shared in the
blessing, for during the period stated, 'out of
230 students then in the College, about one-third
were hopefully converted'.

This happy state of affairs was undoubtedly
helped forward by Timothy Dwight, a grandson
of Jonathan Edwards, who became President of
Yale College in 1795 and remained in office until
his death in 1817. For six months after taking
office he preached incessantly on the Bible as the
inspired Word of God. He also met students in
fair and open discussion on the subject. He

'triumphantly refuted their arguments, proved to them that their statements of fact were mistaken or irrelevant, and to their astonishment convinced them that their acquaintance with the subject was wholly superficial . . . The effect upon the students was electric. From that moment infidelity was not only without a stronghold but without a lurking-place . . . Unable to ensure the exposure of her arguments she fled from the retreats of learning ashamed and disgraced.'

Like Samuel Davies of Princeton, Timothy Dwight was not without poetic talent, and his hymn, 'I love thy kingdom, Lord', became one of the best-loved hymns of the 19th Century. We give three of its verses:

I love thy kingdom, Lord,
The house of thine abode,
The church our blest Redeemer saved
With his own precious blood.

I love thy church, O God!
Her walls before thee stand,
Dear as the apple of thine eye,
And graven on thine hand.

For her my tears shall fall,
For her my prayers ascend;
To her my cares and toils be given
Till toils and cares shall end.

One of the outstanding features of American history in modern times has been the opening up and development of the vast areas of land watered by the Mississippi, Missouri, and Arkansas Rivers. As we said earlier, it had been the ambition of the French, and of the Roman Catholic Church with which they were associated, to claim and retain central North America, but in 1763, after the Seven Years' War, the fortunes of war had disappointed their hopes, and given full scope to the settlers along the Atlantic seaboard to move steadily westwards.

A part of this territory was Louisiana which had been claimed by Spain. But events in Europe had given Napoleon control over it, and it suited his plans 'to turn an uncertain liability in the New World into cash in the Old'. He therefore sold Louisiana to the United States for 15 million dollars in 1803. 'Ol' Man River' thus became American for the whole 4,000 miles of its extent, and a colossal expanse with comparatively few Indian inhabitants challenged both Church and State to occupy it. By 1850 1,000 persons a day were pressing westwards into the new lands.

All denominations made steady advance into the new territory. But their problems were multiplied and became the greater by reason of the new tide of immigration into America from Europe. The latter became so great in fact by the middle of the century that it was more than the entire population of the country in 1790— about four millions—when the first census was taken. Between 1840 and 1869 five and a half million Europeans entered the United States. During the 1840's Irishmen and their families outnumbered other immigrants, especially during the years of the great Irish potato famine of 1845–47. Most of the Irish settlers were Roman Catholics, as also were many of the immigrants from Continental Europe. After the American Civil War of 1863–65 immigrants were mostly Germans, many of them Lutherans in religion, with the result that in many western cities of North America the Lutheran Church became the foremost of the Protestant denominations. The arrival of a million Scandinavians in the latter part of the century increased membership of the Lutheran churches.

Holland too supplied its quota of immigrants.

Princeton Theological Seminary established in 1812 beside the original College of New Jersey where Edwards was President. The College of Jersey changed its name to Princeton University in the 19th century.

During the 1830's a group of Dutch Calvinists, dissatisfied with the government and the doctrinal slackness of their Reformed Church, formed a new congregation calling themselves Christelijke Gereformeerde Kerk (Christian Reformed Church). Some of their members emigrated to the United States of America in 1846 and settled in the State of Michigan. They were led by H. van Raalte. Their ranks were further augmented in the 1880's when another emigration from Holland took place.

As immigrants into America pressed further and further into the great central plain, naturally they came into contact with the country's original inhabitants. Gospel work among the Red Indians required immense patience, ceaseless industry in the task of putting Indian languages into writing, and great skill in the work of Bible translation. From time to time government pressure on the Indians to vacate territory and move ever westwards (as for instance in the case of the Cherokees expelled from Georgia) caused serious friction and even bloodshed. It required great courage for an Indian to settle down to a Christian way of life.

The first Indian of Dakota to become a Christian was Anawangmane (Walks-galloping on). Before his conversion he excelled all others in bravery and had thus risen above Indian law. He had become a law to himself. For three years he was under conviction of sin, but felt that the sixth and seventh commandments of God's law were too strict for him. Finally, grace triumphed over human weakness and at the age of 30 he was baptized and received into the Church. He adopted the name of Simon. To provide for his needs he planted a field with corn and potatoes. But as they passed by, even boys and women pointed at him, the bravest of the Dakotas, saying, 'There goes a man who has made himself a woman'. The bearing of the cross for Christ's sake takes many forms.

One of the chief Christian workers among the Dakotas (sometimes called the Sioux) was a blacksmith's son, Stephen Riggs of Ohio. In 1852 he completed a *Dakota Dictionary* of 16,000 words. At one time he and his friends were in great danger of death at the hands of Indians who hated Christianity, but in 1877, after 40 years of labour, Riggs could write:

The work has been marvellous in our eyes. At the beginning we were surrounded by the whole Sioux nation in their ignorance and barbarism; at the close we are surrounded by churches with native pastors. The entire Bible has been translated into the language of the Dacotas; the work of education has been progressing rapidly. God has been showing us by his providence and his grace that the Red Men too may come into the kingdom.

We have given one typical specimen of Indian work that was carried on in the United States throughout the 19th Century. Among all Indian tribes, broadly speaking there were similar results; for all 'tribes and tongues' find a place in the great family of God.

46

The Faith in the 19th-Century Church: North America (2)

One great problem affecting all branches of the North American Church was that of slavery, common in the Southern States, much less common in the Northern States. The same problem pressed heavily, too, on those responsible for both central and local government.

As we have already seen, negro slavery began in North America in 1619, when a Dutch trading vessel sold 20 'Negars' to planters. The system spread but slowly. By 1776, however, every one of the 13 Colonies held slaves. In the North they were nearly all kept as house-servants and were not very numerous. In the South they were employed as field-hands. Slave owners in the South declared that their livelihood, and that of all dependent on them, necessitated slave labour, for they did not think it possible for rice and tobacco plantations to be cultivated on any other arrangement.

After 1783, when the War of Independence

ended, the Northern States by degrees turned against slavery and began to pass laws giving slaves their freedom. In the South, however, the planters loudly proclaimed that the end of slavery would be the start of economic ruin. Especially was this the case after 1793 when Eli Whitney of Massachusetts, but then resident in Georgia, invented the cotton-gin which revolutionized the 'cleaning' of the cotton fibre (i.e. separating it from the seeds it contained) and this gave rise to a vastly increased growing of cotton and to the establishment of a cotton industry. On the plantations negro labour was invaluable.

In 1807 the United States government forbade any further importation of slaves from abroad. But slavery itself remained. Slavery also remained in the British Empire, but in 1833 the British Parliament passed an Abolition of Slavery Act, at the same time voting £20,000,000 in compensation to slave owners for the loss of their slaves and their services.

In the United States the problem persisted much longer. And there was an additional problem, for as expansion westwards took place the question as to whether States newly added to the Union should be 'free' or 'slave' became acute.

In Britain there had been no problem so far as the homeland was concerned. In 1772 Lord Mansfield (lord chief-justice) had stated categorically that slavery was 'so odious' to Englishmen that on English soil it could not exist. Nothing, he said, could 'be suffered to support it but positive law', and such law did not exist. But the position in respect of North America was quite different. Some, defining slavery as the ownership of one man by another, condemned it outright. Others, in all good conscience, claimed that, while there was neither bond nor free in the kingdom of God, the New Testament permitted slavery to exist in the political and social arrangements framed by man.

Evangelists had to reach their own conclusions. George Whitefield, for example, conscientiously believed in slave labour. In 1751 he wrote, 'As for the lawfulness of keeping slaves, I have no doubt'. At the time of his death in 1770 he possessed 75 slaves whom he employed in the work of the Bethesda Orphan House in the American State of Georgia. On the other hand John Wesley denounced slavery. The last letter he ever wrote —its date was 24th February, 1791—was addressed to William Wilberforce, and commended him for opposing 'that execrable villainy which is the scandal of religion, of England, and of human nature'. American slavery he termed 'the vilest that ever saw the sun'.

The contrasted views of the two evangelists were reflected in those of American Christians at large, the abolitionist viewpoint being heard increasingly in the North in the mid-19th Century. Indeed, in Mrs Harriet Beecher Stowe's *Uncle Tom's Cabin*, it was also to be heard across Britain and Europe. Published in 1852 Mrs Stowe's book was immediately a best-seller and had immense influence. Readers laughed and cried over 'Topsy', 'Eva' and 'Uncle Tom'—for the author included the happier as well as the darker side of slavery—but, in general, tears prevailed and the cry grew for immediate emancipation in the South.

But, North and South, many Christians disagreed with the abolitionists' definition of slavery, believing that the acceptance of that definition imperilled the morality of the Bible where slavery as such is not condemned. Thus one of the best-known Christian journals of the North, *The Biblical Repertory and Princeton Review*, argued that slavery should be defined 'to be a state of involuntary bondage; the state in which one man is bound to labour for another, without his own consent . . . It may be right or wrong, just or unjust, beneficent or cruel, according to circumstances.' 'Consequently,' the writer proceeded, 'the fundamental principle of abolitionists, that all slave-holding is sinful, that slave-holders as such should be excluded from the Christian Church, and that slavery should be everywhere and immediately abolished, is false and unscriptural'.

Yet this was not said to defend slavery as it too commonly existed in the South. Certainly there were in the South outstanding instances of black servitude ameliorated by the Christian devotion of masters. There were not a few who could say of a black servant, with Dr B. M. Palmer of New Orleans, 'he is my brother and my friend'. Nonetheless, built into the system were evils which Christians could not defend for they were plainly contrary to the love which Christ enjoins towards our neighbour. Chief among these evils were laws which forbade teaching slaves to read or write, which authorized the separation of parents and children, of husbands and wives, and which ignored or denied legal marriage to those held as slaves.

While recognizing these evils and encouraging their removal, Christians in the South were generally of the opinion that the sudden emancipation of the black race would not be in the interests of the blacks themselves. More preparation was needed for such a change to be beneficial.

In 1861 time ran out for the voices of moderation. South Carolina put to the test the Southern claim that any State might leave the Union at will,

opposite The first Baptist congregation in America, located at Providence, Rhode Island, and dating from 1638, built this meeting-house in 1775, a year before the Declaration of American Independence. Its steeple, constructed by ship carpenters, withstood hurricanes in 1815 and 1938. Brown University, founded by Baptists, has held 'year-end exercises' in this building for many years.

Robert Lewis Dabney (1820–98), Southern Presbyterian leader and one of the foremost reformed theologians of the 19th Century.

Southern States be explained? As in the case of slavery, it will be well to look at the matter historically. The first American Baptist appears to have been Roger Williams of Providence, Rhode Island. He was baptized by immersion as a believer in 1639. Another of practically the same date was Hanserd Knollys, but he returned to England by the end of 1641.

John Miles, a Welshman from Swansea (and probably the first Welsh Baptist minister ever to cross the Atlantic Ocean), founded a Baptist church in America at Swansea, Massachusetts, in 1649. Before long the government of the colony fined each church member £5 for worshipping God contrary to the established order. For a short time 'bonds and imprisonments', as it were, awaited all Massachusetts Baptists. The Congregational ministers urged on the persecution despite a letter of remonstrance sent from England and signed by such men as Thomas Goodwin, John Owen, and Joseph Caryl. Ultimately, however, liberty of worship was granted.

By the middle of the 18th Century, and especially after the Great Awakening, Baptists were very active in the State of Virginia, but here also persecution was their lot. 'May it please Your Worship' said a prosecuting lawyer to a judge, 'the men are great disturbers of the peace; they cannot meet a man on the road but they ram a text of Scripture down his throat'. The verdict went against them and they were committed to prison. As they were led there they sang cheerfully in the streets a hymn of Isaac Watts:

Broad is the road that leads to death,
And thousands walk together there;
But wisdom shows a narrower path
With here and there a traveller.

if it felt that its interests demanded it. President Abraham Lincoln denied this but six more Southern States stood with South Carolina as the Civil War began. Lincoln then resolved to make slavery a further issue so that the one war might decide the two matters. He made a Proclamation stating that in any State which had not returned to the Union by New Year's Day, 1863, slavery would become unlawful. This was given full effect when the War ended in 1865 with the victory of the North. Over three million negroes were then set free.

Another matter deserves mention. It is sometimes presented as a question: How can the predominance of Baptists in North America's

'Deny thyself and take thy cross'
Is the Redeemer's great command,
Nature must count her gold but dross
If she would gain that heavenly land.

In prison the Baptists preached daily from the windows to the crowds which assembled to hear them. Many were converted. 'So mightily grew the Word of God and prevailed.' In 1768 there were only 10 Baptist churches in Virginia, in 1790 there were 210!

During the 18th Century several Associations of Baptists were formed, notably the Philadelphia Association in 1707. In 1764 Rhode Island (Baptist) College was established which later was renamed Brown University after Nicholas Brown to whose liberality it was greatly indebted.

The 19th Century witnessed 'marvellous progress' among the Baptists. Four reasons for this are given by J. M. Cramp of Nova Scotia in a Baptist History dated 1868:

(1) the immense tide of emigration to North America included many Baptists;
(2) the freedom of Baptist principles was congenial to the mode of government and the state of society;
(3) Baptist ministers in general adapted themselves to the condition and habits of the people;
(4) Baptist churches shared largely in the outpourings of the Spirit, who honoured their 'plain, faithful preaching and their scrupulous adherence to the laws of the King of kings'.

Perhaps it is wise and best to leave present-day Americans to assess the value of these claims. But it is certainly true that Baptists possessed numerical strength, particularly in the Southern States. In 1688 there were only 13 Baptist Churches in North America—7 in Rhode Island, 2 in Massachusetts, 1 in South Carolina, 2 in Pennsylvania, and 1 in New Jersey—but by the mid-19th Century there were upwards of 13,000. With almost mathematical precision 'the little one had become a thousand' (Isa. 60 : 22).

In view of the great variety of sources from which the United States gathered its population, it is not surprising that a variety of heresies appeared in the American scene. For example, in 1792 there arrived in Baltimore a congregation of the followers of the Swedish heretic Emanuel Swedenborg. They had appeared in London nine years previously, and called themselves 'The Church of the New Jerusalem'. Their ideas were quite foreign to Scripture, for they denied the Trinity, the atonement, and the entire message of the gospel.

A second heresy was, however, native to America. Mormonism, or the Church of the Latter-Day Saints, originated in the 1820's and derived from the claim of a certain Joseph Smith that a new revelation of the mind and purpose of God was made on several golden plates to which he had been directed by an angel. As a result of this, believers in this new religion founded Salt Lake City in the State of Utah. The United States government was troubled by the polygamy which was practised by the Mormons and in 1862 the American Congress enacted a law prohibiting it.

A third heresy (though it approached much closer to orthodox Christianity than the two just mentioned) was begun by a certain farmer named William Miller in the 1830's. He announced that the second coming of Christ and the destruction of the world would take place in 1843. But 1843 came and went, and as the event foretold had not taken place, a date in 1844 was announced instead.

The first building to house a Christian Reformed Church in the US, built in the Commerce Street area of Grand Rapids in 1857.

When this also failed Miller retired from the scene, his place being taken by Mrs Ellen G. White who became the founder of the Seventh-Day Adventist Church. It placed great emphasis on prophecy, but its teachings fall short of orthodoxy.

One great feature of the American 19th-Century scene was the growth and importance of the Sunday School. The first quarter of the century was the formative period. About the year 1825 the Sunday School was being organized on a truly national scale. Gradually it became recognized as a most valuable branch of Protestant Christianity. In English Christianity the Sunday School was chiefly intended to be a means of reaching children whose parents had no links with a local church, but in the United States, as in Wales, from the outset it was meant to be a part of the equipment of the local church for the instruction of its own members, children and adults alike. As the century advanced authors and publishers competed in the work of supplying teachers and taught with suitable lesson schemes and literature. The success of the Schools in the Protestant Churches induced the Roman Catholics to follow suit.

Theologically, the United States did not fall behind Europe in producing preachers, Bible scholars and expositors, and able writers. Timothy Dwight has already been mentioned. Charles G. Finney, President of Oberlin College, Ohio, was noted for his strong views on revival—indeed, he was termed a 'revivalist'—and for his policy of calling upon sinners in his audiences to go forward to the 'anxious-bench', and to rise publicly to demonstrate to all present their forming of religious resolutions. Finney's *Autobiography* includes the words: 'Instead of telling sinners to use the means of grace and to pray for a new heart, I called on them to make themselves a new heart and spirit, and pressed the duty of immediate surrender to God'.

Finney's methods were strongly criticized by many of his contemporaries, and especially by those who held to Calvinistic doctrine. In their view Finney's teaching implied, if it did not precisely state, that Christians themselves could 'bring about a revival'. All they had to do was to fulfil certain conditions within their power. Whereas Calvinists believed that revivals had to be looked for from heaven, as the sovereign bestowal of the Spirit of God, and in that sense 'prayed down', Finney's teaching was that they were to be 'worked up'. Calvinists complained also that, whereas the Bible teaches regeneration ('being born again') to be the work of the Holy Spirit, Finney declared it to be an act of the

Charles Hodge (1797–1878), of Princeton Theological Seminary.

human will. There is little doubt that Finney is rightly called the pioneer of 'modern mass evangelism', which is radically different in method, and to a certain extent in doctrine, from the modes of preaching owned and blessed by God in the past.

Among the greatest theologians of the century were Dr Charles Hodge and his son Dr A. A. Hodge of Princeton Seminary, New Jersey. On the male side of their ancestry they were of Scottish–Irish descent, on the female side of Huguenot descent. Dr Charles Hodge produced an outstanding *Systematic Theology* in three volumes; his son an *Outline of Theology* in one volume. But they wrote other valuable works as well.

The latter part of the century saw the rise to fame as an evangelist of Dwight Lyman Moody, once a shop assistant in Boston and later in

Chicago. In middle life he began evangelistic tours in which he was accompanied by Ira D. Sankey who assisted the preaching by his powerful singing of new-style hymns, many of them of American origin. To some of the older hymns choruses were added. The two men held 'campaigns' in Britain in 1873 and 1883. In Chicago a Bible Institute was established by Moody.

Statistics need interpretation and may be misleading, but it is interesting to note that, whereas the total population of the United States in 1890 amounted to 62,622,000 souls, 57 million of these were classed as Christians, 20 million of them being church members. Ministers of the gospel numbered 111,000, divided among 143 denominations and sects.

In one branch of Christian activity the North American Churches played a distinguished part. In general they took to heart the command of the risen Christ, 'Go ye into all the world and preach the gospel to every creature' (Mark 16 : 15). Increasingly as the 19th Century drew to its close they sent out labourers into God's harvest-field. They included many men and women of zeal and activity, and their country's ever-increasing wealth enabled them to subscribe very considerable sums to finance worldwide missionary enterprise. Doubtless they laid to heart the great prophetic word, 'This gospel of the kingdom shall be preached in all the world for a witness unto all nations, and then shall the end come' (Matt. 24 : 14). The divine 'shall' urged them to their various fields of work. To be 'up

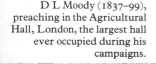

D L Moody (1837–99), preaching in the Agricultural Hall, London, the largest hall ever occupied during his campaigns.

and doing' was a national characteristic.

Arthur T. Pierson, C. H. Spurgeon's immediate successor at London's Metropolitan Tabernacle, and himself an American, closes one of the chapters of his *New Acts of the Apostles* in the following way:

Opportunity never lingers . . . The Emperor of Brazil accounted for the inferiority of Brazil to the great Republic of the North in one sentence. He said, 'My countrymen always say *manana*!— tomorrow, tomorrow! but the United States citizen says *to-day*'.

'Today!' So let it ever be!

A former chapter dealt with Methodism and its impact in Britain and North America. We saw that ultimately it broke away from the Church of England and became a part of Non-conformity. Shortly after it did so it divided into several separate bodies. But Methodism also served to revive evangelical doctrine in the hearts of many who remained within the Established Church, and to confirm that doctrine in others who had never abandoned it. Augustus Toplady, William Romaine, John Newton, John Berridge, William Grimshaw, and John Fletcher are examples of Anglican ministers who exercised powerful ministries in the Church in the later 18th Century. Robert Raikes of Gloucester pioneered the opening of Sunday Schools in order to instruct the children of non-churchgoers in the Christian faith. Thomas Charles of Bala did a similar work in North Wales although in his case the Schools were carried on in places where the influence of

Charles Simeon (1759–1836).

47

The Faith in the 19th-Century Church: The British Isles (1)

Methodism caused the majority of families to attend Church or Chapel worship.

In the same period one of the most prominent of Churchmen was Charles Simeon, vicar of Holy Trinity Church, Cambridge from 1782 to 1836. Macaulay the historian wrote of him: 'If you knew what his authority and influence were, and how they extended from Cambridge to the remote corners of England, you would allow that his real sway over the Church was far greater than that of any primate'. Simeon, in fact, in his day made Cambridge the great centre of English evangelical Christianity, insofar as the Church of England was involved in it.

Foremost in evangelical Anglican circles at this period were the members of the so-called 'Clapham Sect'. Clapham is a south-western suburb of London, and in or around it lived a number of laymen of high repute who worshipped at its parish church, where the Rector was John Venn, son of Henry Venn, both of them outstanding evangelicals. To the 'Sect' belonged William Wilberforce, 'the wittiest and pleasantest of men', who could delight his fellows both by his oratory and his conversational powers. In 1797 he startled his contemporaries by producing a book[1] contrasting the commonly prevailing view of Christianity with 'real Christianity'. In Parliament—he was M.P. for Yorkshire—his influence was very great even over men who did not share his religious views. It was he who led the battle against slavery and the slave trade in Britain's Empire.

Another Claphamite was Henry Thornton, a wealthy banker whose liberality on behalf of causes which evangelicals had at heart was unbounded. Still another was Zachary Macaulay

William Wilberforce (1759–1833), was strikingly converted at the age of 25. In a life spent chiefly in political activities, he maintained an unblemished Christian walk for half a century. His chief efforts were directed to the ending of the infamous slave trade and of slavery in the British Empire. The former was ended in 1807 and the latter in 1833 at a cost to the British Government of £20,000,000. The knowledge that this had been done caused Wilberforce to die happy. 'Few men', it has been said, 'achieved more for the benefit of mankind'.

who had 'much of the old Puritan in him'. He helped to found the Church Missionary Society in 1799, and the British and Foreign Bible Society in 1804. But it is as the father of the famous historian that he is now chiefly remembered. Lord Teignmouth, first President of the Bible Society, and formerly Governor-General of India, did his utmost to promote the preaching of the gospel in that sub-continent.

Later in the 19th Century the 7th Earl of Shaftesbury played a role similar to that of members of the Clapham Sect both in Church and State. He worked hard to reform social conditions that were not in keeping with Christian ideals. A native of Dorset, he received his earliest

[1] *A Practical View of the Prevailing Religious System of Professed Christians in the Higher and Middle Classes in this country contrasted with Real Christianity.*

and deepest impressions of things spiritual from a faithful old servant of his family. A firm evangelical he made it his life-work to ameliorate the conditions of life which obtained among the lower classes of society. For example, he was responsible for the introduction into Parliament of bills which became 'the Magna Charta of the Insane'. He laboured hard to prevent the employment of boy chimney-sweeps who had been forced by their masters to clamber up sooty chimneys innumerable. He played a great part in securing the Mines Act of 1842 by which mine-owners were forbidden to employ women and girls, and boys under ten, underground. He fought hard to limit the employment of women and young persons to ten hours a day, and never tired in helping those who strove for the securing of more humane conditions in factories. Improved housing for the working classes, the establishing of Ragged Schools, and the promotion of all aspects of social betterment all found in him an earnest and untiring supporter. A popular encyclopaedia sums up his career in the words: 'In religious matters he was an out-and-out evangelical and strenuously opposed ritualism, rationalism, and socialism when divorced from Christianity'. The English peerage has never had a better Christian in its ranks.

A group of Churchmen who also wanted to bring about social reform, but who were much less concerned about Reformation doctrine than Shaftesbury, were known as Christian Socialists. The best-known of them are F. D. Maurice and Charles Kingsley. They sympathized with the working-men known as Chartists whose bid for reform failed in 1848, and they wrote sermons, pamphlets and, in Kingsley's case, even novels on their behalf.

The evangelical wing of the Church of England

John Charles Ryle (1816–1900), was converted to God while a student at Oxford University as he listened in church to the reading of Ephesians chap. 2. He became an outstanding evangelical and held livings at Helmingham and Stradbrooke in Suffolk. In 1880 he was appointed first Bishop of Liverpool, a post he held almost until his death. His influence was widespread. He endeavoured to uphold the 'Reformation Settlement' in the Church of England and wrote commentaries on the Gospels, biographies of evangelical leaders, and numerous tracts. His influence through his writings was great in his own day and has persisted throughout the 20th Century.

had a succession of able preachers throughout the 19th Century whose aim it was to maintain Reformation doctrine in its purity and to evangelize at home and to the ends of the earth. Among them J. C. Ryle (1815–1900), created the first Bishop of Liverpool in 1880, was outstanding. He was nominated for the office by Disraeli, Earl of Beaconsfield, and through his influence and devotion to Scripture the Liverpool diocese became noted for its firm evangelicalism. Ryle wrote books and highly popular tracts. It was estimated in 1897 that more than 12 million of the tracts had been sold, and this total did not include the sale of tracts translated into other languages. Ryle gave special attention to the working classes.

Helmingham Church, Suffolk, scene of the ministry of J C Ryle, 1844–61.

languages has been of immense value to the Church of God, and to the work of the missionary. In the first 119 years of its existence it sold 336 million copies of Scripture, in whole or in part, and received almost £20 million of income during the same period. Bibles or portions of the Bible had been issued in 558 languages. All this is apart from the work of other Bible Societies, such as the National Bible Society of Scotland, the Trinitarian Bible Society[1], the Scripture Gift Mission, the Pocket Testament League, and similar agencies.

The 19th Century was a period of great activity in the Church. Alliances, Conventions, and suchlike came into existence to supplement and further the work of the Churches, and in some instances to bring about co-operation between them for such purposes as the relief of persecuted Christians, the promotion of missionary work, and the invigoration of church witness. One such agency was the Evangelical Alliance, formed in 1846 to bring evangelical principles to bear upon problems in Church and State. It held conferences throughout Europe and North America, and both inside and outside the churches the Christian outlook received emphasis.

Another agency of note was the Young Men's Christian Association (YMCA) which also originated in 1846 when George Williams (later knighted) opened a room in St Paul's Churchyard, London, for the use of Christian young men. In 1880 he and others purchased Exeter Hall in the City so that the work of promoting Christian fellowship might be extended.

The responsibility for the care of orphans also stirred the Christian conscience. Muller's Orphanage located at Bristol was one of the first

In the earlier part of the century the establishment of the British and Foreign Bible Society in 1804 was an event of great importance, linked as it is in the minds of many with the story of the Welsh girl, Mary Jones, who walked 25 miles from her home to Bala, to buy a Welsh Bible from Thomas Charles who played a leading part in the formation of the Society. Its work of Bible translation and circulation in all the world's chief

[1] Founded in 1831 by men who left the B. and F. Bible Society in order to be free to give stronger emphasis to the doctrine of the Trinity.

John Elias (1774–1841), preaching in his native Wales. He (a Calvinistic Methodist) and Christmas Evans (1766–1838) were the two greatest preachers of their time, if not of all time, in Wales. They had little formal education but were gifted with pulpit eloquence. They carried into the 19th Century the doctrine and fervour of such men as Howel Harris and Daniel Rowland in the 18th Century. Elias was born in Caernarvonshire and Evans (on Dec. 25th) in Cardiganshire. They visited all parts of the Principality but it was North Wales that felt the full impact of their ministries.

fruits of the conviction that Christians are to show their faith by their works. A similar 'Home' to deal with the 'incredible' conditions in which many young boys existed in London's slums was opened in 1866 by Dr Barnardo. A little later James W. C. Fegan began Ragged School work in London, and established Homes for Destitute Children in various parts of Great Britain. William Quarrier founded similar Homes in Scotland.

It is remarkable how during the 19th Century a host of individual Christians felt moved to engage in philanthropic work of various types. Frederick N. Charrington, born into wealth accumulated by the sale of strong drink, speaks in his writings of witnessing a brutish husband, under the influence of drink, knocking his wife into the gutter, a blow that also 'knocked Charrington out of the drink trade'. Thereafter he used his wealth to promote gospel work in the East End of London. A Miss Daniels established 'Soldiers' Homes', a Miss Agnes Weston opened Sailors' Rest Homes in various ports. An Aged Pilgrims' Friend Society established Homes for the care of elderly believers in need. One and all were gospel-based. Movements were set afoot to reach the Jews with the Gospel. In England the Mildmay Mission was commenced by John Wilkinson; similarly the Hebrew Christian Testimony to Israel by David Baron and C. A. Schönberger. Missionary witness to Gentiles sometimes began by dint of individual effort. And so the work of the Lord was carried forward. But other matters, some of them of a less pleasing character, must next engage our attention.

To a large extent the 19th Century was a time of Christian consolidation. Many believers hoped for the outbreak of revival. The 16th Century had experienced the Reformation; in the following century came the Puritan movement; in the 18th the Methodist Movement. What would the 19th Century produce? But the major hope of the century was disappointed. True, there was a strong movement of the Spirit of God in Ulster in 1858; as also in parts of Wales and Scotland; but nothing happened on a scale comparable to that of earlier times.

Many in the working classes in England, it is to be feared, were much more alert to follow earthly good than heavenly. Not a few came to regard political progress, the extension of the Parliamentary franchise—a vote for every man —as more desirable than evidences of the work of God's Spirit on human hearts. Others began to look upon 'the education of the masses' as the greatest good that could come to the land. Many working men began to regard the growth of trade unions as the thing that would best promote happiness, well-being, and freedom from want. Even so, in a number of ways the Christian Church as a whole appeared to be in a flourishing condition. Great preachers appeared on the scene. A considerable proportion of the population attended church services. Sunday Schools made steady progress. Even if black clouds occasionally gathered on the horizon, the outlook seemed to be set fair.

In Scotland a great upheaval took place, for in 1843 over 400 ministers and their congregations broke away from the Presbyterian Church of the land and called themselves the Free Church. The event is known as 'The Disruption'. It came about because of the patronage system, that is to say, the legal right of a patron, 'who might be an infidel, an atheist, and a foe to godliness', to nominate 'a minister in holy things to a Christian congregation'. This, said the seceders, meant the setting aside of the Lord Jesus Christ as the Head of the Church.

The seceders were led by Thomas Chalmers, one of the greatest of all Scottish preachers. As a young man he had become a minister of the gospel while still ignorant of the saving truth of God, but later, saved by grace, he became a star in the Lord's right hand. Under his guidance the Free Church became firmly established, although troubled later in the century by false teachings.

On the staff of its ministerial College in Edinburgh were several notable professors, chiefly William Cunningham, James Bannerman, James Buchanan, John Duncan and George Smeaton. They all made important contributions to theological literature.

The Faculty at New College, Edinburgh; (left to right) standing, James Bannerman and George Smeaton; seated, James Buchanan, William Cunningham and John Duncan.

48

The Faith in the 19th-Century Church: The British Isles (2)

opposite When Charles Haddon Spurgeon (1834–1892) became pastor of New Park Street Baptist Church, Newington Butts, London, in 1854, he amazed the entire city by his ability as a 'boy preacher' and remained a man of immense influence until his death at the age of 57. It may almost be said that he worked himself to death. His activities were prodigious and his reputation as a preacher of worldwide influence remained unsurpassed and undiminished to the end. Nor has influence passed away: his works 'follow him'.

There is no doubt that, in England, the greatest preacher of the century was Charles Haddon Spurgeon, although William Jay of Bath earlier in the century had many excellent qualities and met with much success. An Essex youth, Spurgeon became minister of a Baptist Church near Cambridge when he was a mere seventeen years of age. At the age of nineteen he accepted the pastoral charge of a declining London congregation, and at one bound he leapt into the public eye. London streets became blocked with traffic in the neighbourhood of his chapel or wherever else he preached in the metropolis. He seemed to be another Whitefield. Buildings were too small to hold his congregations, and in 1861 the Metropolitan Tabernacle was erected. It could hold 6,000 hearers and was always filled to capacity.

Every week during the years 1855 to 1892 a sermon preached and afterwards revised by Spurgeon was printed and sold in very large quantities. So large was the stock of unpublished sermons when the preacher died that the weekly issue continued for another 25 years. In addition to the sermons Spurgeon produced a monthly magazine called *The Sword and the Trowel* (see Nehemiah 4 : 17–18), books by the dozen, and a large Commentary on the Book of Psalms entitled *The Treasury of David*. He founded and maintained an orphanage and a college for the training of ministers and preachers. At the present time the entire series of sermons is in process of reprinting in America, for their value as testimony to and interpretation of, the gospel of God's grace continues unabated.

Spurgeon was a Calvinist in doctrine. Some have called him 'the last of the Puritans', but the phrase is a misfit, for Puritanism is simply another name for vital godliness. During the reign of Queen Victoria 'a Sunday service at Spurgeon's' was one of the attractions of London. The Church to which he ministered must have been one of the largest in regular session since the days of the apostles. During the latter part of his ministry Spurgeon did not enjoy good health and at intervals he had to spend the winter months at Mentone on the Riviera. He died at the age of 57, the entire nation lamenting that his voice was stilled.

Robertson Nicoll, the best known of Nonconformist editors at the turn of the century, paid this tribute to the value of Spurgeon's sermons:

The influence of Spurgeon was not of those that have passed or that can pass away like a dream. Even yet (1898) people will explain his popularity by his voice, his humour, by his oratory, and the like. But the continued life and power of his printed sermons show that his oratory, noble as it was, was not the first thing. Our firm belief is that these sermons will continue to be studied with growing interest and wonder, that they will ultimately be accepted as incomparably the greatest contribution to the literature of experimental Christianity that has been made in this century, and that their message will go on transforming and quickening lives after all other sermons of the period are forgotten.

In the first half of the century events took place in Oxford which constituted what is known as The Oxford Movement, and sometimes as The Tractarian Movement, for its authors produced Tracts for the Times. It originated in the Church of England. Certain Oxford scholars, notably John Henry Newman, F. W. Faber, John Keble, and E. B. Pusey, wished to turn back the Church to the type of churchmanship which prevailed before the 16th Century

Reformation, and accordingly they set themselves to prove that the Church's 39 Articles really bore a different interpretation from that which evangelicals placed upon them, a claim not difficult to disprove. In other words, the movement veered towards Roman Catholicism, and ultimately some of the leaders went over to that Church. Newman was later made a Cardinal. Pusey led the return within the Anglican Church to a ritual scarcely distinguishable from that of Rome; hence the Oxford Movement was often called Puseyism. Evangelical Anglicans and many Nonconformists feared that by means of it Romanism would be revived in England, for it acted as a sacramental leaven within the Anglican Church. We say 'sacramental' because the Oxford Movement placed great stress on the sacraments and on various forms of ritual, and correspondingly less stress upon preaching. Among others, J. C. Ryle of Liverpool spoke and wrote vigorously against it.

Another evil that troubled evangelicals in the second half of the century was Darwinism. In 1859 Charles Darwin, a scientist (though in his youth he thought of becoming an Anglican minister) published a book entitled *The Origin of Species*. He had built up a theory of origins when he sailed round the world as a naturalist in a ship called *The Beagle*. He formulated the theory that all the varied forms of life on earth had evolved from lower forms of life, a main principle determining which forms should survive in 'the struggle for existence' being 'the survival of the fittest'. Certain other writers, notably T. H. Huxley, helped to popularize the theory. Obviously it was in plain contradiction to the teaching of the Book of Genesis that each form of life was created 'after its kind'. Some scientists tried to unite the two teachings, and

later to speak of 'theistic evolution', or evolution directed by the hand of God. Others flatly denied that the evolution in which they believed was any other than the result of blind chance operating over vast periods of time.

When evolutionary theories were applied to the origin of man himself, they again came into violent conflict with Scripture. Evangelicals showed that the most basic doctrines of the Christian faith were bound up with the biblical assertion that a first man, made in the image of God, and not the result of evolutionary descent from lower animals, was placed in the earth by his Creator. If there was no 'first man, Adam', there could not be a 'second Adam', namely, the Lord Jesus Christ, Son of God and Saviour of men.

Furthermore the dogma of evolution denied the Fall of Man. Instead, it spoke of an upward climb and of progressive improvement. Scripture teaches that man was perfect as he came from the hand of his Maker, that sin separated him from his Maker, and that nothing but the redemption effected at tremendous cost by Christ could restore the relationship and render a 'child of wrath' an heir of heaven.

It became evident therefore that the theory of evolution denied the historic Fall and was diametrically opposed to the teachings of both Old and New Testaments. Yet multitudes welcomed the new pseudo-science and virtually conceived of it as a new religion replacing an outworn Christianity. The ideas underlying evolution were applied not only to the question of origins, but ultimately to all aspects of human life. And this legacy from the 19th Century is still with us. It plagues the true Church of God.

Soon after the rise of Darwinism another evil raised its head. It was not unrelated to Darwinism and was known as the Higher Criticism. Literary Criticism is a part of scholarship. Textual Criticism had its part to play in determining the precise and original text of Scripture. Variations occurred in ancient manuscripts and the work of experts was essential in the recovery of the correct readings.

But the Higher Criticism was in a different category. It claimed the power to go behind Bible documents and decide from what sources the Bible's writers derived their material. And the critics rarely, if ever, agreed among themselves. How could they do so when all was conjecture and supposition?

One of the earliest of English Higher Critics was a Cornishman, J. W. Colenso, who had been made Bishop of Natal. In 1862 a book was published in which he denied the historical accuracy of the Pentateuch and the Book of Joshua, and also the Mosaic authorship of the Pentateuch. Later he claimed that Deuteronomy could not have been written until the time of Jeremiah, and that the Books of Chronicles deliberately falsified facts in order to put more power into the hands of priests and Levites. In other words, he claimed that the Old Testament was not a book which could well be termed The Word of God.

Colenso and all who copied his approach to Scripture rejected the ancient teaching, embodied in the Bible itself, that the two Testaments were books inspired by the Holy Spirit, and 'by his singular care and providence kept pure in all ages'; that 'in all controversies of religion the Church is finally to appeal to them'; and that 'the Holy Spirit speaks in the Scripture as supreme Judge of what is right and what is wrong'. All Protestants had been agreed on such matters in the past, but now men arose who

opposite The interior of the Metropolitan Tabernacle where Spurgeon ministered for 30 years. The Metropolitan Tabernacle was opened in 1861 as a place of worship that would seat 6,000 people. It also held a lecture hall, and a schoolroom that would hold up to 2,000 children. It was a hive of ceaseless industry. Visitors from all parts of the English-speaking world supplemented the usual congregation. 'To hear Spurgeon' was one of the activities carried through by most of the visitors to the metropolis from many English, Welsh and Scottish counties, and from overseas. It was Spurgeon's prayer that countless multitudes might be 'born again' as they crowded Tabernacle pews. Sermons preached in the Tabernacle pulpit were printed weekly and finally extended to 62 volumes. 'Here was a Caesar! when comes such another?'

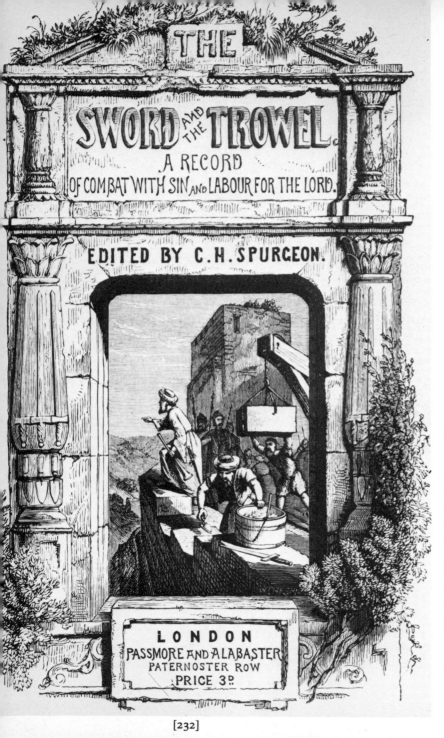

THE

SWORD AND THE TROWEL.

A RECORD

OF COMBAT WITH SIN AND LABOUR FOR THE LORD.

EDITED BY C.H. SPURGEON.

LONDON

PASSMORE AND ALABASTER

PATERNOSTER ROW

PRICE 3D.

argued that the Bible must be treated like all other books, criticized as to its sources, and perchance shown to be inconsistent with itself and in need of correction as if it were the work of fallible men.

The Higher Criticism originated in Germany, but there were men in most of the British Churches who succumbed to it, their influence on evangelical witness being disastrous in the extreme. The new 'German philosophy' penetrated certain religious Colleges as well as the older and newer universities, and shortly evangelical truth was fighting for its life.

One outcome of both Darwinism and the Higher Criticism was what is called The Downgrade Controversy, specially linked with the Baptist denomination and with the name of C. H. Spurgeon. It commenced in the late 1880's when the pastor of the Metropolitan Tabernacle could no longer refrain from calling attention to the ominous signs of departure from 'the faith once delivered to the saints'. He urged all Churches to stand firm on the fundamentals of Christianity. He also denounced the worldliness which accompanied the new heresies. But the evils remained and from year to year appeared to grow worse. Shortly after Spurgeon's death a number of his supporters met together and formed a society called the Bible League in order to continue the fight against doctrinal declension and perverse views of Scripture.

Two 19th-Century additions to what is now known as the Christian denominational spectrum are the Plymouth Brethren and the Salvation Army. The Brethren (they had no particular connection with Plymouth) come first in order of time. They originated during the period 1825–30, claiming that the Christian Church was sadly divided because it had largely departed from the

New Testament pattern. To that pattern, they said, a return must be made. The best-known of the early brethren were J. Nelson Darby, B. W. Newton, Anthony Norris Groves, and George Müller. Müller founded his Orphanage (earlier mentioned) primarily to establish the fact that God was still 'the living God' and able to provide for all human needs. It was a basic principle with Müller not to ask his fellows for financial support; yet he cared for 2,000 children needing daily bread. Unhappily for the Brethren, about 1848 a cleavage in their ranks occurred— Exclusive and Open Brethren separated. Scandal resulted, for Brethren claimed to stand for Christian unity above all other bodies. Later numerous lesser divisions occurred and the whole movement, especially on the Exclusive side, became fragmented. The Open Brethren distinguished themselves by their missionary zeal, for they sent out missionaries to all parts of the world, and gathered many souls into the Kingdom of God.

The Salvation Army originated in 1865 when William Booth and his wife Catherine broke away from their ministerial office in a branch of Methodism called the New Connexion. They believed that the Church at large was doing little or nothing to save the lower classes of the population from vice, misery and unbelief. Hence in their view there must be a radical departure from traditional methods of making known the gospel. New modes of outreach must be adopted if the 'unchurched' and the perishing were to be saved. Later Booth gave his helpers a military organization, he himself taking the title of General Booth, others becoming captains, and so on. Music provided by instrumental bands played a considerable part in attracting attention to the Army and its message. The doctrine held by

George Müller (1805–98) A native of Prussia, Müller came to England in 1829 to fit himself for missionary work among Jews. Before long, however, he and Henry Craik, a Scot, settled at Bristol where they maintained the type of witness associated with 'Open Brethren'. Müller is chiefly remembered as the founder of an orphanage providing for 2,000 children, opened at Bristol in 1835, and for his commencement of The Scriptural Knowledge Institution which promoted Christian Education, Bible circulation, and world-wide missionary activity. Müller was one of the most remarkable Christians of his age.

Booth was strongly Arminian. On the ground that they were divisive the sacraments were not observed, for said Booth, they divided Christian from Christian.

The Army accomplished much social work on behalf of the poor, the outcast, and the down-and-outs. In 1891 Booth wrote a book entitled *In Darkest England and the Way Out*, in which he outlined his plans for the social and spiritual betterment of 'the submerged tenth' of society. Thus the Salvation Army was quite distinct from the normal type of church.

As the century advanced a movement which wanted a revision of the Authorized Version

(King James' Version) of the Bible grew in strength, especially within the Church of England. Versions of Scripture of great antiquity had come to light since 1611 when the A.V. was produced. Great progress had been made in the knowledge of Greek and Hebrew. Many scholars therefore desired a revision of the commonly-used Version.

One of the chief problems facing the appointed revisers of the New Testament concerned Greek manuscripts of Scripture, their age and their degree of reliability. The A.V. had been translated from comparatively few Greek manuscripts. The majority of the revisers, with Bishop B. F. Westcott and Dr F. J. A. Hort as their leaders, urged that the Greek text of Scripture must itself initially be revised before the revision of the A.V. could be made. Dr F. H. A. Scrivener led the opposition to any extensive revision of the underlying Greek text.

Outside the actual revision committee, and intensively active in support of Dr Scrivener and the Greek text behind the A.V., was Dean J. W. Burgon, Dean of Chichester and Gresham Professor of Divinity in Oxford. But the majority of the revision committee accepted the Westcott and Hort views, and the Revised Version duly appeared in the 1880's. It made little appeal, however, to the Christian Church in its day or to the English-speaking world at large. It was judged to lack the literary quality and virility of the A.V., and for all normal purposes the A.V. continued in use.

Before the century closed various heretical sects which have greatly troubled the Christian Church came into existence. We need do little more than mention their names, just as the apostle John made mention in the Book of Revelation, twice over, of the Nicolaitans, without stating their tenets. 19th-Century sects included Christian Scientists, Jehovah's Witnesses (they have used different names at different stages of their existence), Mormons (of whom we have already written in the chapter on North America), and Christadelphians. The first three of these originated in America, the last-named in Birmingham, England. In one way or another each of these sects propagates teachings that depart radically from the Scriptures, even though they all claim to hold to Scripture. Usually great stress is placed upon one or more books written by the sects' founders. Thus they 'draw away disciples after them'. Many of their adherents are full of zeal and show every mark of sincerity, so that Christians and others who know little of the Word of God are readily deceived and easily ensnared. The sects have been thorns in the sides of evangelical churches for many years.

Against the true Church of God the gates of hell will not prevail. Chosen in Christ before the foundation of the world, redeemed in time by the precious blood of Christ, washed and sanctified and justified in the Name of the Lord Jesus and by the Spirit of God, it will appear in glory when earth's foundations melt away. By its means God will show to principalities and powers his manifold wisdom. And as for the success of the gospel the promise stands firm, 'The earth shall be full of the knowledge of the Lord, as the waters cover the sea' (Isaiah 11 : 9).

Church History during the period 1800–1900 brings little pleasure or comfort to the Christian as far as the Continent of Europe is concerned. During the 16th Century the Reformation had brought abundant blessing to lands which had formerly experienced the darkness of the Middle Ages, even if only a minority of their citizens embraced the Protestant creed. France, Germany, Holland, Switzerland, greatly benefited. But, as we have already seen, the Roman Catholic Church spared no effort to recover from its losses, and the Protestant Churches had to fight for their very existence.

The 18th-Century Age of Reason, during which unbelief in a variety of forms resolved to deal a death blow at 'revealed religion', wrought havoc in the Protestant Churches. The world has termed the 18th Century 'The Age of Enlightenment', but under the influence of such men as Rousseau and Voltaire biblical religion was stoutly opposed and held up to ridicule. Voltaire's curse was pronounced upon all religions indiscriminately. 'Crush the infamous thing' was his favourite slogan.

The outbreak of the French Revolution in 1789 also produced intense hostility to religion and the Churches. In 1793 the government and Assembly in France that had replaced the monarchy, and sent king and queen to the guillotine, declared Christianity to be abolished. In its place the Worship of Reason was proclaimed. A certain Mademoiselle Maillard, an opera dancer, wearing the three colours of the new republic, was enthroned as the goddess of Reason upon the high altar of Notre Dame, the Roman Catholic cathedral of Paris, and there she received the homage of the revolutionists. The Christian calendar was abolished and a ten-day week was instituted. Church bells were called 'the Eternal's geegaws' and melted down, cannon and coin being made out of them. Death was declared to be but 'an eternal sleep'. Church services were forbidden, but every tenth day it was arranged that philosophical or political 'sermons' should be preached; alternatively, popular banquets or balls were arranged.

But changes soon came. When Napoleon Bonaparte came to power he soon made peace with the Roman Catholic Church and allowed its former activities to be resumed in France. Even so, the Church had received a tremendous blow from which it never really recovered. Atheism abounded. Few indeed sought the kingdom of God and its righteousness. The Protestant Churches were in a very weak state. A law of 1808 placed Catholic and Protestant on an equal footing as far as the law of the land was concerned, but a time of fearful stagnation set in. Progress towards better things was slow indeed.

At this point of time English Methodism did its best to improve the sad situation. Shortly before the Revolution of 1789 it had planned to make the Channel Islands of Guernsey and Jersey an outpost for the evangelization of France. Dr Coke, mentioned in the chapter on Wesley's Methodism, visited Paris and held a short-lived mission. After the battle of Waterloo in 1815 another Methodist, Charles Cook, began work in France, and when he died in 1858 a vigorous French branch of the Methodist Church had been established. Merle d'Aubigné the historian says of him that 'the work which John Wesley did in Great Britain Charles Cook has done, though on a smaller scale, on the Continent'.

The greatest French Protestant preacher of the century was undoubtedly Adolphe Monod (1802–56), the son of a preacher of the Word at

49

The 19th-Century Church on the Continent of Europe (1)

Adolphe Monod (1802–56).

Copenhagen. As a minister of the gospel he laboured for a time in Naples, then in southern France, but finally he settled in Paris and exercised a vast influence for good by his preaching and his writings. One who knew him well said: 'In the midst of the instability of religious life, everyone looked to him, as the sailor in the storm at the lighthouse'. His brother Frédéric did a similar work, and helped to found the Union of the Evangelical Churches of France.

As for Spain and Portugal, countries where in the 16th Century the doctrine of the Reformation had been quenched and where the cruelties of the Inquisition had been notorious, there was but little evidence of Protestant witness during the 19th Century. The papacy exercised a stranglehold over both monarchy and government, and the Protestant faith was barely represented in the Peninsula.

Yet the English-speaking world possesses a volume of great interest and literary merit in *The Bible in Spain*, written by George Borrow. Born

in Norfolk, and gifted in the acquisition of languages, he became an agent of the British and Foreign Bible Society in Spain, and his book narrates his experiences. From time to time he came under arrest and even feared that he might meet 'the fate of St Stephen'; but he survived his ordeal and bequeathed to posterity a fascinating narrative. Admittedly, in some ways Borrow was a strange character, but the chief of English encyclopaedias guarantees that every page of the account of his adventures in Spain 'glows with freshness, picturesqueness and vivacity'.

Italy, like Spain, remained during most of the 19th Century under the control of the Roman Church, which spared no effort to hinder the work of Protestant Bible Societies. Pope Pius VII in 1816 denounced them as 'pestilences', and ten years later Leo XII warned Catholics that through Bible Societies 'the gospel of Christ had become the word of the devil'. In 1830 Pius VIII described the Protestant Bibles as 'a centre of pestiferous infection' while Gregory XVI in 1846 instructed the priests to tear up all Bibles on which they could lay their hands. Giovanni Diodati of Geneva had produced an excellent translation of the Bible into Italian in the 17th Century but this found no favour in papal eyes and Italians found in possession of it were liable to imprisonment for an undefined period of time or even sent to the galleys.

A translation of Scripture into Italian by Martini had received the approval of the Roman Church, but it was never intended for popular use, even though in 1893 Pope Leo XIII reversed the policy of his predecessors and officially permitted the reading of it. But most parish priests were quite unwilling for their flocks to read Scripture for themselves, and gave no encouragement to those who wished to know the mind of Christ at first hand.

Protestants visiting Italy were invariably struck by the extent of the homage paid to the Virgin Mary. Madonnas abounded. Every church had its Lady Chapel and its images. John Ruskin in his *Stones of Venice* wrote:

It matters literally nothing to a Romanist what the image he worships is like. Take the vilest doll that is screwed together in a cheap toy-shop . . . dress it in a satin frock, and declare it to have fallen from heaven, and it will satisfactorily answer all Romanist purposes. Some have even changed the Lord's prayer to 'Our Mary, who art in heaven'.

In 1854 Pope Pius IX issued a papal bull in which it was stated that Mary had from the moment of her conception been kept free from all stain of original sin—the so-called Immaculate Conception—just as, in 1950, Pope Pius XII proclaimed that after Mary's earthly life ended her soul *and body* were taken up to heavenly glory. But Scripture knows nothing of such doctrines, and for a person's salvation to be made dependent upon a belief in them is a pernicious error.

The Roman Church sustained a great blow from the State during the 19th Century. It lost its temporal power, which caused it to hold on the more grimly to its claim to spiritual power. Through the political intrigues of Count Cavour the Prime Minister of Piedmont, the determination of King Emanuel of Piedmont to unite Italy under himself, and the military prowess of Garibaldi the patriot, the Papal States in Central Italy were taken from the Church and incorporated in the new Kingdom of Italy in the year 1861. The Pope withdrew into the Vatican, and it was not until the time of Mussolini (1929) that

a later Pope came to terms with the State and accepted a settlement. It left him in full control of the Vatican City and gave the Church a very large cash payment for the loss of the Papal States in 1861.

In 1870 Pope Pius IX summoned the first Vatican Council. It decreed that the Pope was endowed with infallibility when he spoke *ex cathedra* (that is to say, when, by reason of his claim to be 'pastor and teacher of all Christians, he defined a doctrine concerning faith and morals to be held by the universal church'). This rendered the division between Roman Catholic and Protestant Churches greater than ever, for the latter cannot agree to ascribe infallibility to the word of a man.

God did not leave himself without Protestant witness during the 19th Century. The Waldensian Church still existed in the shadow of the Alps though, unhappily, it had degenerated. But a 'deliverer' was raised up in the person of Felix Neff (1798–1829), though he had more to do with the French Waldensians than with the Italian. His arduous work cost him his life.

Next we glance at religion in the Swiss cantons. Here, too, there had been the abandonment of Christian orthodoxy and the reception of ideas which were not far removed from those of French rationalists. Natural religion had largely taken the place of biblically revealed truth. The theology of Calvin had long been forgotten. In the late 16th Century an Italian theologian named Sozzini or Socinus had denied the doctrine of the Trinity, and Socinianism became the generally accepted term for what is now known as Unitarianism. The influence of this heresy caused most Swiss pastors in the early 19th Century to question, if not altogether abandon, belief in the Deity of Christ. Paul Bost

left Abraham Kuyper.

right J H Merle d'Aubigné.

who for four years attended a school of theology in Geneva about 1815, but was not converted until later, tells us that the college professors never made use of Old or New Testament in the course of their lectures. Rationalism prevailed.

In 1816, however, Robert Haldane, a wealthy Scotsman who had been converted in 1793 and was now over 50 years of age, arrived at Geneva and opened his rooms to students in the University and various colleges. He expounded to them Paul's Epistle to the Romans, and men who later rose to eminence—Merle d'Aubigné, César Malan, Adolphe Monod, and Louis Gaussen among them—were led by him to adopt evangelical views. His lectures were published in book form in 1819, and during the present century they have been reprinted.

Shortly after 1816 there appeared in canton Vaud a wealthy lady named Madame de Krüdener, who had exchanged a life of Parisian gaiety for the privilege of sitting upon a wooden bench in Vaud and teaching all who came to her

the truths of the Bible and the necessity of a regenerated heart. Despite the strange episodes that belong to her life-story there is no reason to doubt that she was herself a born-again soul, and that her visit to the canton of Vaud was beneficial. Methodist preachers, nicknamed the Momiers, also arrived and helped to carry the work forward. An Evangelical Church was organized, Sunday Schools were opened, and a new school of theology secured staff true to the Scriptures.

Merle d'Aubigné became a leading historian of the Protestant Church, and especially of the Reformation period. Malan travelled and preached not only in Switzerland but also in Germany, France, the Netherlands, and Scotland; he also compiled a much-valued hymnbook. Gaussen is chiefly remembered as a writer, his best known work being *Theopneustia*, a word meaning 'God-breathed' and used of the inspiration of Scripture in 2 Timothy 3 : 16—'all Scripture is given by inspiration of God'. Monod has been mentioned earlier. Two other

Swiss names which deserve to be remembered are those of Alexandre Vinet, a theologian of great repute, but a man who tended to adopt a more personal approach to doctrine and church problems than his fellows; also F. L. Godet, who produced New Testament Commentaries of considerable value.

Moving on to Holland we take particular note of the career of Abraham Kuyper (1837–1920), a Calvinistic theologian, but chiefly remembered by the Dutch nation as a politician. Indeed, from 1901 to 1905 he was Prime Minister of his country. He placed much emphasis upon 'common grace', the kindness of God that is enjoyed by multitudes but which falls short of saving grace. In 1880 he opened a University in Amsterdam free from both Church and State control. Six years later he led 100,000 of his fellow-countrymen from the Dutch Reformed Church to form, with a group of other seceders, the second largest Protestant Church in the Netherlands. He gave a series of lectures in the United States of America in 1898 and they were later published under the title *Calvinism*. Kuyper firmly opposed the Higher Criticism prevalent at the close of the century. He also wished to apply religious truth to all aspects of human life.

Germany presents a rather gloomy picture to the Protestant historian of the 19th Century. As the home of the Reformation in the days of Luther its fine gold had become very dim before that century opened. The earlier part of the century has been called 'the age of Goethe', a writer of immense influence in the German-speaking world. Although not a Roman Catholic he often expressed admiration for the Roman Church, but this was due to his attachment to its old works of art rather than to its theological beliefs. 'Since the Reformation', he wrote, 'something painful, almost evil, characterizes works of art'. Be this the case or not, Goethe's influence on the German nation and its religion was in the main as destructive as if he had written nothing but uncompromising rationalism.

The fact is that Germany, by the mid-19th Century was flooded by unbelief. Its schools and colleges, as well as its churches, contributed to this. Its Protestant hymn-book was revised in order to deprive it of much of its evangelical content. Philosophy replaced theology, and Scripture was dealt with savagely. Miracles ceased to be accounted miracles; they were explained away. Bible prophecies were discredited. Christ was robbed of his Deity. His resurrection, it was said, never took place. Either he did not really die but suffered a fainting fit, or he retreated after his supposed death to some place known only to his disciples. G. F. Strauss startled the world by a *Life of Jesus* (published in 1835–36) which admitted a framework of fact, but claimed that much of the content of the Four Gospels was sheer mythology. Julius Wellhausen achieved notoriety by attacking the orthodox teaching on the authorship, unity and inspiration of the Scriptures, and unhappily many followed in his steps. He was the chief pioneer of Higher Critical views, and under his influence many theologians throughout Western Europe and America questioned or abandoned the authority even of Christ himself.

But not all German theologians were of this type. Exceptionally there were those who maintained an excellent witness to divine truth, as, for example, E. W. Hengstenberg, Professor of Theology at Berlin from 1828 to 1869. He had been educated on rationalistic principles but by grace escaped their pernicious influence, and his Bible Commentaries and other writings, some of them translated into English, are of great value. A theologian of similar type was J. K. F. Keil who had come under Hengstenberg's influence. He excelled as a commentator on the Old Testament.

We must not omit mention of one other German Christian, Johann Gerhard Oncken, who had no place among the scholarly, but who exerted a widespread influence for true godliness in his generation. Born in 1800 he experienced to the full the chilling influences of a formal and decadent Lutheranism, but at the age of 14 a Scottish merchant trading in Germany took him back with him to Scotland. There a Christian lady presented him with, of all books, a copy of James Hervey's *Meditations among the Tombs*! Moving to London he was converted through a sermon on Romans 8 : 1: 'There is therefore now no condemnation to them which are in Christ Jesus'. After a time he returned to Germany and settled at Hamburg. Shortly afterwards he became a preacher of the gospel and an agent of the National Bible Society of Scotland (at first called the Edinburgh Bible Society).

Oncken corresponded with Robert Haldane and under his influence he became a Baptist, but finding it difficult to obtain the services of any Baptist minister in Germany, he was advised by Haldane to baptize himself. He preferred, however, to wait the Lord's time. In 1867, after strenuous labours, he was able to build Hamburg's first Baptist Chapel. The city had a population of over 20,000, but no more than 4,000 attended a place of worship.

C. H. Spurgeon assisted at the Chapel's opening service, and we tell the story of Oncken's triumph over the opposition of the civic authorities as he narrates it:

Burgomaster (Mayor) of Hamburg: Do you see that little finger, Mr. Oncken ? While I can move that little finger, I will put the Baptists down.
Oncken: With all due respect to your little finger, Mr. Burgomaster, I would ask you another question: Do you see that great arm ?
Burgomaster: No, I do not see it.
Oncken: Just so, but I do see it, and while that great arm moves, you cannot put us down, and if it comes to conflict between your little finger and that great arm, I know how it will end.
Spurgeon: It was my great joy to see the Burgomaster among the audience that listened to my sermon at the new Chapel. The little finger had willingly given up its opposition, and the great arm [of the Lord] was made bare among us.

To ministerial students whom Oncken had gathered together, Spurgeon said, 'Preach not only so that the people can understand, but so that they cannot misunderstand if they wish'. It was by means of such men as Johann Oncken that evangelical truth was revived in 19th-Century Germany. While such men as Bismarck were pursuing a 'blood and iron policy' to unify Germany, and making war upon Austria and France who stood in the path of their ambition, Oncken and his friends were proclaiming salvation by 'the blood of the cross' and extending the bounds of the kingdom of God.
And soul by soul and silently her shining bounds
increase
And her ways are ways of pleasantness and all
her paths are peace.

We move on to Poland, a stronghold of Roman Catholicism. During the 19th Century it did not exist as an independent State, for it had been partitioned by its neighbours, Russia, Prussia and Austria during the previous century. In any case the Protestant faith was very poorly represented within its borders. The Reformation had not taken root there to any great extent, despite its proximity to Germany and Lutheranism. On the contrary it had become a centre of Socinianism (Unitarianism) which spared no effort to overthrow evangelical religion.

But there was promise that Bible truth might make progress in Poland after 1815. The Czar Alexander I of Russia was confirmed in the possession of central Poland by the great European Peace Treaty of Vienna of that year, and he had great respect for the Scriptures. Furthermore, as Poland lacked true geographical frontiers, gospel preachers from Germany could obtain easy access to its towns and villages, and frequently did so, Oncken being one of them. In 1863 a Polish Revolt gave Alexander II considerable trouble in its suppression. He offered safe asylum in Russian Poland to Poles living in German Poland if they would take his side against the rebels. In consequence hundreds more Polish believers came under his jurisdiction. Most of them were Baptists and Oncken went to St Petersburg on their behalf in 1864 to ask for full toleration. The official whom he encountered said to him: 'There is only one difficulty in the way of your sect being acknowledged; and that is, you are making proselytes. This is not allowed in Russia, but strictly forbidden.' Nevertheless, in several centres, especially Lodz, Baptists flourished.

And so we move on into Russia, or rather, into 'all the Russias' for it was as if several Russias were comprised in the vast territory which lay stretched between the Baltic Sea in the west, the Black Sea in the south, the Arctic in the north, and the Pacific in the east, a territory larger than the whole of Africa. At one time it was called Holy Russia, as if it were a territorial and racial 'ecclesia' (church). Every Russian was required to belong to the Greek Orthodox Church which, in many ways was like the Roman Church. It claimed to hold sway over the souls of men. But whereas in the Roman Church images played a considerable part, their place in Russia was taken by ikons or holy pictures. An Englishman of the days of Queen Elizabeth I, visiting Russia, reported of it:

The house that hath no god, or painted saint
within,
Is not to be resorted to; that roof is full of sin.
The ikons were a source of great idolatry.

Superstition was a characteristic of life in Russia. Just as in 20th-Century Britain people often say, 'I'm keeping my fingers crossed', so in Russia a yawn necessitated the making of the sign of the cross in front of the gaping mouth lest the devil should seize the opportunity of entering the person by way of his throat. A threefold sneeze required some kind bystander to say 'God bless you', failing which, it was believed that disaster would ensue.

There was no liberty of worship in Russia in 1800. Notwithstanding, there were groups of widely-scattered believers called Molokans. The name means 'milk-eaters' and was given in derision to people who did not keep the fast days decreed by the Orthodox Church, but ate their curds and cheese as on other days. But they cheerfully accepted the term, quoting in their defence the words found in 1 Peter 2 : 1 :

50

The 19th-Century Church on the Continent of Europe (2)

A view of Russians, young and old, in 1929.

'Desire the sincere [unadulterated] milk of the word that ye may grow thereby'.

The Molokans' worship was of the simplest kind—Bible reading, prayer, psalm singing, and even the singing monotonously of chapter after chapter of Scripture. In 1805 Czar Alexander I gave them official permission to worship according to their consciences.

In 1812 Napoleon Bonaparte marched into Russia, reached Moscow and required Alexander's surrender. It was the greatest mistake of the Frenchman's career, for the Czar had retreated beyond Moscow after robbing the area of all food supplies, and in their turn the invaders had to retreat under vile wintry conditions. Most of them perished as they plodded westwards. Thereafter the Czar was one of the participants in the peace settlement at Paris and later at Vienna. In the former city, and earlier still in a German city, he came under the influence of Madame de Krüdener whom we have already mentioned. She opened her home for meetings in which the New Testament was studied, and the Czar attended them. He had been studying Scripture, and before her, he, 'the most powerful man in Europe, sat, his face buried in his hands, sobbing like a child, until at last he declared that he had found peace'. In 1816 we find him writing:

To lead back the lost sheep to the fold cannot be done by force, this being quite contrary to the doctrine of the Saviour who came to seek and to save the lost. True faith is a work of grace and can only be effected in the soul by instruction, gentleness and, most of all, by good example.

The Church must neither use force nor permit violence against the erring ones, even should it not approve of their separation (i.e. from the Established Church). It is utterly opposed to the spirit of the Divine Head, when he said, 'But if ye had known what this meaneth, I will have mercy and not sacrifice, ye would not have condemned the guiltless'.

Signed by His Majesty's own hand,

ALEXANDER.

The Czar now became anxious for Christian teachers and preachers to get to work in his vast dominions. The British and Foreign Bible Society was able to send its agents, and before long 280 'branches' supplying Bibles had been opened. But in 1825 Alexander died and was succeeded by his brother Nicholas who condemned the Society's work as revolutionary and likely 'to shake the foundations of religion and of the State'.

'What were the results of such Bible-reading as had taken place?' said one English visitor to a priest of the Orthodox Church. 'Who can tell?' was the reply; 'you plant the acorn; your descendants sit beneath the oak'.

In 1855 Alexander II became Czar of all the Russias, and after six years he conferred freedom on Russian serfs, twenty-two and a half million of them, by his Edict of Emancipation. At the same time the Bible Society re-appeared, but under a new name. It was now The Society for the Encouragement of Moral and Religious Reading.

By this time Russian Christians outside the Orthodox Church were also known by a new name. They were called Stundists, a word derived from the German 'stunden', meaning 'hours'. The name referred to their practice of setting apart certain hours for prayer and Bible reading. Despite sundry persecutions, local not national, Stundists became active and steady progress seemed to be in sight, especially in the Ukraine—southern Russia—where German and Dutch settlers, including Mennonites and Baptists, were found in considerable numbers. The chief difficulty was that the Orthodox Church still forbade the making of disciples. In 1879 an increased measure of liberty was given to believers and to immigrants in particular.

So long, however, as the old laws against proselytism remained in force the position was similar to that of a man driving a vehicle with the brakes on. But it was hoped that one degree of toleration would lead to another, depending, humanly speaking, on the character and disposition of the ruling Czar. The words of a stirring German hymn were often sung by believers at this time (here quoted in translation):

Ye who bear his sacred Name,
Follow him through flood and flame;
Where our Head has gone before us
We will tread, his banner o'er us!

Tragedy befell the land in 1881. Alexander II was brutally killed by bombs thrown at his carriage as he drove through the streets of St Petersburg. In consequence the new Czar, Alexander III, lived under the shadow of death, and hardened his heart against any extension of liberty, whether civil or religious, and indeed against such extension of liberty as had already been conceded.

The body responsible for the control of religious affairs was The Holy Governing Synod. It dated from the reign of Peter the Great centuries earlier. To it the Czar now appointed Constantine Pobiedonostzeff, a University Professor of great decisiveness of character. 'Severely logical, pitilessly absolute, and tremendously in earnest' he made it his policy to act mercilessly to all who were outside the State Church. Historians have called him the 'lay pope' of Russia. Persecution recommenced, not against Baptists and Stundists only, but also against Jews. Over a million Jews are said to have fled from Russia during the years 1881 and 1882. Many of them found refuge in the United States of America.

Pobiedonostzeff was a religious man. He well illustrates the saying that 'No tyrant is so remorselessly tyrannical as the religious fanatic'. Like Saul of Tarsus he believed that, as he breathed out threatenings and slaughter, he was doing God's service. Often he could be seen 'walking around the gardens of St Petersburg's Winter Palace, Prayer Book in hand, attending to his devotions'. Sometimes he would retire to a monastery for the purpose of fasting and would even beat his forehead against the stone floor as he knelt in prayer. Such was the man who organized and executed one of the greatest religious persecutions of modern times. He held office from 1881 to 1905.

In 1894 Nicholas II became Czar and after the great civil unrest which followed Russia's defeat in a war against the Japanese he made concessions to his subjects both civil and religious. Yet the lot of the person who failed to conform to the Orthodox Church and its requirements remained far from comfortable.

It was customary for prisoners of State to be sent into the wilds of Arctic Siberia where the severity of the climate and the intolerably harsh conditions under which prisoners served their sentence usually broke their spirit. Siberian prisons have been described as 'a hell upon earth'. Such visitors from the west as were permitted to visit them looked, as it were, down into 'the crater of a lurid volcano of human misery, agony and despair'. No such message as that of the gospel of divine grace ever reached that land of woe.

Occasionally, however, Christians from the west would be allowed to travel to Siberia. One such person was Dr Frederick William Baedeker, a cousin of the Baedeker of Guide Book fame. Born and bred in Germany where 'the doctrine of baptismal regeneration was the shroud in which lay the corpse of the religious life of that land', he came to England and at the age of 43 was soundly converted at a meeting held in Weston-super-Mare. Lord Radstock, a member of Britain's peerage, and a man who paid periodical visits to Russia for evangelistic purposes, was the preacher. Describing his experience, Dr Baedeker wrote: 'I went into the meeting a proud, rebellious infidel and came out a humble believing disciple of the Lord Jesus Christ'. Up to that point of time his health had been precarious, but as a man now dedicated to God, he began a career of 40 years' Christian witness which took him to many parts of Europe, and to Russia in particular. He wanted to preach the gospel to 'every creature' and to strengthen the hands of believers wherever he found them. He spoke English, German and French, and mastered the Russian language sufficiently well to preach in it if occasion demanded it, but ordinarily he searched for 'brethren in Christ who were able to translate his words into Finnish, Fris, Russ, Lett, Georgian, Armenian, Esthonian, or any other of the bewildering multiplicity of languages spoken within Russia's frontiers.' 'To visit the prisons,' he said, 'and to minister to the poor souls who are under the awful power of sin and darkness, is to me better than angels' food'.

Sometimes Dr Baedeker met with believers in high society. One such was Princess Lieven who welcomed into her home in the Russian capital all gospel preachers, one of them being George Müller of Orphanage fame. Colònel Paschkoff, a wealthy nobleman and an officer of the Imperial Guard, was another who let his light shine brightly before men. His reward from men was a sentence of exile. 'Never set foot upon Russian soil again' was the message he received from Czar Alexander III.

Dr Baedeker ended his Christian life where he began it, at Weston-super-Mare. He called his house *Wart Eck*, German for 'Waiting Corner', by which he meant that he was 'looking

Frederick William Baedeker (1823–1906) Some time after his conversion at the age of 43, Baedeker settled for three years at St. Petersburg where he mingled with all classes of society. Among members of the upper classes he played a leading part in the so-called 'drawing room awakening'. Later he travelled in all parts of Scandinavia, visiting universities and prisons, and mingling with high and low in his preaching of the Gospel. In Russia he carried 'the good news' from the Caucasus to Siberia. In 1899, despite the opposition of Pobiedonostzeff, he obtained permission to preach and distribute Bibles in all Russian prisons, and there were many of them! This permission (renewed biennially) he continued to receive until his death. In England his associations were mainly with 'Open Brethren'.

for that blessed hope and the glorious appearing of our Lord and Saviour Jesus Christ'.

An ancient name for southern Russia was Scythia, and in Colossians 3 : 11 the apostle Paul introduces that place-name. Macedonia, Greece, Dalmatia, Italy, Spain, and Scythia all find mention in the New Testament, thereby reminding us that the Church of Christ is gathered out of all nations, kindreds, people and tongues. The divine work still continues; it is not yet complete though it hastens to its consummation. And meanwhile, as Horatius Bonar of Scotland sang last century:

Far down the ages now,
Much of her journey done,
The pilgrim church pursues her way
   Until her crown be won;
The story of the past
   Comes up before her view;
How well it seems to suit her still—
   Old, and yet ever new!

'Tis the repeated tale
   Of sin and weariness;
Of grace and love yet flowing down
   To pardon and to bless:
No wider is the gate,
   No broader is the way,
No smoother is the ancient path
   That leads to light and day.

No sweeter is the cup,
   Nor less our lot of ill;
'Twas tribulation ages since,
   'Tis tribulation still:
No slacker grows the fight
   No feebler is the foe,
Nor less the need of armour tried,
   Of shield and spear and bow.

Thus onward still we press,
   Through evil and through good;
Through pain and poverty and want,
   Through peril and through blood:
Still faithful to our God,
   And to our Captain true,
We follow where He leads the way,
   The Kingdom in our view.

Index

Further Reading from the Present Publishers

General

HISTORY OF CHRISTIAN DOCTRINES, *Louis Berkhof*
HISTORICAL THEOLOGY, *William Cunningham*
GOD MADE THEM GREAT (FOR YOUNG PEOPLE), *John Tallach*

Sixteenth Century

WRITINGS OF JOHN BRADFORD
SERMONS ON EPHESIANS, *John Calvin*
LETTERS OF JOHN CALVIN
MAN OF GENEVA (THE LIFE OF CALVIN FOR YOUNG PEOPLE), *E. M. Johnson*
THE REFORMATION IN ENGLAND, *J. H. Merle d'Aubigné*

Seventeenth Century

THE PILGRIM'S PROGRESS, *John Bunyan*
THE GREAT WORKS OF CHRIST IN AMERICA, *Cotton Mather*
THE PURITAN HOPE, *Iain Murray*
WORKS OF JOHN OWEN (16 volumes)
LETTERS OF SAMUEL RUTHERFORD
THE GOLDEN TREASURY OF PURITAN QUOTATIONS, *I. D. E. Thomas*
THE SHORTER CATECHISM (AN EXPOSITION), *Thomas Vincent*
THE LIVES OF PHILIP AND MATTHEW HENRY, *J. B. Williams*

Eighteenth Century

THE LIFE OF GEORGE WHITEFIELD, *Arnold Dallimore*
THE LOG COLLEGE, *Archibald Alexander*
THE WORKS OF JONATHAN EDWARDS
WILLIAM JAY, AN AUTOBIOGRAPHY
LETTERS OF JOHN NEWTON
CHRISTIAN LEADERS OF THE 18TH CENTURY, *J. C. Ryle*
THE GREAT AWAKENING, *Joseph Tracy*
GEORGE WHITEFIELD'S LETTERS
GEORGE WHITEFIELD'S JOURNALS

Nineteenth Century

MEMOIRS AND REMAINS OF R. M. M'CHEYNE, *Andrew Bonar*
LIFE OF M'CHEYNE, *Andrew Bonar*
LIFE AND LETTERS OF JOHN ELIAS
LIFE OF R. L. DABNEY, *R. C. Johnson*
ADOLPHE MONOD'S FAREWELL
THE FORGOTTEN SPURGEON, *Iain Murray*
LIFE OF J. H. THORNWELL, *B. M. Palmer*
CHARGES AND ADDRESSES, *J. C. Ryle*
C. H. SPURGEON, AN AUTOBIOGRAPHY:
    VOLUME I—THE EARLY YEARS;
    VOLUME 2—THE FULL HARVEST
METROPOLITAN TABERNACLE PULPIT (VOLUMES 28–31 AND 34–37), *C. H. Spurgeon*
THE LIFE OF NETTLETON, *B. Tyler and A. Bonar*